Steven Spielberg's Style by Stealth

James Mairata

Steven Spielberg's Style by Stealth

palgrave
macmillan

James Mairata
Charles Sturt University
Sydney, NSW, Australia

ISBN 978-3-030-09868-1   ISBN 978-3-319-69081-0   (eBook)
https://doi.org/10.1007/978-3-319-69081-0

© The Editor(s) (if applicable) and The Author(s) 2018
Softcover re-print of the Hardcover 1st edition 2018
This work is subject to copyright. All rights are solely and exclusively licensed by the Publisher, whether the whole or part of the material is concerned, specifically the rights of translation, reprinting, reuse of illustrations, recitation, broadcasting, reproduction on microfilms or in any other physical way, and transmission or information storage and retrieval, electronic adaptation, computer software, or by similar or dissimilar methodology now known or hereafter developed.
The use of general descriptive names, registered names, trademarks, service marks, etc. in this publication does not imply, even in the absence of a specific statement, that such names are exempt from the relevant protective laws and regulations and therefore free for general use.
The publisher, the authors and the editors are safe to assume that the advice and information in this book are believed to be true and accurate at the date of publication. Neither the publisher nor the authors or the editors give a warranty, express or implied, with respect to the material contained herein or for any errors or omissions that may have been made. The publisher remains neutral with regard to jurisdictional claims in published maps and institutional affiliations.

Cover illustration: REUTERS / Alamy Stock Photo
Cover design by Henry Petrides

Printed on acid-free paper

This Palgrave Macmillan imprint is published by the registered company Springer International Publishing AG part of Springer Nature
The registered company address is: Gewerbestrasse 11, 6330 Cham, Switzerland

For Eli and Ish

Contents

1 Introduction: Setting the Scene — 1

Part I Origin — 21

2 Fundamentals of Classical Narration — 23

3 Spielberg as Filmmaker — 53

4 Continuity Editing as System — 79

Part II Function — 103

5 Deep Space Composition and Staging — 105

6 Space and the Wide Reverse Strategy — 151

7 The Wide Reverse and Extended Variation — 189

Part III	Effect, Affect and Precedent	239
8	The Wide Reverse, Cognition and Affect	241
9	Manifestations of the Wide Reverse in Mainstream Narrative Cinema	275
10	Conclusion: Style by Stealth	331
Index		341

List of Figures

Figs. 4.1a-c	*Bridge of Spies* (2015)	81
Fig. 4.2	Conventional shot, reverse shot	82
Figs. 4.3a-c	Simulation, 4.3d/4.3b, *Amistad* (1997)	83
Figs. 4.4a-h	*Empire of the Sun* (1987)	86
Figs. 4.5a-l	*Munich* (2005)	91–92
Figs. 4.6a-b	*The Private Lives of Elizabeth and Essex* (1939)	95
Figs. 4.7a-b	*Detective Story* (1951)	95
Figs. 4.8a-b	*Murder by the Book* (1971)	96
Figs. 4.9a-d	*Jurassic Park* (1993)	97
Figs. 4.10a-d	*Kingdom of the Crystal Skull* (2008)	98
Figs. 5.1a-b	*Eyes* (1969)	113
Fig. 5.2a	*Murder by the Book* (1971)	114
Fig. 5.3a	*Duel* (1971)	114
Fig. 5.4a	*The Sugarland Express* (1974)	114
Fig. 5.5a	*Raiders of the Lost Ark* (1981)	114
Fig. 5.6a	*Minority Report* (2002)	115
Figs. 5.7a-b	*Murder by the Book* (1971)	116
Figs. 5.8a-b	*Always* (1989)	116
Figs. 5.9a-c	*Raiders of the Lost Ark* (1981)	116
Figs. 5.10a-d	*Murder by the Book* (1971)	117–118
Figs. 5.11a-b	*The Sugarland Express* (1974)	119
Figs. 5.12a-b	*Always* (1989)	119

x   List of Figures

Fig. 5.13a	*Eyes* (1969)	120
Fig. 5.14a	*Citizen Kane* (1941)	121
Fig. 5.15a	*Duel* (1971)	121
Fig. 5.16a	*The Color Purple* (1985)	123
Fig. 5.17a	*Bezhin Meadow* (1935)	123
Fig. 5.18a	*The Last Crusade* (1989)	123
Fig. 5.19a	*Always* (1989)	124
Fig. 5.20a	*Hook* (1981)	124
Fig. 5.21a	*Schindler's List* (1993)	124
Fig. 5.22a	*Saving Private Ryan* (1998)	124
Fig. 5.23a	*Amistad* (1997)	125
Figs. 5.24a-b	*Minority Report* (2002)	125
Fig. 5.25a	*Catch Me if You Can* (2002)	125
Fig. 5.26a	*The Terminal* (2004)	125
Fig. 5.27a	*Munich* (2005)	126
Fig. 5.28a	*Lincoln* (2012)	126
Fig. 5.29a	*Bridge of Spies* (2015)	126
Figs. 5.30a-g	*Jaws* (1975)	128–129
Figs. 5.31a-h	*Raiders of the Lost Ark* (1981)	131
Figs. 5.32a-g	*Catch Me if You Can* (2002)	132–133
Figs. 5.33a-e	*Close Encounters of the Third Kind* (1977)	134–135
Figs. 5.34a-c	(enlargement of 5.34b)	136
Figs. 5.35a-b	*The Royal Tenenbaums* (2001)	137
Figs. 5.36a-l	*The Sugarland Express* (1974)	139–141
Fig. 5.37	Portable toilet sequence. Overhead view, *The Sugarland Express* (1974)	142
Fig. 6.1	Wide reverse coverage	152
Figs. 6.2a-e/f	*Close Encounters of the Third Kind* (1977)	154–155
Fig. 6.3	Roy Neary's close encounter—overhead view—initial shot reverses, *Close Encounters of the Third Kind* (1977)	156
Figs. 6.4a-l	*Jaws* (1975)	162–163
Figs. 6.5a-f	*Saving Private Ryan* (1998)	166
Figs. 6.6a-c	*Raiders of the Lost Ark* (1981)	169
Figs. 6.7a-d	*Raiders of the Lost Ark* (1981)	171
Figs. 6.8a-f	*Raiders of the Lost Ark* (1981)	172–173
Figs. 6.9a-e	Production still *Jaws* (1975)	174
Fig. 6.10	Ferry scene—overhead view—wide reverse, *Jaws* (1975)	175

List of Figures   xi

Figs. 6.11a-f	*Empire of the Sun* (1987)	176–177
Figs. 6.12a-c	*Saving Private Ryan* (1998)	179
Figs. 6.13a-g	*The Terminal* (2004)	180–181
Figs. 7.1a-c	*Murder by the Book* (1971)	192
Figs. 7.2a-d	*Duel* (1971)	193–194
Figs. 7.3a-b	*The Sugarland Express* (1974)	195
Figs. 7.4a-b	*The Sugarland Express* (1974)	196
Figs. 7.5a-c	*Jaws* (1975)	196
Figs. 7.6a-c	*Jaws* (1975)	197
Figs. 7.7a-c	*Close Encounters of the Third Kind* (1977)	198
Figs. 7.8a-c	*Raiders of the Lost Ark* (1981)	199
Figs. 7.9a-f	*1941* (1979)	201
Figs. 7.10a-f	*Schindler's List* (1993)	203
Figs. 7.11a-e	*Jurassic Park* (1993)	205–206
Figs. 7.12a-c	*Jurassic Park* (1993)	208
Figs. 7.13a-d	*Jurassic Park* (1993)	209
Figs. 7.14a-e	*Jurassic Park* (1993)	210–211
Figs. 7.15a-b	*Jurassic Park* (1993)	212
Figs. 7.16a-f	*Duel* (1971)	214–215
Figs. 7.17a-d	*A.I. Artificial Intelligence* (2001)	216
Figs. 7.18a-d	*Minority Report* (2002)	218
Figs. 7.19a-d	*Catch Me if You Can* (2002)	219
Figs. 7.20a-d	*Munich* (2005)	220–221
Figs. 7.21a-d	*Saving Private Ryan* (1998)	222
Figs. 7.22a-g	*Empire of the Sun* (1987)	223
Fig. 7.23	Dr. Rawlins warns Jim – overhead view, *Empire of the Sun* (1987)	225
Figs. 7.24a-f	*The Sugarland Express* (1974)	226
Fig. 7.25	Tanner speaks with Clovis—overhead view, *The Sugarland Express* (1974)	227
Figs. 7.26a-i	*War of the Worlds* (2005)	228–229
Figs. 7.27a-h	*The Terminal* (2004)	230–231
Figs. 7.28a-c	*Munich* (2005)	232
Figs. 7.29a-b	*War of the Worlds* (2005)	233
Figs. 7.30a-b	*War Horse* (2011)	234
Figs. 8.1a-b	*The End of Summer* (1961)	247
Figs. 8.2a-k	*Jurassic Park* (1993)	267–268
Figs. 9.1a-b	*Ladies Skirts Nailed to a Fence* (1900)	277

List of Figures

Figs. 9.2a-b	*Giant* (1956)	286
Figs. 9.3a-c	*Belly of an Architect* (1987)	287
Figs. 9.4a-c	*The Insider* (1999)	289
Figs. 9.5a-c	*The Shining* (1980)	290
Figs. 9.6a-b	*La chinoise* (1967)	291
Figs. 9.7a-c	*The General* (1926)	292
Figs. 9.8a-c	*Day of Wrath* (1943)	295
Figs. 9.9a-c	*Day of Wrath* (1943)	297
Figs. 9.10a-c	*Ordet* (1955)	298
Figs. 9.11a-b	*The Man Who Knew Too Much* (1956)	301
Figs. 9.12a-c	*Vertigo* (1958)	302
Figs. 9.13a-b	*Caught* (1949)	304
Figs. 9.14a-b	*Caught* (1949)	305
Figs. 9.15a-b	*La Ronde* (1950)	307
Figs. 9.16a-b	*Lola Montes* (1955)	308
Figs. 9.17a-c	*Blind Husbands* (1919)	309
Figs. 9.18a-c	*Peggy Sue Got Married* (1986)	310
Fig. 9.19a	*Orpheus* (1949)	310
Fig. 9.20a	*The Reckless Moment* (1949)	310
Fig. 9.21a	*La Ronde* (1950)	311
Figs. 9.22a-f	*Madam de…* (1953)	313
Figs. 9.23a-b	*A Hen in the Wind* (1948)	314
Figs. 9.24a-d	*Tokyo Story* (1953)	316
Figs. 9.25a-d	*Late Spring* (1949)	317
Figs. 9.26a-h	*The Story of Floating Weeds* (1934)	318–319
Figs. 9.27a-g	*Floating Weeds* (1959)	321–322
Figs. 9.28a-c	*An Autumn Afternoon* (1962)	324

List of Tables

Table 6.1   Golden idol chamber—coverage and angles *Raiders of the Lost Ark* (1981)   170

Table 8.1   Associative Point of View (AP) and Optical Point of View (OP) in wide reverses (Chap. 6)   252

1

Introduction: Setting the Scene

Now well into his fifth decade as a film director, Steven Spielberg has established himself as the world's most popular and financially successful feature filmmaker and various box office statistics illustrate this dominance. Six of the films he has directed feature in the all-time top 100 box office revenue list including two in the top ten (Box Office Mojo 2017). *Jaws* (1975), his second feature as director, was the first film to make 100 million dollars at the United States box office in its initial release while the huge profits from his next film, *Close Encounters of the Third Kind* (1977), literally rescued Columbia Pictures from bankruptcy (Phillips 1991).[1] Overall, the films he has directed have earned almost 10 billion dollars at the box office (Forbes 2017).

Published at the end of the 1970s, Michael Pye and Lynda Myles' *The Movie Brats* identified six directors—Francis Coppola, Martin Scorsese, George Lucas, Brian De Palma, John Milius and Spielberg—and characterised them as the new heirs to Hollywood. The label arose from their collective youth, box office successes and high degree of cine-literacy. The authors also suggested that these six were 'pure' filmmakers, from film schools (except Spielberg) and not sullied by a previous career in television like many of the other directors working in Hollywood at the time.[2] Together with his movie brat, 'New Hollywood' contemporaries,

© The Author(s) 2018
J. Mairata, *Steven Spielberg's Style by Stealth*,
https://doi.org/10.1007/978-3-319-69081-0_1

Spielberg's unprecedented early box office success helped to financially reinvigorate Hollywood after its decline in the late 1960s, when the recession of 1969 had precipitated some 200 million dollars in losses and widespread retrenchments. This deterioration continued into the following decade with 1971 recording the industry's all-time lowest box office revenue while Universal and Columbia teetered on the edge of insolvency, and MGM, Warner Brothers and United Artists all changed management (Cook 2000, pp. 9–14).

Spielberg's early popularity was so spectacular that it has evolved into almost mythical status. With *Jaws* (1975), Spielberg is widely perceived to have initiated the blockbuster phenomenon that now dominates the American industry (Shone 2004). Yet Sheldon Hall and Steve Neale (2010) claim that while *Jaws* was the most successful blockbuster, it was not the first. Box office takings for 1974—the year before *Jaws*—set an all-time record with the strong performance of *The Exorcist, Chinatown, That's Entertainment* and the disaster films *Earthquake, The Towering Inferno* and *Juggernaut* (all 1974). The year 1974 also saw the highest average weekly attendances in ten years: 'Variety [the Hollywood trade paper] referred to the industry as now being "devoted to the blockbuster business" with "blockbuster pictures" and "blockbuster advertising campaigns"' (Hall and Neale 2010, p. 212). Ironically, Spielberg's first feature, *The Sugarland Express* (1974), had been released in the middle of this period. Minimal marketing and other factors[3] meant that it was quickly overwhelmed by the blockbusters and other hits such as *Serpico* (1973), *The Exorcist* (1974), *The Sting* (1974), *Papillon* (1974) and *American Graffiti* (1974). *Jaws* had originally been budgeted at 3.5 million dollars, approximately the average for a studio feature during this period, but the cost tripled (Bart 1999, p. 124) because of the often-reported production difficulties generally attributed to a combination of the added difficulty of shooting at sea and the malfunctioning special effects sharks. The decision to open the film in wide release backed by an aggressive television advertising campaign rather than the then-customary practice of gradually increasing the number of cinemas showing the film was made by Universal Studio's then owner, Lew Wasserman, not Spielberg (Shone 2004, p. 26). This pattern of wide release coupled with a saturation advertising campaign had already been used the year before for the re-release of *Billy Jack* (1974). David Cook (2000, p. 42) notes that this kind of saturation booking had actually been applied since the 1940s on 'stiffs', films that were expected to perform poorly and so were quickly given wide release to recoup as much revenue as possible before word-of-mouth and poor reviews compromised admissions.

Further colouring the perception of the movie brats and Spielberg as all-conquering, Peter Kramer (1998) notes some inconsistency over which period 'New Hollywood' actually represents:

> ...in different critical contexts 'New Hollywood' may refer to the period 1967–75 as well as to the post-1975 period, to the aesthetic and political progressivism of the liberal cycles of the earlier period as well as to the regressiveness of the blockbusters of the later period. (p. 303)

He also queries the 'newness' of the 'New Hollywood' era by pointing out that 'juvenilzation', the role of technology in enhancing cinematic presentation, and the emphasising of spectacle over narrative had all been going on since the 1950s and were as such part of a longer term cycle that predated the 1970s revival. Geoff King (2002, pp. 12–13) isolates the period in Hollywood from 1967 to the mid to late 1970s as the 'Hollywood Renaissance' period that arose due to a conjunction of social, industrial and stylistic change. Thomas Schatz (1993, p. 9) argues that the 'sustained economic vitality' of the 'blockbuster syndrome' since the mid-1970s justifies the 'New Hollywood' label. Thomas Elsaesser (1998, p. 191) identifies three elements that defined the 'New Hollywood', namely, a new generation of movie directors that included the movie brats, new marketing strategies relating to distribution and exhibition of the 'high concept' blockbuster, and the corporate takeover of the studios and the rise of the star/film packaging system. Noël Carroll (1998a, p. 257) adds that the conditions that enabled the rise of the New Hollywood as a phenomenon had begun with the decline of the audience from the mid-1940s, the theatre-antitrust action, the multiple box-office failures of expensive films in the mid-1960s and the passing of the studio moguls.

Yet there is no denying that as each of his contemporaries has fallen by the wayside, Spielberg's critical esteem, power and influence within the film industry have continued to grow. Of the original movie brats, only

Scorsese and Spielberg are still releasing features regularly. Despite the enormous impact of the *Star Wars* films on popular culture, Lucas has directed only six features and in 2013 announced his retirement from directing. Other contemporaries who enjoyed popular success during the 1970s such as Peter Bogdanovich (his recent work is mostly in television) and William Friedkin (he has directed two features in the past ten years) failed to preserve their popular success beyond that decade. Even Robert Zemeckis—considered a Spielberg protégé and the nearest rival in all-time box office earnings—has failed to sustain the popularity he enjoyed with a string of box office hits during the 1980s and 1990s. Though not considered part of the mainstream industry, only Woody Allen[4] surpasses Spielberg in terms of volume as a director, managing to consistently release a low-budget feature almost every year since the 1970s.

If we go beyond Spielberg's work as a director and consider all of the film industry production in which he has had some kind of involvement, his output can only be described as prolific. In addition to the 30[5] features he has directed, he has amassed more than 150 producing or executive producing credits for features, television series, documentaries and video games; has written three produced feature screenplays[6] and received numerous story credits for features and television series; is the long-time head of Amblin Entertainment—itself responsible for more than 500 individual productions—and was co-head of DreamWorks Pictures for 11 years until its sale in 2005.[7] This, together with the enduring popularity of both his previous and newer films and their related promotion and marketing, has helped ensure that Spielberg's presence within popular culture remains ubiquitous. His reputation as a box office titan is so well established within the realm of entertainment culture that mainstream filmmakers in other countries who experience a run of repeated box-office success are quickly labelled after him—Luc Besson as the French Spielberg, Tsui Hark the Hong Kong Spielberg and so on.[8]

Not only does Spielberg clearly know how to direct films that almost always attract a wide audience, he has managed to do so consistently for more than 40 years—a sustained period of popular success unmatched in Hollywood. In terms of combining success and longevity, John Ford likely comes the closest with a career that spanned six decades and some 130 films though he never really achieved the spectacular box office with individual films in the way that Spielberg has. Similarly, a number of other directors including Alfred Hitchcock (53 features over six decades) and Howard Hawks (40 features over four decades) enjoyed long careers that included extended periods of popularity and success.

Following on from the uncertainty and multiple box-office failures of the late 1960s, Cook (2000) points out that Hollywood returned to the relative safety of the genre film in the 1970s. This study cannot devote the required space to adequately consider the complex area of genre study such as the debate surrounding 'pure' genre (Staiger 2000, p. 65). Therefore, the following represents some 'basic' definitions of genre in relation to Spielberg and classical cinema. Thomas Schatz (2004) notes that at a rudimentary level, film genre represents an understood 'contract' between filmmaker and the audience. Drawing on the analogy with language, he isolates three basic levels of genre: the characteristics common to all genre film and therefore to all genres, the characteristics common to the films in one genre and, third, the characteristics that separate one genre film from all other films. Schatz specifies the significance of the arrangement and combinations of character, setting, plot structure and conflict within a given film 'It is this system of conventions—familiar characters performing familiar actions which celebrate familiar values— that represents the genre's narrative context, its meaningful cultural community' (pp. 692–699). Steve Neale (2000) proposes an even broader, more generalised sense of genre:

> …'genre' and 'generic' are multifaceted concepts and terms: if genre can mean 'category', generic can mean 'constructed or marked for commercial consumption'; If genre can mean 'corpus', generic can mean 'conventionally comprehensible'; if genre can mean 'formula', generic can mean 'those aspects of representation that entail the generation of expectations'; and so on. (p. 252)

The genre film proved less risky for studios and could be more easily packaged, promoted and marketed worldwide. Genre film provided an audience with an immediately recognisable experience and clear differentiation between types of films, a condition most clearly realised in the related rise of the sequel, remakes and the movie series (Neale 2000,

p. 27). New Hollywood examples have included two *Jaws* sequels, remakes of *King Kong* (1976/2009), movie series such as the *Dirty Harry* (1973–83) sequels and the on-going James Bond 'franchise' (1962-present). Sequels, remakes and 'spin-offs' are now produced so frequently that a feature like *The Hulk* (2003) can be remade only five years later as *The Incredible Hulk* (2008), though this pales in comparison to the numerous Spiderman sequels and remakes and multiple character and plot combinations created for the Marvel and DC Comics movies. Story concepts are conceived as multiple films as with *The Lord of the Rings* (2001–2003), *Harry Potter* (2001–2011), *The Hobbit* (2012–2014) and the *Star Wars* (1976–present) 'universe'. Spielberg has been a key participant in the rise of the sequel via the *Indiana Jones* (1981–2008) films—currently at four released titles—and the *Jurassic Park* (1993–2015) series, which will expand to five films with the scheduled release of a new title in 2018.[9]

Carroll (1998a, p. 269) also identifies the return of the genre film as directly related to the arrival of the movie brats and characterises the audience for these films as fitting into two categories: a young (largely youth) audience[10] and the 'connoisseur' viewer, knowledgeable of the embedded references to other films or contexts. Carroll has labelled this concept of an awareness of cinema, of a 'cine-literacy' as 'allusionism'.

> …an umbrella term covering a mixed lot of practices including quotations, the memorialization of past genres, the reworking of past genres, homages, and the recreation of 'classic' scenes, shots, plot motifs, lines of dialogue, themes gestures, and so forth from film history, especially as that history was crystallized and codified in the sixties and early seventies. (p. 241)

Allusionism was central to the relationship between the movie brat directors, the films they were making and audiences. As the term movie brats implies and like their audiences, all of these directors where young in the 1970s—all under 30 at the time of their first feature with Spielberg the youngest at 25 for *The Sugarland Express* and still under 30 at the release of *Jaws*. Also important was the role played by television in exposing both the emerging filmmakers and audiences to the history of Hollywood cinema.

...television's 'archiving' of classical cinema by constantly recycling studio-era film helped to form the new Hollywood historical consciousness—that unique sense of retrospection that informs the work of nearly every major figure of the 70s from Altman through Spielberg—becoming a major part of demarcation between the 'old' Hollywood and the new. (Cook 2000, p. 173)

As with many of the American '1960s auteur' directors that were heavily influenced by the influx of European art-cinema occurring around the same time,[11] the movie brats also claimed to be similarly influenced.[12] Spielberg was the exception and he has often expressed an affinity for Hollywood's golden period 'I'm really interested in films from around 1933 to 1954. And then I sort of go off films for a while—you know, from the mid-fifties until the early seventies' (Taylor 1994, p. 12). This suggests a further correlation between the types of films he was making in the 1970s and the audiences for them. Spielberg's popular success continued into the 1980s with *Raiders of the Lost Ark* (1981) and *E.T.* (1982), still his most successful film. With the exception of two *Raiders* sequels the remainder of the 1980s proved to be a lean period by Spielberg standards. This changed in 1993 with the critical and commercial success of *Schindler's List* (1993) and the enormous popularity of *Jurassic Park* (1993). The 1990s continued to be a successful decade with a popular *Jurassic Park* sequel in 1997 and a second Academy Award for the popular *Saving Private Ryan* (1998). The 2000s also saw a number of strong performers at the box office with *Minority Report* (2002), *Catch Me if You Can* (2002), *War of the Worlds* (2005) and another *Raiders* sequel in 2008.

Spielberg's directing career can essentially be divided into three stages: *Commercial*—from early television until *Raiders of the Lost Ark* (1981). This includes his first successes where his repeated claims of wanting to appeal to a mass audience are most fully realised. *The Sugarland Express* (1974) is the aberration in this group and was really a result of the earlier 'Hollywood Renaissance' period from the mid-1960s that was so heavily influenced by European art-cinema. *1941* (1979), contrary to expectation, was not popular. The second stage is the *Search for Respect* and begins with the unexpected success of *E.T.* (1982) and ends with the critical and industry recognition for *Schindler's List* (1993). Films like *The Color Purple* (1985) '…my first grown-up film…' (Schickel 2007) and *Empire of the Sun* (1987) were attempts by Spielberg to demonstrate that he was capable of dealing with 'adult' subject matter. The third stage is *Authoritative* and covers the period after *Schindler's List* until the present. Having achieved the desired industry recognition, Spielberg has consolidated his power and influence in Hollywood by seeking to generate a more eclectic variety of projects—both commercial and small scale—that display a range of subject matter and genre versatility. Included here is his first foray into directing feature animation with *The Adventures of Tintin* (2011), together with the more traditional concept-driven, action-based, commercial fare of *Jurassic Park* (1993), *Minority Report* and *War of the Worlds*. Also interspersed are the character-centred dramas of *Amistad* (1997), *A. I.* (2001), *Catch Me if You Can*, *The Terminal* (2004), *Munich* (2005), *War Horse* (2011), *Lincoln* (2012), *Bridge of Spies* (2015) and *The BFG* (2016). These later films have also tended to not attract the kind of box office traditionally associated with Spielberg and this decline is best exemplified with *The BFG*, Spielberg's least profitable film since the expensively produced *Hook* (1991).

Yet why have so many of Spielberg's films enjoyed such great popularity? King (2002) offers a fairly typical, culturally based explanation:

> A coincidence of the personal concerns of the director and wider issues in the society might be one way of explaining the degree and consistency of box-office success enjoyed by a figure such a Spielberg. (p. 108)

Also significant is the highly formalised, Hollywood production system that exists purely to maximise audience reach.

> Spielberg' blockbusters, contrary to much contemporary Hollywood practice, cater for a wide audience, offering different pleasures to children (for the last decade much less so), teenagers, parents, 'serious' adult filmgoers and knowledgeable fans, which partly explains their profitability. Furthermore, blanket promotion, comparatively cheap per capita, exploits this potential and supports more specialised marketing to targeted subgroups, and creates a media 'event'. (Morris 2007, p. 378)

Before an audience even sees a film, marketing undertakes the complex construction of 'preferred readings' and 'preferred meanings' via the generation of 'paratextual' (Cook 2000) and 'pre-compositional' (Bordwell 1989, p. 376) information utilising a complex range of publicity structures across multiple delivery platforms and forms. Bordwell cites sources, influences, clichés and received forms as all impacting on the audience's perception of a film before they view it. Steve Neale (2000, p. 39) draws on John Ellis' term 'narrative image' to describe the intended, preconceived perception of a film through publicity. Even less tangible factors such as '…tapping into a national trend or sentiment…' (Wyatt 1994, p. 15) can significantly modify preconceived viewer perception. Caldwell (2008, pp. 299–306) points to the evolution of publicity in the internet age that now bypasses the newspaper, magazine and television editors and reviewers—the 'gatekeepers' of traditional media—in favour of 'viral marketing', the 'leaking' of gossip, reviews, fake reviews and even the embedding of additional online content relating to new releases. Integral to this process is 'wunderkind director Steven Spielberg' (Schatz 1993, p. 17), not only as filmmaker but as a brand.

Then there are the films themselves, their subject matter, genre and context within the marketplace—how they compare and/or contrast to other releases and to Spielberg's own films. Their consumption upon release also creates an additional set of discourses that can confirm, complement or contradict the already 'pre-prepared' interpretations. Much has already been written about these aspects of Spielberg's films together with the many reviews and essays based within an interpretive context, which examine narrative signification centred on thematic, cultural and/or ideological perspectives and their role in popularising the films and why they connect with an audience.

Little study has been devoted to exploring the contribution of style in determining how the films are constructed and how this may contribute to their popularity. This may be due in large part precisely *to* Spielberg's popularity. Writing about Hollywood in the early 1970s, V. F. Perkins (1993) observed:

> …the notion that the cinema offers two distinct phenomena, one important, called art, and the other, trivial, known as entertainment. In its crudest

form it amounts to the belief that the quality of a film is inversely proportional to the size of its audience. (p. 162)

Kristin Thompson (1988, p. 8) similarly identifies the high art, low art distinction in relation to neoformalism and the historically imbued sense that low or popular art lacks aesthetic sophistication largely because of its popularity and therefore does not qualify for serious consideration. That the brief, late 1960s Hollywood flirtation with art-cinema was—to some extent—terminated by the movie brats of which Spielberg's wildly popular 'bubblegum blockbusters'[13] played a large part, can only have further intensified the artistic disdain levelled at his cinema, and his earlier films in particular. His expressions of populist sentiment would likely also have contributed to the sense of critical derision: 'I want everybody to enjoy my films' (McBride 1997, p. 155), and 'I've always made the kinds of films that I as an audience would want to see' (Dialogue on Film 1988). Considering *Raiders of the Lost Ark, E. T.* and a number of other popular films, Stanley J. Solomon (1989) writes:

> The narrative elements in such films are chronologically arranged incidents that, given the premises, could happen but have no tragic or comic necessity for happening—the causes stemming not from story but from an available mixed bag of general emotions, special effects and faith in production values. So, ultimately, these films do not matter because they are rooted not in the patterns of life but in the fantasies of daydreams designed to embody a sentiment. (p. 65)

This perceived lack of artistic sophistication is further magnified when one factors in the dominant perception of Hollywood film as already lacking in any kind of stylistic artistry other than that generated by visual effects and expensive action sequences.

> Individual filmmaker's agency is not usually considered in explaining style—style is often not considered at all—and mainstream commercial filmmakers less so. (Bordwell 2005)

Is there some aspect or aspects of Spielberg's directing technique—effectively his use of style—that contributes in some way to making his films popular and more accessible to an audience? If so, what are these strategies and how does he actively (intentionally) manipulate style to achieve intended outcomes? While critical response has long acknowledged the role of style in Spielberg's films (often without realising its actual function), just how significant this role is has always been either glossed over, considered in a derogatory way or both. From Pauline Kael's (1994) review of Spielberg's first feature *The Sugarland Express* (1974) where she questions whether '…he [Spielberg] may be so full of it that he doesn't have much else' (p. 559); to James Monaco's (1979) labelling of the blockbuster phenomenon as having a 'Bruce esthetic',[14] '…machines of entertainment, precisely calculated to achieve their effect' (p. 50); to an examination of the 'realness' of *Saving Private Ryan* (1998) that asserts 'According to some reviewers, Spielberg was also successful in achieving one of his other aims, of abandoning his famed sentimentality and manipulative style…' (Haggith 2002, p. 334). King (2002) weighs in with a general summary: 'His films tend to be filled with very smooth transitions and slick visual matches, coupled with dynamic use of continuity editing patterns' (p. 106).

Part of the objective of this study is to reverse the perception of these often uninformed and somewhat clichéd criticisms of Spielberg's films in relation to his application of style. I instead argue that the very narratives that are '…precisely calculated to achieve their effect…' or that have '…manipulative style…' actually suggest the operation of complex levels of narrative construction. As Spielberg has expressed 'Everything about movies is manipulative; when you walk into the theatre you're buying a ticket to manipulation!' (Ebert and Siskel 1991, p. 76). For Spielberg, the level of craft in his film is so highly developed, so carefully 'polished' as to be largely rendered transparent. Critics instead grasp at the thematic and symptomatic components of the films to produce a range of clichéd perceptions of his films—and of him—as child-like, naïve and sentimental. This preoccupation with seeing him in the film or the film in him only further distracts from appreciating the significant role of style.

Logically, breaking down a narrative should assist in our understanding of how and why it functions: 'Unravelling the form of a film explains how it is capable of making its intended points and actualizing its purposes' (Carroll 1998b, p. 399). I argue that a key component in this unravelling involves understanding how Spielberg constructs scenographic space. Spielberg often constructs space in a unique way through a combination of deep space compositions and the use of reverse masters in a system that I describe as *wide reverses*. I further contend that this system of constructing space has important implications for how an audience cognitively perceives a narrative constructed using this wide reverse strategy. Understanding how stylistic strategies such as wide reverses contribute to spectator comprehension may also assist in understanding how certain stylistic devices function cognitively.

Essentially, this study has three key objectives: To identify and define how Spielberg uses style and specifically constructs scenographic space utilising a combination of deep space composition, staging and the wide reverse as strategy; to understand how this functions to assist in narrative construction; and to understand how this operation encourages a more immersive, more 'complete' form of audience comprehension and affective engagement. Additional objectives include understanding how Spielberg is able to mobilise these strategies within the 'confines' and 'restrictions' of classical practice and convention and positioning him within an historical context of classical practice that explains why and how he has appropriated existing classical devices and modified them into an essentially unique set of stylistic strategies.

The ten chapters in this book are divided into three sections. Part I: Origin includes Chaps. 2, 3 and 4 and establishes the fundamentals required for this study. In Chap. 2, I define and elaborate on the methodological approach that I employ in the examination of Spielberg's style. My focus is on the aspect of cinematic poetics that includes Bordwell's 'constructivist' account of how narratives are created, how they function and how they have evolved—all key elements in the operation and understanding of style. As mainstream style is concerned principally with constructing narrative, a definition of this type of narration is required and I consider a range of definitions ranging from Bordwell's canonical, cause-effect model, to criticisms of it as well as variations and alternatives. Also necessary is an explanation and definition of style itself as it exists in the mainstream—what it is, and what it does. I conclude the chapter with a consideration of the significance of scenographic space and off-screen space in classical cinema.

Deducing how Spielberg constructs narrative requires an understanding of what it means to call Spielberg the *director* of feature films and this is examined in Chap. 3. Critical perception—due undoubtedly to his success—automatically assumes his role is as author—auteur—of his films. This also has implications for degrees of intentionality and the notion of Spielberg as rational-agent. Is it possible to definitively accord him auteur status while also acknowledging his career-long collaboration with key creatives such as film editor Michael Kahn, composer John Williams, producer Kathleen Kennedy and his later association with stars like Tom Cruise and Tom Hanks? Spielberg's financial pragmatism also plays a significant role in how he makes his films, informing, for instance, his preference for shooting quickly but with extensive coverage. This is then sometimes reflected in scene construction where the integration of multiple masters is evident. Spielberg's celebrity inevitably permeates through his films and I argue that this manifests at the level of narration with the identification of the filmmaker as camera. This creates a direct conflict with the traditionally suppressed visibility of style in classical cinema and also explains why Spielberg compensates through the use of the wide reverse and its additional function relating to the implied absence of the camera and therefore of the author.

The analysis of Spielberg's style begins in Chap. 4 where I consider the classical continuity system and demonstrate how Spielberg's style appears to function conventionally within the accepted norms of the shot, reverse shot and point-of-view arrangement. The analysis of a scene from *Munich* (2005) underlines Spielberg's preference for shooting multiple masters but also reveals the potential for innovative variation with his unique, two-stage process derived from (1) deep space and (2) wide reverse constructions.

The next three chapters are grouped into Part II, Function, and examine Spielberg's style in detail. Chapter 5 initially examines the historical development of deep space composition and staging in classical cinema and how its use has declined since the advent of the New Hollywood in the early 1970s. Spielberg is one of the few active filmmakers in the classical sphere who has consistently embraced deep space configurations and this aspect of his practice in itself sets him apart from most of his contemporaries. The remainder of the chapter identifies and examines a total of seven variations in deep space compositions that Spielberg utilises across his cinema.

Considering the second stage (wide reverses) occupies the next two chapters. Chapter 6 examines how Spielberg has adapted the continuity principles of the conventional shot, reverse shot system to create the wide reverse. Together with the integration of deep space compositions, Spielberg is able to use wide reverses to construct a comprehensive scenographic space that creates a more 'complete' and thus convincing world of the film. Through the examination of eight instances of wide reverses categorised as type A, I detail the system's additional perceptual advantages including the erasing of the camera's presence and therefore also of the narrator, thus permitting greater spectator immersion; the negating of Kuleshov's pyramid and a greater role for foregrounding; an improved perception of shape in objects; and the punctuation of events made possible via the 'cine-tableau'.

The second set of wide reverse variations are considered in Chap. 7. Type B variations retain many of the characteristics found in the type A wide reverses but are structured as single reverses and single shot reverses. The former involves isolated pairs of shots in which the first shot is then reversed by the second. The latter is constructed out of a single, moving shot that alters the angle seen at the beginning of the shot, gradually reversing the vista so that a 180-degree reversal is achieved by the end of the shot.

Chapters 8 and 9 make up the final section, Part III: Effect, Affect and Precedent. In Chap. 8 I employ cognitive theory and emotion 'theory' to determine how the wide reverse is perceptually processed and how it contributes to generating spectator affect. Divided into two sections, the first examines how the wide reverse mobilises a number of functions including match-on-action cutting and what I label as *associative point-of-view* (AP) perspectives to help 'disguise' the perceived presence of editing. Films are popular primarily because of their success in stimulating emotional responses from audiences (Plantinga 2009, p. 5; Carroll 2013, p. 85). The second section studies how Spielberg uses style to generate affect and here also devices such as AP and repeated referencing of character faces features as important strategies.

Chapter 9 traces the origin of the wide reverse in mainstream cinema and surveys the narratives of other filmmakers that display instances of wide reverses to determine the relative uniqueness of Spielberg's own system. While isolated examples exist in the films of directors such as Peter Greenaway, Takeshi Kitano, Michael Mann, Stanley Kubrick and Buster Keaton, more extensive instances appear in films by Alfred Hitchcock, Carl Theodore Dreyer and Max Ophuls. Yasujiro Ozu—unlikely as it may seem—exhibits the greatest similarity in his application of wide reverses with those of Spielberg, although Ozu's display far fewer variations.

Joseph McBride (2009) argues that the recent re-evaluation of Spielberg's films has led to a new-found appreciation of the level of craft. He notes that Spielberg has suffered the same fate as Hitchcock and Hawkes, who were not initially respected as artists because of their popularity. Barry Salt (2006) maintains that three elements should be considered when evaluating the 'value' of a film: how well the filmmakers realise their intentions; the level of narrative and stylistic complexity and/or intricacy; and the influence the film exerts on other films (2006, pp. 21–22). If we instead apply these criteria to Spielberg's skills as director then the enduring popularity of his films answers the first and third points. Explaining the second criterion with an emphasis on stylistic explication is the task of the following chapters.

Notes

1. Philips, producer of *Close Encounters*, provides an account of the film's ballooning budget and the studio's deteriorating financial situation.
2. This seemingly glosses over Spielberg's own origin in television.
3. Spielberg identifies three factors that contributed to the film's failure: perception of it was confused and it was lumped together with the 'thematically similar' and similarly poor performing *Badlands* (1974) and *Thieves Like Us* (1974); it was released during one of the most highly competitive seasons seen for many years; the film was poorly marketed with a campaign that tried to exploit the comedic star appeal of Goldie Hawn, which also misrepresented the nature of the film itself. Nigel

Morris (2007, p. 40) also notes that any momentum from the film's mostly positive reviews was largely lost when Universal delayed its release some five months so that it not compete with their own *The Sting*.
4. Allen's unique contract stipulates only that he produce at least one feature per year within a certain budget. All other factors including all creative aspects are controlled entirely by him (Bjorkman 1993, p. xii).
5. *Duel* (1971) is included as it was lengthened for cinema release.
6. *Close Encounters of the Third Kind* (1977), *Poltergeist* (1982) and *A.I. Artificial Intelligence* (2000).
7. Spielberg also serves as the chairman of Amblin Partners. Formed in late 2015, the company is a partnership among Dreamworks Pictures, Participant Media, Reliance Entertainment and Entertainment One.
8. The comparison of Besson and Tsui to Spielberg extends beyond popularity and includes commonalities such as genre (action/adventure), style, success at a young age, and involvement in writing and producing of their own and others' productions.
9. Disney has announced that both Spielberg and star Harrison Ford will return for a fifth Indiana Jones film to be released mid-2019 (McClintock 2016). Spielberg directed only the first two *Jurassic Park* films, *Jurassic Park* (1993) and its sequel, *The Lost World: Jurassic Park* (1997).
10. By 1977, 50% of the cinema-going audience was under the age of 25 and a large proportion of these were teenagers (Carroll 1998a).
11. Among them: Bob Rafelson, John Cassevettes, Arthur Penn, Robert Altman, Hal Ashby, William Friedkin and John Boorman. Boorman laments the passing of the mid-1960s to early 1970s period of Hollywood 'experimentation' (Carroll 1998a, p. 269), which saw the rise and fall of the studio sanctioned, European influenced, American art-cinema. 'What changed everything was the success of Spielberg's and Lucas's films, because the studios suddenly realised that the audience was composed of teenagers, and they went after that audience, and suddenly they knew what their function was' (Cowie 2004, p. 229).
12. George Lucas claimed that the characters R2D2 and C3PO from the *Star Wars* films were in fact inspired by the two comic peasants in Kurosawa's *The Hidden Fortress* (1965).
13. This label is attributed to critic J. Hoberman (Cook 2000, p. 23) and further exemplifies the critical condescension directed at the modern Hollywood cinema.
14. Bruce was the name given by Spielberg to the mechanical shark in *Jaws*.

References

Bart, P. (1999). *The Gross*. New York: St. Martin's Griffiin.
Bjorkman, S. (1993). *Woody Allen on Woody Allen*. New York: Grove Press.
Bordwell, D. (1989). Historical Poetics of Cinema. In R. B. Palmer (Ed.), *The Cinematic Text* (pp. 369–398). New York: AMS Press, Inc.
Bordwell, D. (2005). *Figures Traced in Light: On Cinematic Staging*. Los Angeles: University of California Press.
Box Office Mojo. (2017). *All Time Domestic Grosses* (Adjusted for Inflation). Retrieved from http://www.boxofficemojo.com/alltime/adjusted.htm
Caldwell, J. T. (2008). *Production Culture: Industrial Reflexivity and Critical Practice in Film and Television*. Durham: Duke University/Durham Press.
Carroll, N. (1998a). *Interpreting the Moving Image*. New York: Cambridge University Press.
Carroll, N. (1998b). Film Form: An Argument for a Functional Theory of Style in the Individual Film. *Style, 32*(3), 385–401. Retrieved from EBSCOhost Academic Search Premier.
Carroll, N. (2013). *Minerva's Night Out: Philosophy, Pop Culture, and Moving Pictures*. Malaysia: Wiley Blackwell.
Cook, D. A. (2000). *Lost Illusions: American Cinema in the Shadow of Watergate and Vietnam 1970–1979*. Los Angeles: University of California Press.
Cowie, P. (2004). *Revolution! The Explosion of World Cinema in the Sixties*. New York: Faber and Faber Inc.
Dialogue on Film: Steven Spielberg [Print Interview]. (1988). *American Film, 13*(8), 12–16.
Ebert, R., & Siskel, G. (1991). *The Future of the Movies*. Kansas City: Andrews & McMeel.
Elsaesser, T. (1998). Specularity and Engulfment: Francis Ford Coppola and Bram Stoker's Dracula. In S. Neale & M. Smith (Eds.), *Contemporary Hollywood Cinema* (pp. 191–208). London/New York: Routledge.
Forbes/Profile/Steven Spielberg. (2017). Retrieved from https://www.forbes.com/profile/steven-spielberg/
Haggith, T. (2002). D-Day Filming: For Real. A Comparison of 'Truth' and 'Reality' in Saving Private Ryan and Combat Film by the British Army's Film and Photographic Unit. *Film History, 14*(3/4), 332–353. Retrieved from http://www.jstor.org/stable/3815436
Hall, S., & Neale, S. (2010). *Epics Spectacles and Blockbusters*. Detroit: Wayne State University Press.

Kael, P. (1994). *For Keeps: 30 Years at the Movies*. New York: Plume/Penguin Books.

King, G. (2002). *New Hollywood Cinema: An Introduction*. London: L.B. Tauris.

Kramer, P. (1998). Post-Classical Hollywood. In J. Hill & P. C. Gibson (Eds.), *The Oxford Guide to Film Studies* (pp. 289–309). New York: Oxford University Press.

McBride, J. (1997). *Steven Spielberg: A Biography*. New York: Simon and Schuster.

McBride, J. (2009). A Reputation: Steven Spielberg and the Eyes of the World. *New Review of Film and Television Studies, 7*(1), 1–11. Retrieved from https://doi.org/10.1080/17400300802602833

McClintock, P. (2016). Harrison Ford, Steven Spielberg to Return for Fifth 'Indiana Jones' Movie. *The Hollywood Reporter*. Retrieved from http://www.hollywoodreporter.com/news/disney-announces-fifth-indiana-jones-875794

Monaco, J. (1979). *American Film Now: The People, The Power, The Money, The Movies*. New York: Oxford University Press.

Morris, N. (2007). *The Cinema of Steven Spielberg Empire of Light*. London: Wallflower Press.

Neale, S. (2000). *Genre and Hollywood*. London/New York: Routledge.

Perkins, V. F. (1993). *Film as Film: Understanding and Judging Movies*. New York: Da Capo Press, Inc.

Phillips, J. (1991). *You'll Never Eat Lunch in This Town Again*. New York: New American Library.

Plantinga, C. (2009). *Moving Viewers: American Film and the Spectator's Experience*. Berkeley/Los Angeles: University of California Press.

Salt, B. (2006). *Moving Into Pictures*. London: Starword.

Schatz, T. (1993). The New Hollywood. In J. Collins, H. Radner, & A. P. Collins (Eds.), *Film Theory Goes to the Movies*. Abingdon: Routledge.

Schatz, T. (2004). Film Genre and the Genre Film. In L. Braudy & M. Cohen (Eds.), *Film Theory and Criticism* (pp. 691–702). New York: Oxford University Press.

Schickel, R. (Writer & Director). (2007). *Spielberg on Spielberg* [DVD documentary]. United States: Turner Classic Movies.

Shone, T. (2004). *Blockbuster*. London: Simon and Schuster.

Solomon, S. J. (1989). Aristotle in Twilight: American Film Narrative in the 1980s. In R. B. Palmer (Ed.), *The Cinematic Text: Methods and Approaches* (pp. 63–80). New York: AMS Press Inc.

Staiger, J. (2000). *Perverse Spectators: The Practices of Film Reception*. New York: New York University Press.
Taylor, P. M. (1994). *Steven Spielberg*. London: B. T. Batsford Ltd.
Thompson, K. (1988). *Breaking the Glass Armor: Neoformalist Film Analysis*. Oxford: Princeton University Press.
Wyatt, J. (1994). *High Concept: Movies and Marketing in Hollywood*. Austin: University of Texas Press.

Part I

Origin

2

Fundamentals of Classical Narration

To understand how Spielberg utilises style to construct narrative, we first need to consider the theoretical components relevant to this study. Contained within the over-arching theory of poetics are fundamental systems such as narration, style and scenographic space. Each needs to be defined and contextualised within the formal system that is mainstream classical cinema.

Cinematic Poetics

Related to the 'underestimation' or disregard for Spielberg's cinema as in any way technically innovative or progressive is the 'interpretive school' (Bordwell 2008, p. 12) nature of the interrogation of cinematic narratives. This is based largely, as Bordwell points out, on literary and linguistic traditions that favour implicit or symptomatic readings that best accommodate the theory with which it is being associated (Psychoanalysis, Marxism, etc.). 'Ideally, our hypotheses are grounded in a theoretical activity rather than a fixed theory' (2008, p. 20). This tradition in cinema studies had functioned to further 'distract' from the legitimate study of

© The Author(s) 2018
J. Mairata, *Steven Spielberg's Style by Stealth*,
https://doi.org/10.1007/978-3-319-69081-0_2

style in mainstream filmmakers. Bordwell's 'poetics of cinema' addresses this with a conception of film theory that is designed to directly consider both 'texts and contexts'. Bordwell draws on a tradition that began with Aristotle's Poetics and has continued through to the Russian formalists and to Kristin Thompson and Bordwell's own reconfiguring of formalism into neoformalism. From the Russian formalists, Victor Shklovsky, Yuri Tynianov and Boris Eikhenbaum, Bordwell appropriates the conception of a focus on style and the 'dominant' as a set of formal organisational principles that govern both individual and sets of artworks; from the Structuralists, Jan Mukarovsky's 'aesthetic norm' as a set of filmic 'conventions' that define a type of filmmaking but which are also susceptible to variation and change; from musicologist Leonard Meyer, Bordwell adapts the idea of filmic style as evolving or developing in different ways and directions (as opposed to the common conception of development as always progressing in a specific direction—such as V.F. Perkins' assertion that progress is about making cinema more 'realistic'); from art-historians Heinrich Wolfflin and Erwin Panofsky, the role of history in contextualising cinematic change; and from E.H. Gombrich the notion of the problem-solution model as driver of change in artworks.

> Any inquiry into the fundamental principles by which artefacts in any representational medium are constructed, and the effects that flow from those principles, can fall within the domain of poetics… poetics is characterised by the phenomena it studies (films' constructional principles and effects) and the questions it asks about these phenomena—their constitution, functions, purposes and historical manifestations. (2008, pp. 12–23)

Bordwell avers that 'traditional poetics' normally considers three areas: thematics, the isolation of themes and subject matter; large scale form, the analysis of how narrative is organised; and stylistics, '…the materials and patterning of the medium as components of the constructive process' (p. 19). He adds that all three areas can be considered but that usually one dominates. Bordwell's own programme distils this into two categories: analytical poetics—the 'principles' fundamental to how films are constructed and the effects they generate; and historical poetics—understanding how and why these 'principles' have changed. Bordwell defines 'principles' as the '...underlying concepts governing the sorts of material that can be used in a film and the possible ways in which it can be formed' (p. 16).

Crucial to my own application of poetics to Spielberg's cinema is Bordwell's incorporation of the rational-agent and problem-solution elements into his model. The former acknowledges the potentiality of the filmmaker as an 'intentionalist' force (p. 16) in the filmmaking process '...most textual effects are the result of deliberate and founding choices, and these affect form, style, and different sorts of meaning' (1989, p. 269). This implies responsibility for certain constructional strategies that shape the narrative as opposed to traditional theories that position cinema within an ideologically or teleologically preordained pathway of evolution and development. The problem-solution component likewise identifies the filmmaker as capable of targeting and responding to certain complexities in constructing narrative and replacing or modifying prior practices with revised ones. Central to Spielberg's stylistic innovation is his application of the well-established convention of the deep space composition; his modification and application of the shot, reverse shot convention—now expressed as wide reverse—and the 'novelty' arising from the *combining* of both these 'norms' and the effect this has on the construction and perception of scenographic space and meaning. André Bazin traced the development and use of both editing (montage[1]) and deep space in classical cinema in what Bordwell describes as a 'narrational dialectic'—two stylistic systems that construct narration via different means. Bazin cited Orson Welles as an American example of a director who combined both systems in his narratives. The domination of editing in contemporary classical narration has seen a corresponding decline in the use of deep space decoupage.[2] Spielberg is one of the very few directors working in the classical system who similarly and consistently draws on two established classical systems to construct scenographic space. He ascribes to his own version of a narrational dialectic through his strategy of 'fusing' wide reverses and deep space compositions.

The context provided by an historical poetics is also expressed through an understanding of how and why these conventions functioned within mainstream narrative and the craft tradition that was Hollywood prior to Spielberg. Providing a 'before and after' will further illustrate the nature of his innovation and allow us to ask '...how does the work fit into a tradition and how does it repeat, reuse or reject its forerunners?' (Bordwell 2008, p. 22). The influences of a highly codified industry dynamic and the systemised practice of Hollywood filmmaking on Spielberg's craft choices need to be considered as significant factors in the shaping of his use of style. Also relevant to the application of Bordwell's poetics to Spielberg is the study of systems relating to spectator cognition. While poetics draws on the formalist concept of the active spectator, it includes cognitive theories that provide links between how narrative is constructed and how this directs spectator comprehension. Bordwell orders spectator activity in terms of three processes: perception, comprehension and appropriation, noting that the filmmaker exercises the least control over the latter process. Writing about the cinema of Yasujiro Ozu, Bordwell (1988) affirms the filmmaker as an agent for constructing narrative that imprecisely directs the spectator to perform certain 'activities'.

> Here a film is taken not as 'text' to be 'read' but an artefact to be *used* by the spectator to produce certain *effects*, of which 'meaning' in its most elevated sense (themes, implicit messages) is only one. The work prompts a range of perceptual, emotional and cognitive effects—guidance of attention, establishment of expectations, thwarting of hypothesis, retroactive reconsideration of information—which are essential to the work's uniqueness. (p. 140)

Narration

Within the context of his poetics, Bordwell has identified four 'modes' or historically inflected types of narration that are defined in part by their appropriation of style: classical, art cinema, historical materialist and parametric. The concern of this study only necessitates a consideration of classical narration though some references will be made to art cinema. While Bordwell and his co-authors helped to popularise the term classical narration and classical cinema through their influential text *The Classical Hollywood Cinema* published in 1985, Bordwell notes that the term classical had been applied to Hollywood cinema as early as the 1920s by French critics and filmmakers such as Jean Renoir. This continued into the 1930s with Bazin's (1985) declaration that Hollywood cinema had all the characteristics of a 'classical art', expressed through his famous description of Hollywood as '…the genius of the system, the richness of its ever-vigorous tradition and its fertility, when it comes into contact with new elements…' (p. 258). Bordwell (Staiger and Thompson) provides a justification for the continuing adoption of the term classical to describe mainstream Hollywood narration.

> It seems proper to retain the term in English, since the principles which Hollywood claims as its own rely on notions of decorum, proportion, formal harmony, respect for historical mimesis, self-effacing craftsmanship, and cool control of the perceiver's response—canons which critics in any medium usually call 'classical'. (1985, p. 3)

In *Narration in the Fiction Film*, Bordwell asks a number of questions about the nature of cinematic narration that are pertinent to this study including: how does cinematic narration work and what features and structures solicit narrative construction? Before contemplating these, we first need to arrive at a definition for narration. At its simplest, Edward Branigan (1992) distinguishes between narration and narrative with the former as the telling of a story—how it's told—while the later concerns what is said. 'Narrative—construed narrowly as *what* happens in the story—is then seen as the *object* or end result of some mechanism or process—narration' (p. 65). Bordwell identifies narration as evolving from either the diegetic—a telling—or the mimetic—a showing, in the Aristotelian tradition. Bordwell and Thompson (2008) characterise narrative as the '…chain of events in cause-effect relationship occurring in time and space' (p. 75). Noël Carroll (1988, p. 171) argues for an account of narration based on Pudovkin's question/answer dynamic. Stressing that his 'erotetic' version applies only to mainstream narrative, Carroll contends that popular narratives consist largely of scenes that ask a question or questions, which are then answered in subsequent scenes. This system of question and answer provides a more precise set of potential alternatives than the conventional cause-effect chain that Carroll feels lacks comprehensiveness in explaining how unfolding scenes are explained by causation. Instead, he suggests that in the course of watching narratives, spectators construct a range of possible outcomes that are in fact questions. He then presents an example of an 'idealized erotetic' narrative that can include up to six types of scenes: an establishing scene whose function seems largely expositional; a questioning scene, which may incorporate multiple questions; an answering scene, which may also answer multiple questions; a sustaining scene, which further develops a question or provides more clues to an answer; an incomplete answering scene and an answering/questioning scene where an answer is immediately followed by another question or questions. Carroll further divides the question-answer dynamic into large-scale narrative and 'macro-questions' that may take the entire film to answer and 'micro-questions' that are answered immediately or within a few scenes (p. 178). Tom Gunning (2004) draws on literary critic Gerard Génette and identifies three separate components for narrative: the language of the text telling the story, the events—real or fictitious—that make up the story and the act of someone narrating a story. Echoing Bordwell's mimetic/diegetic distinction, Gunning emphasises filmic narration's prioritising of showing over telling. 'The filmic narrator shapes and defines visual meanings'. Bordwell (2008, p. 90) in turn divides narrative into three separate dimensions: the world of the story including the elements that constitute it, the arrangement of the narrative into a whole and the narration—the process of conveying story information.

> The narration, then, is the force which guides the viewer in the reorganization of the plot into the story, or the construction of the story on the basis of the plot. Moreover, a narration may be usefully described in terms of three principal qualities: knowledgeability, communicativeness, and self-consciousness. (Smith, M. 1995, p. 74)

Attributing the origin of their own definition to Meir Sternberg, Bordwell (Staiger and Thompson 1985, p. 25) similarly describes the significance of the 'three spectra' of mainstream narrative: (1) the level of self-consciousness communicates the degree to which a film recognises it is addressing an audience. (2) Level of knowledge refers to how much a character may know. (3) Level of communicativeness concerns how much the narration is prepared to tell the spectator at any given time about any given incident. Self-consciousness tends to be greater during opening and closing credits where the titles and concentrated exposition function to more or less directly address an audience. A detective may have little knowledge about the circumstances surrounding a crime and must piece together the events—unless recounting the story as a flashback in which case that character as narrator has full knowledge. Likewise, the detective will gradually reveal information to the spectator in the course of the narrative, thus maintaining a limited level of communicativeness to the spectator. The level or degree of the three spectra can vary during the course of a film. In *E.T.* (1983), we know as much about E.T. as does Elliot until the intoxication sequence, where the crosscutting between the two characters permits a high level of communicativeness with the audience having greater knowledge of the event than Elliot. Likewise we always know more about the existence of E.T. and his presence in the house than does Elliot's mother—and part of the humour stems from our greater knowledge and the uncertainty relating to how E.T. manages to remain undetected. In *Close Encounters of the Third Kind* (1977) we only ever know as much as the protagonist, with the level of communicativeness increasing only at the film's climax when the alien ship and its occupants are revealed. Also derived from Sternberg is the process of hypothesis-forming that constitutes a key part of the spectator's activity in processing mainstream narration: 'Hollywood narration asks us to form hypothesis that are highly probable and sharply exclusive' (p. 38). Sternberg isolates three variations in terms of hypothesis creation: that a certain outcome is more or less likely ('boy will get girl'), that there may be multiple, simultaneous hypotheses or that a relatively fixed set of options or potential variations are likely.

Telling a story is the fundamental function of classical narrative and the canonical story dominates as form. Kristin Thompson (1981) notes the Russian formalists' identification of devices in the artwork designed to add complexity to story development. 'Staircase' or 'stair-step' construction involved the use of various techniques such as retardation '…in order to keep them [the artwork] from ending prematurely…they must be delayed, and the devices used to do this tend to turn the action away from a straight path' (p. 34). Along with the Aristotelian requirement that a story have a beginning, a middle and an end, classical narration incorporates a highly structured set of norms that include a goal-orientated plot with character(s) as the central causal agent and motivation as the principle for action.

Paisley Livingston (1996) defines a character 'agent' as '...any entity capable of performing an intentional action' and '...for there to be an actual event or episode of characterization, some actual agent or agents must perform the right sort of representational action'. In a Spielberg film, characters are usually human—though there are some exceptions including Duel, Jaws, *Close Encounters of the Third Kind, E.T., Jurassic Park* (1993), *Jurassic Park: The Lost World* (1997), *A.I.* (2001), *War of the Worlds* (2006), the period film *War Horse* (2011) and *The BFG* (2016). In *Always*, the main character appears for most of the film as a ghost.

Human or not, character behaviour is always motivated 'realistically' as is mise en scene, space and time. Thompson identifies three types of motivation that function to logically justify an action or object: realistic motivation—as relatable to the real world; compositional motivation—derived from the work's specific structure; artistic motivation—where the device itself becomes overt. This type is rarely seen in classical narration and never in a Spielberg narrative. Related to this is the Russian formalists' concept of 'baring the device' where a technical element becomes prominent. Thomas Elsaesser (2012) emphasises both causal logic and character rationality in relation to how narration progresses in a way that is consistent and reflective of the spectator's understanding and experience of 'real' life.

> Hollywood rigorously respects and adheres to a first-level verisimilitude, in which any change of time, of place and action, as well as of a protagonist's goal or purpose is internally motivated, and communicated to the audience through a cinematic language primarily destined to follow, as closely as possible, the dramatic, causal and psychological exigencies of the action. (p. 90)

Related to this is Bordwell's (2008. p. 112) referencing of Marie-Laure Ryan's 'Principle of Minimal Departure', which suggests that we apply our own knowledge and experience of reality to a text unless it directs us otherwise.

Branigan (1992, p. 4) also draws on an Aristotelian concept of film narrative for his explanation: 'Narrative is a way of experiencing a group of sentences or pictures (or gestures or dance movements, etc.) which together attribute a beginning, middle, and end to something'. He further elaborates by citing philosopher Tzvetan Todorov's 'theory of narrative' equilibrium model with its five basic stages. Branigan (pp. 86–87) expands this and Susan Lanser's six levels to eight: (1) an 'abstract' that 'primes' the spectator to construct expectations—encouraged by devices such as the title and the establishing shot; (2) an 'orientation', usually provided by expository devices that establish the present situation but also contextualises relevant past events; (3) the 'initiating event' or 'point of attack' that changes the equilibrium; (4) articulating a 'goal' in response to the initiating event; (5) the rise of the 'complicating action' that creates obstacles and delays; (6) the 'climax' where the goal is achieved; (7) the 'epilogue' where equilibrium is restored. Branigan's (2006) eighth element also seeks to explain the process by which we acquire knowledge as we comprehend the events of an unfolding scenario: 'Generally the spectator engages the text in multiple ways, assuming a variety of roles for different contexts at different times'. Representing a 'hierarchy of relative knowledge', the eight levels are able to accommodate comprehension at both the explicit and implicit as well as account for a range of implied authorial positioning. The eight levels can exist across the range of narrative scale such that all eight can potentially occur in a shot, sequence, scene and so on through to the entire film. He further isolates three 'fields of knowledge'—the narrator, actor and focalizer—as 'agents' that variously share the load of how knowledge is being 'presented' to an audience (1992, p. 106).

Hollywood practice has tended to manifest this narrative process structurally by representing them in sections as acts. Well-known screenplay 'teachers' such as Syd Field and Robert McKee have traditionally advocated the typical Hollywood narrative scenario as consisting of three acts. Act one sets up the characters and introduces the plot, usually together with a 'complicating action' or the initiating event. Act two develops the various lines of action, complete with obstacles and revelations, while the third act brings the story to a climax and restores equilibrium. Thompson (1999, p. 28) argues that the three-act model is not specific enough and that many Hollywood narratives fall more easily into four or five parts. Thompson labels the four-section narrative as setup, complicating action, the development and the climax. Of key importance, as Branigan (1984) notes, is the way Hollywood films strive to be both comprehensible and unambiguous.

Also seemingly subscribing to the question-answer dynamic,[3] Elsaesser identifies variations in the types of narrative logic as applied to cinema. One is the Bordwell narration model, similarly expressed by Branigan and again drawn from Aristotle, with its prioritising of goal-orientated drive, act structures, and developing and resolving action. A second type characterises Hollywood narrative as '…free-standing, self-explanatory, self-sufficient' (Elsaesser 2012, p. 110), which implies that it does not require 'learning' to be understood and that comprehension is largely universal. Elsaesser ascribes this type to Vladimir Propp and his assertion that popular narrative is easily understood[4] partly because of its inherently high degree of repetition and redundancy.

Referencing the Russian formalist division of plot and story, Bordwell (1985, p. 49) uses the terms fabula to describe all of the elements that constitute a complete story and syuzhet[5] as the elements that make up the plot as it is presented in the narrative together with style where style represents the tools used to construct the plot. Bordwell further identifies three areas that relate syuzhet to fabula. The first involves narrative logic, the spectator's activity in recognising and connecting events based on causation; second is temporality where fabula events may be presented in any sequence, order, duration or frequency; third, space where any location depicted and presented by the syuzhet relates directly to fabula space. The syuzhet-fabula division also allows for the easy identification of style's role in narration.

> I take narration to be the process by which the film prompts the viewer to construct the ongoing fabula on the basis of syuzhet organisation and stylistic patterning. (2008 p. 98)

Style is thus a crucial element in the process of narration creation—featuring prominently as the principal component in plot construction that then in turn leads to story coherence and the formation of the narration itself. Yet a key function of classical style depends on its ability to 'hide' behind narration such that the workings of the narration itself become imperceptible, unobtrusive or 'invisible' as Bazin described it. Noël Burch (1973) identifies this feature of classical narration as the 'zero point of cinematic style' (p. 11), with elements such as camerawork supposedly responding to action not initiating it, and editing as unobtrusive and 'seamless'. Early Hollywood established and encouraged this concealment of the artifice to facilitate a sense of 'reality', with the spectator positioned as an 'ideal observer' (Bordwell, Staiger and Thompson 1985, p. 37). Gunning (2004) notes that the intention was to create a sense that '…events seem to narrate themselves…' (p. 478). Geoff King (2002) similarly notes 'Classical conventions invite us, much of the time, to surrender to the pleasurable illusion that we are merely witnesses at the scene, rather than that the scene has been fabricated for us' (p. 41). The implication then is that the world of the film exists independently and regardless of any mediation.

> By virtue of the handling of space and time, classical narrative makes the fabula world an internally consistent construct into which narration seems to step from the outside. Manipulation of mise-en-scene (figure behaviours, lighting, setting, costume) creates an apparently independent profilmic event, which becomes the tangible story world framed and recorded from without. This framing and recording tends to be taken as the narration itself, which can in turn be more or less overt, more or less 'intrusive' upon the posited homogeneity of the story world. (Bordwell 1985, p. 161)

One method of reinforcing the notion that the world of the film exists whether the spectator is present or not is to commence a narrative in medias res, a tactic often employed by Spielberg.[6] Generally, in the textual analysis of the work of individual filmmakers, one searches for evidence of difference or variation from the collective norm. In examining narration in Spielberg the reverse is true. His narration never strays from the conventions and norms that characterise classical cinema and he always deploys a strictly limited range of narrational devices. Yet it is through examining the choices that he makes at the level of narration and the strictly limited stylistic parameters that he operates in that the first clues relating to a unique, overall strategy of narration creation emerge. All of his films employ canonical stories that always deliver clear resolutions.[7] Realistic motivation always defines character psychology and behaviour likewise adheres to 'normal' rationality. The degree of spectator knowledge usually matches that of the protagonist[8] as does the level of communicativeness. In these areas, Spielberg's presentation of plot and story information remains utterly conventional. As King notes (2002):

> Spielberg's work can also be identified stylistically, however, if only in terms of the sheer skill and aplomb with which he deploys certain techniques available from within the dominant conventional repertoire. Such qualities are not always easy to pin down, the whole point of the classical style being its relative invisibility-through-familiarity. (p. 106)

Morris (2007) argues that critical rejection of his narratives can arise because at specific moments '…Spielberg's films evidence artificiality, foreground the apparatus, which they always invoke in relation to perception and desire, and narrate self-consciously' (p. 379). I contend (and will demonstrate) that the opposite is true and that Spielberg almost always chooses the most restrictive presentational devices to minimise the level of self-consciousness.

The highly self-conscious montage sequence, an historical favourite of Hollywood cinema, and that Bazin (1967) claimed '…played tricks with time and space…' (p. 36), rarely appears in a Spielberg film. *Amblin'* (1968) and *Duel* (1971), two instances early in Spielberg's career, utilise montage, while *The Terminal* (2004) and *Lincoln* (2012) also include a brief montage. Championing the deep space composition, Bazin argued that the close-up distracted from the perceptual 'reality' of the mise en scene and was therefore highly self-conscious because it '…makes the audience conscious of the cutting…' (p. 32). Known for his judicious use of the close-up, Spielberg instead often applies them as the foreground for deep space compositions and the implications of this practice are examined in Chap. 5. Other devices that suggest self-consciousness, such as fades, wipes and dissolves,[9] are prudently applied, with 'straight' cuts the norm. In the bulk of Spielberg's narratives, temporality is presented in linear fashion and only *The Color Purple* (1985), *Hook* (1991), Amistad

(1997), Minority Report (2002), Munich (2005) and *The BFG* (2016) include flashbacks.[10] This calculated restriction on the overt presence of self-consciousness further reinforces Spielberg's strategy of suppressing traces of authorial 'activity' and contributes to the sense of the narration as unfolding independently of any guidance or benevolent control.

Spielberg's adherence to classical convention seemingly reinforces the accuracy of Bordwell's definition for classical narration. Yet a number of theorists contend that classical narration has evolved markedly since the demise of the studio era circa 1960 and that these changes are not acknowledged in Bordwell's account. Arguing for the validity of a post-classical, Elizabeth Cowie (1998) criticises Bordwell and Thompson's definition of classical narration as being too 'elastic' claiming that their definition includes '…virtually all possible deviations, so that every exception therefore proves the rule' (p. 178). Cowie adds that elements such as genre, stars, spectacle and 'spectacular effects' may not necessarily be important to the narrative itself but are significant components of the 'package' that constitutes the Hollywood, studio generated film and its desire for 'profitability'. Challenging the significance of causality and echoing Carroll's concern, Cowie suggests that Hollywood films are not always causally driven and that causality sometimes plays a minimal role and she provides examples from films by John Ford. Cowie also questions the significance of motivation and suggests that in *The Big Sleep* (1946), spectator interest is more than adequately sustained by the romance rather than by its infamously incoherent plot. Rick Altman (2008, p. 12) similarly argues that definitions of classical narrative tend to underestimate the importance of character and that 'narrative drive'[11] can be lost or blocked by the distraction created by characters and/or actors. The post-modern shares similar characteristics with the post-classical and is typically related to cinema in three areas. One is industrial and considers the transition from the studio system to the independent 'packaging' structures; another relates to thematic concerns such as shifts in the depiction and treatment of authority and technology; a third identifies a more overt role for style, greater self-consciousness and as with post-classical, an acknowledgment and referencing of other films and styles.

Utilising poetics and based on an interrogation of a number of specific cinematic texts, Eleftheria Thanouli (2006) suggests that the post-classical be added as a fifth mode into Bordwell's four types of narrational norms. Thanouli claims to identify explicit differences in recent films in the areas of narrative logic, including the inclusion of a greater number of characters resulting in more complex interactions, the disruption of a clear goal-orientated plot and a greater likelihood of unresolved endings. The overt presentation of extended hallucinatory character experiences also undermines classical norms relating to realistic motivation while historical self-awareness and parodying distorts the conventional role of artistic motivation. Thanouli introduces the concept of 'digital logic' in relation to space where the richness of the imagery contributes to faster cutting while 'spatial logic' results in '…blurring the distinction between the space 'in frame' and 'out of frame' and breaking down the logic of one screen/one image'. Thanouli posits this fusing of off- and on-screen space as an innovation of the post-classical 'form' yet Bazin (1974, p. 89) had made exactly this observation of Jean Renoir's films of the 1930s, claiming that off-screen and on-screen space existed 'simultaneously'. All of the films chosen by Thanouli can hardly be described as mainstream narratives and more easily fall into the category of art-cinema for which Bordwell (1979) has observed distinctive characteristics such as complex characters, lack of goal orientation and ambiguity as common traits—the very elements Thanouli ascribes to the post-classical. Like Thanouli, Elsaesser (1998) also argues that the post-classical narrative displays more prominent instances of complex, temporal manipulation, more open endings as well as a greater exploration of character psychology. Elsaesser cites *Back to the Future* (1985), among others, as an example of a temporally complex narrative. I would suggest the sequel, *Back to the Future Part II* (1989), manipulates time even more intricately yet actually only replicates the narrative structure and plotting of Frank Capra's much earlier *It's a Wonderful Life* (1946).

In noting the highly developed degree of classical narrative craft in *Jurassic Park*, Angela Ndalianis (2004, p. 3) elevates it to 'superclassical' status. In this vein, Ndalianis argues for a 'neo-baroque poetics' that encapsulates recent Hollywood cinema and points out the baroque influence present in set design and costumes of 1920s Hollywood and the films of Griffith, von Sternberg and von Stroheim. Essentially extending beyond the conventional 'restrictions' of classical narration with its canonical story and linear narrative, the neo-baroque addresses the evolving potentiality of the blockbuster's presence in multiple platforms and technologies. These range from the theme park ride to the computer game, endless storylines (the *Star Wars* films and related animated television series, novels and comics, etc.), and the prioritising of spectacle and exhibitionism.

Bordwell (2006) rejects the significance of these differences claiming that '…critics have exaggerated the novelty of current developments' (p. 9) and points out that in accentuating the blockbuster, one tends to downplay the historical tradition of change and variation that has always characterised Hollywood narrative. Thompson (1981) similarly argues that classical narrative has incorporated numerous 'small changes' through its history but that it has retained a 'basic standardisation of approach' (p. 54). King (2002) points out that a small number of Hollywood films have always attracted a disproportionately large level of interest given Hollywood's substantial output. He is speaking specifically of the small group of films that constitute the 'Hollywood Renaissance' but notes that a significant number of film noir's from the 1940s and 1950s also featured '…doubt, cynicism and bleak endings…' (p. 47), characteristics also applied to the post-classical. Instead, Bordwell (2006, p. 121) proposes a series of style-based changes that he argues largely account for the development of mainstream narration since the 1960s but which still fall within the paradigm of the classical. Labelled as 'intensified continuity' and more accurately described as evolutionary rather than innovative, the four, style-based areas of change identified by Bordwell include: shorter shots, the editing together of disparate focal length shots, greater use of tighter framing and a highly mobile camera. While the elements identified as post-classical, post-modern and neo-baroque bare little relevance to Spielberg's narratives (other than as points of difference), the principles of intensified continuity can be clearly seen as operating to some degree in all Spielberg narratives and therefore require more detailed consideration. It is also important to note that the four changes tend to manifest a degree of relatedness in the sense that the change of one directly affects the functioning of the others.

First evolution—shorter shots: Drawing on the programme first initiated by Barry Salt involving measuring the length in seconds of shots in films to produce an average shot length (ASL) for individual, groups and eras of films, Bordwell (and Salt) have noted that the ASL for Hollywood films made between the 1930s and 1960s hovered in the 8 to 11 second range. With each successive decade the ASL has steadily decreased and by the end of the century stood at three to six seconds. Clearly, the pace of editing in classical films has substantially accelerated in the past 50 years. This finding of a trend to shorter shots is also supported by Cutting, DeLong and Nothelfer (2010).

Second evolution—contrasting focal lengths: studio-era Hollywood practice generally mandated the use of lenses of similar focal lengths when filming specific scenes with longer focal length lens often reserved for close-ups or wide exteriors. The increased use of the long lens in European productions from the 1960s and the already discussed influence of these films on the New Hollywood filmmakers resulted in the greater use of the long lens in Hollywood practice from the mid-1960s. This quickly evolved into the mixing of both wide angle and long focal length lens shots within a scene. Bordwell (2006, pp. 127–128) specifically mentions Spielberg's use of this strategy in *The Sugarland Express* (1974) and *Jaws* (1975). Even earlier instances are evident in *Amblin'* (1968) and *Duel* (1971).

Third evolution—greater use of close-ups: the increased cutting rate has meant that wider framed compositions have declined in popularity as contemporary filmmakers compensate for the shorter screen time of individual shots with tighter framings that more clearly convey information. This functions as the reverse of Burch's concept of 'legibility' (Thompson 1981, p. 41) where the more information contained in the shot, the longer the shot needs to be for the spectator to adequately absorb the required detail. Within the context of intensified continuity, if the shot cannot be made longer then the only other way to convey the required information is by privileging the relevant detail with a more tightly framed composition or close-up.

Bordwell notes that the traditional wider, establishing type shot now tends to appear both less frequently and later in a scene with its application additionally functioning as a form of punctuation. The reduced use of wider shots that also previously assisted with spatial orientation has meant that greater emphasis is now placed on conventions such as the shot, reverse shot and the eye-line match to perform these duties. Conversely, the preference for tighter shots has also presented editors with the opportunity to cut even more rapidly.

Fourth evolution—a more mobile camera: Bordwell suggests that this practice evolved largely because of two factors: the development of camera movement that followed the technical restrictions imposed by early sound recording in the 1930s and the greater camera mobility evident and made possible by the reduction in camera size and weight during the 1960s and seen in the French New Wave, vérité and Direct Cinema movements. Intensified continuity further underlines the crucial and intimate role of style in syuzhet, fabula and narration creation. Yet, as mentioned earlier, convention dictates that classical style should not be 'seen or heard'.

> …as viewers we treat the presentational vehicle (the medium and its patterning) as secondary; we 'look through' the HOW and concentrate on the WHAT. (Bordwell 2008, p. 111)

Andrew Sarris (1968, p. 36) also focussed on style and Bordwell notes his definition for mise en scene as sounding very similar to that for style: 'The art of the cinema is the art of an attitude, the style of a gesture. It is not so much WHAT as HOW. The WHAT is some aspect of reality rendered *mechanically* by the camera. The HOW is what the French critics designate somewhat mystically as mise-en-scene'. It is the consideration of the 'how'—of the workings of style in the cinema of Spielberg—that will occupy the remainder of this chapter and of the next six chapters.

Functions of Classical Style

> Let me say this to you. I put first and foremost cinematic style before content. Most people, reviewers, you know, they review pictures purely in terms of content. I don't care what the film is about. I don't even know who was in the airplane attacking Cary Grant. I don't care. So long as that audience goes through that emotion! Content is quite secondary to me—Alfred Hitchcock (1995, p. 292).

In his perception of the role for style, Hitchcock may be employing some of the hyperbole for which he was renown later in his career, but the intention is clearly to emphasise the significance of style in constructing narrative and generating affect. As with narration, a definition for classical style is required.

> I take style to be a film's systematic and significant use of techniques of the medium. Those techniques fall into broad domains: mise-en-scene (staging, lighting, performance, and setting); framing, focus, control of color values, and other aspects of cinematography; editing; and sound. Style is, minimally, the texture of the film's images and sounds, the result of choices made by the filmmaker… (Bordwell 1997, p. 4)

John Gibbs (2002) offers a similar definition when considering mise en scene: '…the contents of the frame and the way that they are organised…' and '…encompasses both what the audience can see, and the way in which we are invited to see it' (p. 5). Bordwell and Thompson (2008, pp. 306–309) suggest four necessary steps in analysing classical style: establishing and considering the form of the text—in this instance classical style and the tradition of extrinsic norms and conventions that shape it, specifying the relevant stylistic elements as agents, and exploring how they occur and the effect they have on narration. Tom Gunning (2004) likewise isolates three different levels that function to transform what he describes as the showing of narration into telling: the profilmic or mise en scene—the specifically chosen and arranged items photographed by the camera; the 'enframed' image, or how the images are 'prepared' for the frame through the utilisation of perspective; camera movement, distance and angle, composition, lenses, exposure and so on; and editing for the construction of space and manipulation of temporality, most commonly expressed through the continuity of action between shots.[12]

Barry Salt's[13] 'quantitative stylistic analysis' programme surveys films from the beginning of Hollywood through to the end of the twentieth century. Salt's (2006) survey of Hollywood cinema targets six technical aspects of style: shot length; type of shot (close-up, long shot etc.); camera movement and angle in each shot; whether the shot is subjective or objective; noting the main objects and action in the shot; and the type of shot transition. While it is simplistic to describe Salt's consideration of the six areas as constituting his definition of classical style, they do consider relevant cinematographic factors that directly impact on the construction of classical narration.

Given the formal and traditional links cinema shares with theatre, Noël Carroll (1996, p. 84) develops his theory of the functioning of classical style by initially considering why cinema is fundamentally easier to follow than theatre. Unlike theatre, film narrative is usually made up using multiple shots, often taken from different positions and spatial perspectives—all of which suggest that comprehension is likely to be challenging. In contrast, theatre features a narrative that unfolds from a single perspective and within the same, easily comprehended space. Carroll brings together three stylistic devices under the umbrella of what he calls 'small scale visual narration' to explain how style facilitates comprehension. First, the film spectator is always directed to relevant information. The act of the camera filming something or moving towards or with an object(s) is described as 'indexing'—or similar to the act of pointing. Indexing further leads to 'bracketing' where the information off-screen is excluded and therefore seen as less significant. The third ostensible device is known as 'scaling' and relates to the size of an object in the frame and how this can be altered by making the object larger or smaller and therefore more or less significant. These three techniques constitute Carroll's conception of 'variable framing' and function to direct the spectator's attention to significant narrative elements and thus assist in achieving 'cognitive clarity'.

At the same time, Carroll qualifies his conception of bracketing by noting that sometimes off-screen space can be considered as significant. In fact, part of the construct of the classical continuity system is that space, the world of the story, be seen to continue off-screen or off-camera. Noël Burch (1973) emphasises the significance of his six zones of off-screen space while André Bazin (1974) has noted Jean Renoir's constant 'acknowledgement' of off-screen space in his narratives. In some genres, such as horror or the thriller, off-screen space is often accorded greater importance than on-screen space in the sense that the location of the alien, monster or murderer is withheld and we are instead shown the unsuspecting victim. Spielberg's wide reverses and the 360 degree coverage are examples of the extension of scenographic space to include 'outside' the frame (Chap. 6).

Related to Bordwell's how and what is Carroll's (1998) 'content is the matter, form is the manner'. Carroll adds: 'The form of a film is whatever functions to advance or realise whatever the film is designed to bring about. The form of the individual film is what enables it to realise its point or purpose'. Bazin (1967) similarly points out the relevance of understanding the process of narration construction in the creation of meaning '…as good a way as any towards understanding what a film is trying to say to us is to know how it is saying it' (p. 30). Carroll uses form and style interchangeably and, like Bordwell, positions style as the main driving component responsible for the creation of narration. Drawing on Richard Wollheim's 'individual style', 'general style' distinction (Gaiger 2002), Bordwell, Thompson and Carroll identify multiple instances of 'types' of style. Carroll re-labels Wollheim's 'individual style' as 'personal style' and this includes notions of the filmmaker's 'personal expression' as manifest in their films—much like an auterist conception of the artwork. Yet Carroll observes that isolating a particular element in the work of a filmmaker does not mean that the whole film will include this element and this is certainly an important point in relation to Spielberg and his stylistic variation. Carroll (1998, p. 387) takes 'general style'—or classical Hollywood style—and further divides it into four sub-categories: 'universal style', 'period style', 'genre style' and 'movement style'. The implication with each of these categories is that they uniquely impact style.

Spielberg is both a product and an exponent of a dominant style and his career longevity has permitted him to work in multiple genres. As already discussed, he began his career during the New Hollywood period and was therefore influenced by movements like the French New Wave (literally realised by his casting of Francois Truffaut in *Close Encounters of the Third Kind*). Spielberg is also heavily influenced by past or earlier Hollywood style and by directors from the 1930s and 1940s in particular. Carroll (1998) also notes that 'The project of a specific film will present the filmmaker with various specific problems to that film that will inevitably differ to other film…' (p. 388). Evidence of the different demands of different films on style can be seen in Salt's (2006, p. 323) observation of the ASL for Spielberg's films and the way they vary from film to film.

Observing that Spielberg's ASL tends to be longer than the Hollywood norm, he also notes that specific films like *Schindler's List* have an extremely long ASL while only the *Raiders* films have a cutting rate that is equivalent to the industry average. The overwhelming inferences to be considered from these findings are twofold: the significance of genre in shaping style and the importance of considering the elements of style as they occur in the individual films of the same director.

Bordwell (2005, p. 36) suggests that classical style has four main functions and I would argue that two of them—denotation and the expressive—relate most directly to Spielberg's work. The denotative role for style is clearly crucial as it depicts characters behaving in logically motivated ways, in clearly defined situations—all of which is unequivocally presented to the spectator. Echoing Hitchcock, the expressive relates to using style to encourage an emotional engagement with the spectator. This is also a key component in Spielberg's narration and is expressed through his construction of scenographic space, how he 'inserts' close-ups to signal emphasis into his deep space and wide reverse compositions,[14] and the essential role of music. Bordwell's third function is symbolism and some critics seem able to take this to extremes when considering a Spielberg narrative—such as Morris' (2007, p. 380) claim that in one shot in *Empire of the Sun* the tail of an aircraft symbolises a shark fin. One legitimate instance occurs in *Always* where Pete is briefly illuminated angelically in a soft, white light, seemingly from a refrigerator, and this anticipates his death and return as a guardian angel in subsequent scenes.

The fourth function, style as decorative, also rarely occurs in Spielberg's films despite claims to the contrary as noted earlier. Yet Spielberg does actively engage in the elaborate use of style to create visually complex shots but he always prioritises narration by 'disguising' the artifice, instead promoting a 'narrator-less' narration through his application of classical continuity devices that encourage 'invisible' storytelling. In a 1992 essay, Adrian Martin draws on Richard Jameson's observations about the changing dynamic of style in classical narration and suggests that style has increased in prominence, labelling it as 'stylishness' and 'designer style'—which evokes similar claims of the post-classical position. Martin identifies three categories of style in classical narration ranging from: the conventional position of style as wholly subservient and motivated by narrational requirements, a more overt presence for style that still services narration and what he calls 'mannerist films' where style is artistically motivated and exists beyond narrational demands. Martin also raises the form, content distinction—or 'container/contents'—as he describes it, and suggests that thematic concerns should be considered as part of a group of formal elements that includes space, time and 'narratological systems'.

Further expanding on the relationship between syuzhet and style and its overarching function as vehicle for the transmission of fabula information, classical style therefore relies on a specific set of devices, conventions and norms that it uses and reuses in various combinations that are recognisable to spectators. If we recall the definition for narration as events in a cause-effect chain occurring in time and space and consider it from the perspective of style, this can then be divided into three stylistic systems dealing with narrative logic, temporality and spatial configurations. Each of these systems is in turn determined by sets of devices of which continuity editing functions as both device and also as system. In its most basic sense, or small scale, to use Carroll's term, continuity editing relates to the matching together of character action or motion across edits—also known as match-on-action editing—the principal function of which is to preserve the illusion of a continuous time and space. Just as style tends to be subordinated by narration, space similarly is usually motivated by the requirements of narrative logic and the cause-effect chain. And just as style tends (or is in fact designed) to be overlooked by the spectator, so is the operation that determines the construction of space by the classical continuity system.

Scenographic Space

Bordwell (1985, p. 113) defines scenographic space as the 'imaginary space of fiction, the "world" in which the narration suggests fabula events occur…' and observes that space in classical cinema is perceptually constructed out of three aspects of classical style.

1. Shot space: in classical narrative the intention is always to simulate three-dimensional space by employing; perspective (such as converging and vanishing points); 'prototype schemata', where our life experience and familiarity with objects assists in our understanding of the size and distance of objects in the frame—Jacques Aumont (1997, p. 32) labels this as 'perceptual constancy'; overlapping contours that cue an object as being in front of another; camera movement that alters the relation between framed objects or 'monocular movement parallax'; figure movement, light and shade, cast and attached shadows and selective focus. Spatial 'devices' include the persistent use of centred compositions[15] that draw on conventions of post-renaissance art and include the balanced dividing up of the frame (the rule of thirds) and the prioritising of 'frontality'[16]—of privileging the human face and enabling spectator access to a performer's eyes and mouth.
2. Editing space: the 180 degree rule assists with perceptual orientation of space which the spectator constructs using memory and anticipation to create a 'cognitive map' of the depicted space and location of relevant objects in that space. The shot, reverse shot arrangement should be disorientating given the dramatic shift of up to 180 degrees in perspective between edits. Overlapping space and cues such as eye-line matching, 'ear-line matching' and recognition of objects such as a character's shoulder positioning assist in introducing a high degree of spatial and figure repetition that reconfirms a continuous time and space, disguises the editing and encourages the piecing together of the 'cognitive map'.[17]
3. Sonic space: speech is usually privileged for foregrounded characters and mixed in a way that is consistent with cues relating to distance of the sound source as it appears in the frame. Sound is also constructed according to principles of ideal spectator comprehension that works to minimise the artifice, and this is realised through synchronised sound, clear dialogue (recorded and mixed carefully to overcome location or background noise), the application of sound to smoothen transitions (sound bridges) and the use of compositionally motivated, emotively intentioned music.

Mary Ann Doane (1986) also emphasises the role of sound in the spatial consideration of cinema and argues that space cannot be separated from sound and vision. Considering the existence of space from the spectator's perspective, Doane considers three distinct types of space in cinema: the diegetic space of the film as a 'virtual space', the screen space or screen surface as 'receptor' of the image where sound does not emit from the screen itself but from speakers and the space of the auditorium where sound 'envelops' the audience. Classical cinema actively operates to legitimise only the first type of space through its 'representational illusion'.

Despite Bordwell's (1985, p. 130) observation that classical film usually establishes space before narration, Mark Garrett Cooper (2002) argues that Bordwell still underestimates its importance. Discussing early Lumiére film, Cooper claims that 'The story does not happen *in* space so much as *to* space'. Eisenstein (Nizhny 1979) also emphasised the importance of conceiving and constructing distinct spaces as part of the storytelling process.

> When you face a scenario task…you must work out a scheme of where and on what spaces—zones of action—each section is to be played. The division between the sections of the story must also be rendered spatially: each action-fragment or section must have its own allotted space and develop on it. (p. 34)

Stephen Heath (1976) considers off-screen space as integral to the construction of space in classical narrative and argues that off- and on-screen space alternate such that off-screen can change to on-screen and then change again to off-screen and so on. This alternating process needs to be realistically motivated and integrated into the narrative or 'narrativised'. Burch (1973, p. 17) has isolated six zones of off-screen space: left and right of the frame, below and above the frame, behind the space depicted in the frame and the area in front of the frame and taken up by the camera. Bordwell differentiates between off-screen space and non-diegetic off-screen space, or the space that is not part of the world of the film—also known as the fourth wall and which is occupied by the camera.

Important to Bordwell's (Buckland 2000, p. 31) constructivist account of narrative is the sense that the spectator's conception of the unfolding story—the fabula—is a dynamic process rather than a fixed one. The spectator is encouraged to infer significance and meaning but also to constantly revise, abandon and/or modify their understanding of the unfolding story. In *Making Meaning* Bordwell (1989, p. 170) elaborates on the spectator's interpretive process with his 'bulls-eye schema'. He likens narrative comprehension to three concentric circles with the innermost circle consisting of characters, their traits, actions and relationships, with the next outer circle including scenographic space and style occupying the outer circle. This representation prioritises character agency as central to spectator comprehension but also integrates the significance of setting and style in constructing meaning. It also reinforces the perception of style as invisible while simultaneously demonstrating that characters, action and causality determine its role.

As a form, classical narrative dominates cinema (and television) production worldwide. Its pervasiveness, easy comprehension across multiple cultures and seeming lack of variation have undoubtedly contributed to the sense of it as being simplistic and technically (and therefore artistically) deficient. The work of scholars such as Bazin, Bordwell and Thompson, Carroll, Branigan and others has shown that the processes involved in constructing and perceiving classical narrative are complex. The successful classical filmmaker (where success is defined by popularity) must coherently engage with highly codified conventions such as the canonical story and structure, plot driven narrative and the character as causal agent. At the same time, the filmmaker must also effectively facilitate the spectator's activity by successfully manipulating elements such as narrative logic, motivation, causality, levels of knowledge, communicativeness and cues for hypothesis forming—all to maximise spectator comprehension.

The successful filmmaker deploys style in precise ways to achieve these fundamental principles of narration. Just as Bordwell proposes the place for style with his 'bulls-eye schema', we can similarly represent the elements constituting style as two concentric circles. The inner circle contains the technical elements relating to mise en scene, composition, lighting, staging, design, and so on. Also included is the convention of classical cinema as commercial industry practice with established craftspeople such as the cinematographer, the gaffer, costume designer, production designer, producers, directors and so on all functioning collaboratively within the industry to create a highly recognisable, specific form of narrative.

The outer circle includes the 'filmmaker's activity'. This contains concepts relating to the filmmaker as rational agent and capable of identifying 'problems' and resolving them (Gombrich's problem-solution model). The filmmaker makes choices about how to construct narrative using style and is at the same time influenced by both current and past industry practice and convention as well as on-going evolutionary influences such as the post-classical and/or stylistic variations described in Bordwell's intensified continuity. Also included are the conventions relating to the place of classical style as unobtrusive, Burch's 'seamless' or Bazin's 'invisible'. As a filmmaker Spielberg must precisely calibrate his use of style, juggling all its components and traversing the fine line between success and failure. Before proceeding to examine how he achieves this, it is necessary to first consider what is meant by Steven Spielberg as filmmaker and director and this is examined in the following chapter.

Notes

1. Editing is termed montage in the French context and is not to be confused with the Americanised montage sequence.
2. Découpage in its French definition refers to the '…realisation of the story as images…', essentially the construction of the narrative (Bordwell et al. 1985, p. 60).
3. Elsaesser seems to fuse causality with the question-answer model in contrast to Carroll's assertion that the cause-effect model lacks specificity in explaining narrative development or 'drive' and is therefore inferior to the question and answer explication.
4. The cognitive implications of this notion of classical cinema as easily and widely comprehended are examined in Chap. 8.
5. Barry Salt (1992, p. 29) criticises Bordwell's apparent incorrect use of the term syuzhet, claiming that it is a Russian derivative of the French 'sujet', which means theme.

Fundamentals of Classical Narration

6. *Close Encounters, 1941*, the *Raiders* films, *E.T.*, *Always*, the *Jurassic Park* films, *Amistad, Minority Report, Catch Me if You Can, Lincoln* and *Bridge of Spies* all begin this way.
7. The single exception is *The Adventures of Tintin* and the open ending likely relates to plans for an intended sequel rather than for any specific desire at difference.
8. *Always* (1989) is the exception with the female protagonist, Derinda, never actually aware (in a literal sense) that Pete is always nearby as a ghost. At the same time, we only ever know as much as Pete, the principal protagonist.
9. The epilogue in *Saving Private Ryan* (1998) utilises a 'morph'/dissolve transition from the young Ryan to the elderly Ryan at the cemetery. *Raiders of the Lost Ark, The Temple of Doom, The Color Purple, Empire of the Sun, The Last Crusade, Amistad, A. I.* and *The Kingdom of the Crystal Skull* have one dissolve. *Duel, Jaws, Always* and *War Horse* have two dissolves. *Bridge of Spies* has three. Spielberg does make extensive use of superimposed titles—usually to identify locations and time. While acknowledging the audience and therefore increasing the level of self-consciousness, this is outweighed by its practice as classical convention and likely demonstrates Spielberg's preference for prioritising narrative clarity.
10. *Saving Private Ryan* is bookended by contemporary scenes and so the majority of the syuzhet is technically constructed as a flashback. *Catch Me if You Can* similarly is structured with the majority of the narrative as a flashback. *Munich* contains 4 sustained flashbacks that appear to be motivated by the thoughts of Avner, the protagonist.
11. 'Narrative Drive' in Altman's context refers loosely to the logic of the cause-effect chain or Carroll's question-answer system that propels the narrative forward.
12. Gunning also includes the role of sound.
13. Salt (Burnett 2008, p. 136) prefers the term 'continuity cinema' to 'classical' partly because of his belief in the greater potential for individual agency than is traditionally associated with the 'classical' as codified form.
14. In Chap. 6, I identify and explain an additional variation of subjective point-of-view that wide reverses permit and that I label as associative point of view.
15. Bordwell et al. (1985, pp. 51–55) note that centred compositions also function to divert attention from frame edges and that edge framing is rarely employed in classical compositions.

16. Bordwell (1997, p. 171) avers that 'frontality' is a powerful device for directing spectator attention in the frame, with spectators drawn to the potential for expressivity and information available only from the human face. The emotive significance of the face is examined in Chap. 8.
17. The perceptual relevance of the 180-degree rule and of 'hiding' edits is examined in Chap. 8.

References

Altman, R. (2008). *A Theory of Narrative*. New York: Columbia University Press.
Aumont, J. (1997). *The Image* (C. Pajackowska, Trans.). London: British Film Institute.
Bazin, A. (1967). *What Is Cinema? Volume 1* (H. Gray, Trans.). Berkeley/Los Angeles: University of California Press.
Bazin, A. (1974). *Jean Renoir* (W. W. Halsey II & W. H. Simon, Trans.). London: W. H. Allen.
Bazin, A. (1985). On the politique des auteurs. In J. Hiller (Ed.) & P. Graham (Trans.). *Cahiers du Cinema The 1950's Neo-Realism, Hollywood, New Wave*. Cambridge: Harvard University Press.
Bordwell, D. (1979). The Art Cinema as Mode of Film Practice. *Film Criticism, 4*(1), 56–64. Retrieved from Academic Search Premier.
Bordwell, D. (1985). *Narration in the Fiction Film*. London: Routledge.
Bordwell, D. (1988). *Ozu and the Poetics of Cinema*. New Jersey: Princeton University Press.
Bordwell, D. (1989). *Making Meaning*. Cambridge: Harvard University Press.
Bordwell, D. (1997). *On the History of Film Style*. Cambridge, MA/London: Harvard University Press.
Bordwell, D. (2005). *Figures Traced in Light: On Cinematic Staging*. Los Angeles: University of California Press.
Bordwell, D. (2006). *The Way Hollywood Tells It: Story and Style in Modern Movies*. Los Angeles: University of California Press.
Bordwell, D. (2008). *The Poetics of Cinema*. London: Routledge.
Bordwell, D., & Thompson, K. (2008). *Film Art*. New York: McGraw Hill.
Bordwell, D., Staiger, J., & Thompson, K. (1985). *The Classical Hollywood Cinema: Film Style and Mode of Production to 1960*. New York: Routledge and Kegan Paul.
Branigan, E. (1984). *Point of View in the Cinema*. Berlin: Mouton Publishers.

Branigan, E. (1992). *Narrative Comprehension and Film.* London/New York: Routledge.
Branigan, E. (2006). *Projecting a Camera: Language Games in Film Theory.* New York: Routledge.
Buckland, W. (2000). *The Cognitive Semiotics of Film.* New York: Cambridge University Press.
Burch, N. (1973). *Theory of Film Practice.* London: Secker & Warburg.
Burnett, C. (2008). A New Look at the Concept of Style in Film: The Origins and Development of the Problem-solution Model. *New Review of Film and Television Studies, 6*(2), 127–149. Retrieved from Taylor & Francis Journals Complete
Carroll, N. (1988). *Mystifying Movies: Fads and Fallacies in Contemporary Film Theory.* New York: Columbia University Press.
Carroll, N. (1996). *Theorizing the Moving Image.* Cambridge: Cambridge University Press.
Carroll, N. (1998). Film Form: An Argument for a Functional Theory of Style in the Individual Film. *Style, 32*(3), 385–401. Retrieved from EBSCOhost Academic Search Premier
Cooper, M. G. (2002). Narrative Spaces. *Screen, 43*(2), 139–157. Retrieved from http://screen.oxfordjournals.org/
Cowie, E. (1998). Storytelling: Classical Hollywood Cinema and Classical Narrative. In S. Neale & M. Smith (Eds.), *Contemporary Hollywood Cinema* (pp. 178–190). London/New York: Routledge.
Cutting, J.E., DeLong, J., & Nothelfer, C. E. (2010). Attention and the Evolution of Hollywood Film. *Psychological Science, 21*(3), 432–439. Retrieved from http://pss.sagepub.com/content/21/3/432
Doane, M. A. (1986). The Voice in the Cinema: The Articulation of Body and Space. In P. Rosen (Ed.), *Narrative, Apparatus, Ideology: A Film Theory Reader* (pp. 335–348). New York: Columbia University Press.
Elsaesser, T. (1998). Specularity and Engulfment: Francis Ford Coppola and Bram Stoker's Dracula. In S. Neale & M. Smith (Eds.), *Contemporary Hollywood Cinema* (pp. 191–208). London/New York: Routledge.
Elsaesser, T. (2012). *The Persistence of Hollywood.* London/New York: Routledge.
Gaiger, J. (2002). The Analysis of Pictorial Style. *British Journal of Aesthetics, 42*(1), 20–36. Retrieved from Oxford University Press Journals Current
Gibbs, J. (2002). *Mise-en-scene: Film Style and Interpretation.* Wiltshire: Wallflower Press.

Gunning, T. (2004). Narrative Discourse and the Narrator System. In L. Braudy & M. Cohen (Eds.), *Film Theory and Criticism* (6th ed., pp. 470–481). New York: Oxford University Press.

Heath, S. (1976). Narrative Space. *Screen, 17*(3), 68–112. Retrieved from http://screen.oxfordjournals.org/

Hitchcock, A. (1995). *Hitchcock on Hitchcock: Selected Writings and Interviews* (S. Gottlieb, Ed.). Berkeley/Los Angeles: University of California Press.

King, G. (2002). *New Hollywood Cinema: An Introduction.* London: L.B. Tauris.

Livingston, P. (1996). Characterization and Fictional Truth in the Cinema. In D. Bordwell & N. Carroll (Eds.), *Post-theory: Reconstructing Film Studies* (pp. 149–174). Wisconsin: The University of Wisconsin Press.

Martin, A. (1992). Mise-en-scene Is Dead, or the Expressive, the Excessive, the Technical and the Stylish. *Continuum, 5*(2), 87–140. Retrieved from https://doi.org/10.1080/10304319209388230

Morris, N. (2007). *The Cinema of Steven Spielberg Empire of Light.* London: Wallflower Press.

Ndalianis, A. (2004). *Neo-baroque Aesthetics and Contemporary Entertainment.* Cambridge: The MIT Press.

Nizhny, V. (1979). *Lessons With Eisenstein* (I. Montagu & J. Leyda, Eds. & Trans.). New York: Da Capo Press.

Salt, B. (1992). *Film Style and Technology: History and Analysis.* London: Starword.

Salt, B. (2006). *Moving Into Pictures.* London: Starword.

Sarris, A. (1968). *The American Cinema, Directors and Directions 1929–1968.* New York: Dutton and Co. Inc.

Smith, M. (1995). *Engaging Characters.* London: Oxford University Press.

Thanouli, E. (2006). Post-Classical Narration. *New Review of Film and Television Studies, 4*(3), 183–196.

Thompson, K. (1981). *Eisenstein's Ivan the Terrible. A Neoformalist Analysis.* New Jersey: Princeton University Press.

Thompson, K. (1999). *Storytelling in the New Hollywood: Understanding Classical Narrative Technique.* Cambridge: Harvard University Press.

3

Spielberg as Filmmaker

Filmmaker as Author

In attempting to understand the degree to which a filmmaker controls the construction of narrative (Bordwell's 'intentionality'), we also need to ascertain which agent or agents are responsible for specific parts of a film: the director, the producer, the writer, the star, etc. A contrasting perspective can be seen in Janet Staiger's (2003, p. 31) consideration of W. K. Wimsatt and M. C. Beardsley's 'intentional fallacy' where the emphasis on the meaning in the narrative is placed with the spectator. Gregory Currie (1995, pp. 245–249) forgoes his 'Real Author Intentionalism' for 'Implied Author Intentionalism' suggesting that how works are interpreted is more important than authorial intention. Torben Grodal (2004) considers the links between intentionality, consciousness and free will and the claim that these are superseded by '… language, culture, discourses, or unconscious traumas' (p. 27). Arguing for the role of intentionality in the creative process he points out 'Somehow, the fact that the function of consciousness and intentions are influenced by non-conscious factors has been interpreted as if consciousness has no role whatever'. Staiger (2000, pp. 37–39) constructs 'perverse spectators'—her term for audiences that do not necessarily perceive or react as expected. Criticising

© The Author(s) 2018
J. Mairata, *Steven Spielberg's Style by Stealth*,
https://doi.org/10.1007/978-3-319-69081-0_3

the 'normative description' as a blanket definition for the nature of the audience, she lists seven instances of inaccuracies in the way audiences are defined. These range from their artificial construct at the hands of scholars to a lack of recognition in audience variety, erroneous assumptions about why audiences watch films and inaccuracy in the assumed knowledge of audiences.

Peter Woollen (2003, p. 71) also questions the significance of intentionality and includes the 'system' (or industry) as an important agent. Paisley Livingston (2005, p. 71) draws on Foucault's '*What is an Author?*' essay and the idea of the 'author function'. Livingston employs the term 'condition' to similarly suggest the concept of an intentional plan by the author. David A. Gerstner (2003) references the poststructuralist repositioning of the reader as author noting the significance of '...the way in which a text is consumed, appropriated and reproduced given the complicated relationships of production, reception and spectatorship' (p. 5). Another key element in the consideration of a work is Boris Tomashevsky's (1965, pp. 61–98) description of the author as 'biographical legend'. He argues that audience knowledge about a filmmaker also influences how they perceive the filmmaker's narrative. This has particular relevance for Spielberg's work given his enormous presence in popular culture as noted in the introduction.

Writings about Spielberg's films invariably position him as more-or-less solely responsible for their form and content. As already mentioned, this usually centres around thematic concerns.

> In *E.T.* the father of Eliot (Henry Thomas) is absent, estranged from the mother. Substitute father figures are found in the shape of *E.T.* itself—although the alien is also figured at times as child-like—and an empathetic scientist paired with the mother at the end. Similar thematic patterns are found in many of Spielberg's other films, from his first theatrical feature *The Sugarland Express* (1974) to *Jurassic Park* (1993) and many more in between (King 2002, p. 105).

On the odd occasion that analysis does turn to an examination of form, notions of authorial responsibility are still automatically attributed to Spielberg. Gary Bettinson's (2009) reappraisal of *Always* (1989), one of

Spielberg's few commercial disappointments, details the stylistic skill evident in the assembly of the first bar scene but then follows with an extended examination of what he contends is the narrative's 'organic unity':

> In all, Spielberg's purposive distribution of character goals undercuts conventional goal-orientation, derails expectations, compels the viewer to retread prior action, and discloses the narration's restrictedness. Frustrating for a mainstream audience this may be; but there is no denying the bold ingenuity of Spielberg's narrational tactics. (p. 45)

Bettinson describes narrative elements usually attributed to the screenwriter and seems to direct responsibility for them entirely to Spielberg. This negation of the writer's influence is further emphasised by Spielberg's own assertion that '…I'm not a writer and I don't enjoy writing. I'd much rather collaborate' (Pizzello 1997). While he would have been heavily involved in the writing process including approval of the final script, Spielberg does not receive a writing credit. *Always* is a remake of *A Guy Named Joe* (1942), which Spielberg (Listal 2012) has commented is one of his favourites. The original was directed by Victor Fleming and written by Dalton Trumbo. Spielberg's remake was in gestation for some ten years—a not unusual development period for a Hollywood film. Bettinson mentions the film's credited screenwriter—Jerry Belson—only once in his essay and that acknowledgment seems largely dismissive. At the same time, King's declaration that the estranged parents of *E.T.* and substitute father figures can be '…found in many of Spielberg's other films…' suggests that the very life experience of the director is reflected in his films.[1] Both Bettinson and King apply 'classic' auteurist interpretations in their interrogation of Spielberg as filmmaker. Bettinson seemingly takes for granted that all creativity comes from the director while King echoes André Bazin's seminal study of Welles and his implicit biographical reading that the character of Charles Foster Kane reflects Welles' own unhappy childhood. The auteur as not only responsible for the creative text but also that his or her own personality is somehow reflected in it; effectively tracing the 'author in the text' (Bordwell 1989, p. 45). This also then has implications for characterising the text as worthy of study as Staiger (2003) explains:

If individuals impart aesthetically sophisticated insights through movies, then art exists. Conversely, if scholars find such insights in movies, sentient beings are assumed to have put them there. (p. 34)

This then opens the way for the rehabilitation of Spielberg as artist and therefore worthy of 'serious' consideration. Steve Neale (2000, p. 11) points out that François Truffaut's influential *La Politiques des Auteurs* essay posited auteurism as positioning the director as artist and therefore as author. Truffaut argued that the personal and individual expression of the filmmaker could be glimpsed in the work of some classical Hollywood directors—despite the industrialised, commoditised nature of classical production. Truffaut and the *Cahiers* critics applied the auteur predominantly to European art-cinema directors with consideration of Hollywood limited to a small core set of directors including Orson Welles, John Ford, Howard Hawks, Alfred Hitchcock, Otto Preminger and a few others. In his response to Truffaut, Bazin (1985) described cinema as '…an art which is both popular and industrial…' (p. 251) and further positioned auteurism within the context of Hollywood commercial practice via the already mentioned '…the genius of the system'. Peter Wollen (1998, p. 50) notes that the customary definition of the auteur functions within an examination of two categories: the revealing of the filmmaker through the thematic motifs present in their films and the analysis of a distinctive style and mise en scene. Bordwell (2008, p. 260) recounts Andrew Sarris' belief that the 'distinguishable personality of the director' should be glimpsed through the way the director utilises style in their cinema. Steve Neale (2000, p. 11) adds a third element of the auteur in the Hollywood context that relates to identifying auteurs in classical cinema—as Andrew Sarris realised in his categorisation of American directors in *The American Cinema: Directors and Directions 1929–1968*. Bordwell (1979) observes that the application of auteurism to Hollywood was essentially about applying '…art-cinema reading strategies to the classical Hollywood cinema' (p. 59).

On the basis of these 'definitions' one would imagine that Spielberg qualifies on all counts. Yet Dudley Andrew (1993) points out that the *Cahiers du Cinema* incarnation of the auteur carried with it an '…aura of elitism…' (p. 77) while Noël Carroll (1988) comments similarly

'Auteurism was not really much of a theory; it was actually a form of connoisseurship' (p. 3). This hints at an explanation for the on-going reluctance to anoint Spielberg as auteur in the *Cahiers* tradition. Even when he is described as an auteur, the inevitably added qualification usually devalues and obscures the 'artist' as in Spielberg as not just auteur but more specifically as 'blockbuster auteur' (Shone 2004, p. 83). The emphasis here is with Spielberg as a commodity, reduced to a signature with 'crass' commercialism as the overriding inspiration—not artistry. 'Cinema is part of the media economy that has reduced the auteur to a sign, indeed precisely to a signature' (Andrew 1993, p. 82).[2]

While a consideration of Spielberg's work may invoke the notion of him as author, his popular success seemingly disqualifies him as artist. This conception of Spielberg also accommodates Michel Foucault's 'author-function' (Rabinow 1984, p. 107) and the idea that the work can be classified as 'Spielbergian', which does privilege his work in the sense that it is differentiated from that of other filmmakers—that it at least stands out. Similarly, Bordwell (1989, p. 158) mentions that a key function of the auteur theory is that it 'personifies' the filmmaker. One of the difficulties of the perception of the filmmaker as author of a 'type' of filmmaking is that the labelling function can both generalise and simplify the 'actual' skills of the filmmaker. As James Naremore (1999, p. 9) observed of famous directors like Eisenstein and Hitchcock, their name '…has come to signify not only persons but also traditions, theories and genres'. Yet even these filmmakers are known predominantly for their innovative mastery of style. In the case of Eisenstein it was as a pioneer of Soviet montage practice and theory (in all its variation)—itself largely an exploration of aspects of style. For Hitchcock, 'the master of suspense', it was for having carved out his own 'genre'—through his unique control of style.[3] As noted above, Wollen isolates the mobilisation of style as one of two key 'identifying' characteristics of the auteur. For the *Cahiers* critics, style was, in the hands of an auteur, a crucial tool for shaping the kind of exceptional narrative for which that auteur was recognised. Andrew Sarris represented the features of the American auteur as three concentric circles with technical proficiency occupying the inner circle, a recognisable personality the next outer circle and the 'deepest significance' of the narrative occupying the outside circle. Wollen (1998) singles out the career of

Howard Hawks whose many films across a variety of genres could nevertheless apparently be found to contain '...the same thematic preoccupations, the same recurring motifs and incidents, the same visual style and tempo...' (p. 53). Based on the earlier comments of King and Bettinson, Wollen's observations could just as easily apply to Spielberg's narratives.

Rather than repeat their (seemingly valid) reasons one could point to Bazin and the original *Cahiers* critics who 'rediscovered' or 'rehabilitated' the image of the leading practitioners of classical cinema—Wyler, Ford, Hawks, Hitchcock [with the benefit of some self-engineered legitimacy (Kapsis 1992)] relatively late in their careers and elevated them to auteur status. Bordwell (2011, pp. 69–72) points out that this calculated re-evaluation and promotion of filmmakers was sometimes initiated by the filmmakers themselves and that this practice has a long tradition in Hollywood. D. W. Griffith apparently claimed credit for '...the close-up, powerful suspense, restrained acting, "distant views" (presumably picturesque long shots of the action), and the "switchback," his term for cross-cutting...' This perception of Griffith as stylistic innovator was widely accepted as accurate until the late 1970s when film scholars revealed that most of the techniques either predated or appeared in other films at around the same time as Griffith. Bordwell further considers William Wyler, Orson Welles and cinematographer Greg Tolland's own publicity promoting the value of their long takes and deep focus compositions—and their claims that these techniques fostered a greater sense of cinematic 'reality'. Remarkably, Bordwell connects this publicity to Bazin's subsequent seminal writing that championed the use of long takes and deep space to create 'reality' in the films of these very filmmakers.

The refusal to accept Spielberg as 'genuine' auteur can be traced back to the beginnings of his career as feature director and the critical reception of his debut film *The Sugarland Express*. Reviewing the film in 1974, Pauline Kael (1994) captured the kind of ambivalence toward Spielberg as artist that still persists today.

> In terms of the pleasure that technical assurance gives an audience, this film is one of the most phenomenal debut films in the history of movies. If there is such a thing as a movie sense—and I think there is...—Spielberg really has it. But he may be so full of it that he doesn't have much else. (p. 559)

Kael's suggestion of the potential concept of a kind of 'all style and no substance' was actually identified in some early Hollywood filmmakers by the *Cahiers* critics. Truffaut labelled these 'second tier' auteurs as *metteur-en-scéne* and they were generally considered to be good technical directors although their films were perceived as lacking in authorial individuality and/or an exceptional style, thus disqualifying them from auteur status. Bazin (1985, p. 255) agreed with Truffaut and the *politique des auteurs* claim that even a good film by a non-auteur was usually considered inferior to an 'ordinary' film by a designated auteur.

Michael Curtiz was one director categorised as *metteur-en-scéne*. Wollen (2003, p. 64) notes that Curtiz was one of the most successful and powerful directors in Hollywood during the 1930s and 1940s largely because of a string of hits that included *Captain Blood* (1935), *The Charge of the Light Brigade* (1936), *The Adventures of Robin Hood* (1937) and *Angels With Dirty Faces* (1938). All but *Angels with Dirty Faces* featured the pairing of Errol Flynn and Olivia De Haviland, both of whom would also have contributed to the films' popularity. With a reputation as a perfectionist and for being highly demanding on set, as well as a prolific career that spawned 67 films at an average of three a year, Curtiz was nevertheless never accorded auteur status by the *Cahier's* critics or even later by Andrew Sarris. Wollen argues that this may in large part have been due to most of Curtiz's success as having come from swashbucklers, costume dramas and historical romances, genre combinations seen as 'unworthy' and not recognised by the *Cahiers* critics. Even *Casablanca* (1942) and *Mildred Pierce* (1945), two further hits for Curtiz, escaped clear genre categorisation and Wollen claims that this would have hurt his recognition as an artist given the tendency of auteurism to favour specific genres.

Substantial popular success, working in a mixture—and mix—of genre, a competent but nondescript narrative style, features accorded to Curtiz but also some 30 years later to Spielberg—a point not lost on Spielberg himself.

> I would serve the screenwriter and I would be a good storyteller but I wouldn't impose—I don't feel I have a style but Hitchcock had a style and Scorsese has a style and certainly Welles had a style. But Curtiz I identify

with more, people like Victor Fleming and Michael Curtiz, I identify with more because they didn't have styles either. But they were chameleons and they could quickly adapt, they could go from a story about heaven and an afterlife to the civil war and to *Gone With the Wind* and they could do a lot of different subjects and they could do them well because they were good craftsmen and they were good with actors and they could draw out good performances but they didn't impose kind of who they were on what that was and I always felt I was more in their game. (AFI 1995)

While promoting *Saving Private Ryan* Spielberg again draws on the comparison to Curtiz:

> The preparation period for this film was not unlike an average year in the life of a 1930s, 1940s director. And I did want to do that at one point in my life, I did want to see what it was like for John Ford or Howard Hawks or Michael Curtiz to make three films in a single year which they did several times—more than several times. (Bouzereau 2004)

His claim of a certain kinship with directors like Victor Fleming and Curtiz does seem to be reinforced by his own use of style. His career-long espousal of deep space staging and compositions—noted earlier as unusual in the present era—recalls the 1940s when such staging was common. Spielberg's awareness of Hollywood's studio-era industrial practice is further reflected in his often-repeated claim of a self-imposed discipline that prioritises the importance of finishing a film on time and on budget. While detailed information about the true production cost of the films is not reliably available, five of them—*Jaws, Close Encounters of the Third Kind, 1941* and *Hook* (1991)—are commonly reported (and acknowledged by Spielberg) to have substantially exceeded their schedule and budget. For a director with some 30 feature credits this does not seem excessive, particularly as all have since become profitable[4]—and in the case of the first two titles—also among the most profitable ever made. Commenting in a 1981 interview:

> I just found that by not doing 15 takes on each shot, but by doing only, let's say, three to five takes, I was able to get a lot more spontaneity into the film with less self-indulgence and pretentiousness. I didn't have a lot of

time to try different things, but I think I've made enough movies that involved horrendous logistics—*Jaws*, *Close Encounters* and *1941*—for me to finally receive my diploma, graduate with both honour and infamy, and get into the field where I could make a movie responsibly for a relatively medium budget that would appear to be something more expensive. That was the challenge. (Spielberg 1981)

His apparent desire to conform to this classical method explains some of the logic behind his supposedly 'style-less' style. Paradoxically, Spielberg's frequently stated preference for an anonymous style, or style that transparently services a particular narrative, is to some extent undermined by his commodification as successful filmmaker. He claims to prefer to 'disappear' into the narrative but his extraordinary success and celebrity prevents any real degree of authorial anonymity. This 'difficulty' results in Spielberg trying even more aggressively to suppress authorial presence and the result contributes to the manifestation and implementation of the wide reverse strategy.

Collaboration

Patrick Colm Hogan (2004) argues that, because film production is highly collaborative, the potentiality exists for 'multiple authorship' and numerous degrees of intentionality. He contends that determining authorship is essentially an empirical issue—who makes the greatest contribution to the narrative? Hogan goes on to propose a cognitive-based explanation of the 'uniqueness' and/or innovation of aspects of the work of the auteur as realised in *creative cognition theory*. He argues that for an 'act' or 'idea' to be considered creative, it needs to differ from those previously used and 'An innovation is appropriate in our experience when we are able to process the innovation in a way that furthers relevant purposes of the film—emotional effect, thematic understanding, or whatever'. At the same time, any innovation '…relies on principles that are largely shared among filmmakers and viewers…'. Therefore, even though an innovation exhibits distinctive characteristics, it still needs to observe '…standard cognitive structures, processes, and contents' (pp. 72–73). This conception of the filmmaker as connected to an 'innovation' accords with my proposition of Spielberg and the wide reverse as stylistic innovation that still manages to conform to, and function within, classical convention.[5]

A significant 'effect' of auteurism has been its role in helping to elevate the status of the director to the position of sole author. This may have been more accurate in the smaller European productions for which the concept of the cinematic auteur was conceived, but its wholesale transference to Hollywood industrial practice has been more problematic. As noted earlier, and regardless of whether or not auteurism may be under consideration, critics are quick to lay creative responsibility for seemingly all visible aspects of a production at the feet of the director where the reality relating to authorial responsibility may often be more intricate. Casper Tybjerg (2004, p. 62) avoids the term 'authorship' precisely because of the attached preconception that implies one person as responsible for all creativity and instead prefers 'filmmaker'. This complexity is illustrated in the long running feud that began during the making of *The Godfather* (1972) between producer Robert Evans and director Francis Coppola. Evans (1994, p. 326) claimed that the film's celebrated ending, which depicts a series of assassinations intercut with a christening, was 'invented' by one of the film's editors—a claim hotly contested by Coppola.

In the classical Hollywood cinema, collaboration is a crucial production strategy, and understanding how Spielberg operates within this process is an important aspect in comprehending the extent of his creative control as author. Longtime Hollywood producer John Wells (Caldwell 2008) notes:

> ...pride and egotism are in the final analysis counterproductive and self-destructive. Building long term, personal trust in a closely knit group of individuals proves to be a far more successful move, both artistically and commercially. (p. 384n)

Spielberg also claims to value the contributions of those working for him.

I don't know that I've become more creative or collaborative—I'm very collaborative with everybody on the set—Spielberg. (Head 2002)

Few directors have managed to establish the kind of multiple, long-term, key professional relationships that Spielberg has. This is undoubtedly partly due to the longevity of his career and the related opportunities this has generated for developing extended associations. Film editor Michael Khan has edited all but one[6] of Spielberg's films since *Close Encounters of the Third Kind* (1977) and is one of his longest serving collaborators. At the same time, in attempting to determine the influence of the editor in the feature film, Barry Salt (2011) has concluded that the individual editor usually exerts little stylistic impact. Taking a sample of films, Salt surveyed the cutting patterns in the dialogue scenes comparing their 'A length' and 'B length'—the number of frames from the point the dialogue ends to the cut in the former, and the number of frames from the cut to the point the dialogue begins in the latter. Comparing different films cut by the same editor, Salt determined little distinct similarity from film to film. At the same time, he noted that films by a particular director did display editing similarities, citing writer/director M. Night Shyamalan for the unusually long pauses during the dialogue scenes in his films.[7] Salt also observed that for films released in 1999, the dialogue scenes tended to be cut more tightly, supporting his own earlier conclusions about the generally shorter shots in more recent Hollywood films (and considered in relation to intensified continuity in Chap. 2).

Spielberg 'discovered' Janusz Kaminski working as a cinematographer in television and employed him to shoot *Schindler's List*. Their collaboration continues to the present and Kaminsky has shot every one of Spielberg's films since *Schindler's List*. Yet, Spielberg is clear about who makes the creative decisions: 'I set the camera. I do all the blocking. I choose the lenses. I compose everything. But Janusz, basically, is my lighting guy. And he's a master painter with light. And he sort of, you know, made tremendous contributions to my work through his art' (Head 2002).[8] Production Designer Rick Carter has worked steadily with Spielberg since his initial work on the television series *Amazing Stories* (1985). His subsequent production design for Spielberg has included

Jurassic Park, *Amistad*, *The Lost World: Jurassic Park*, *A.I. Artificial Intelligence*, *War of the Worlds*, *Munich*, *War Horse*, *Lincoln* and *The BFG*.
Spielberg has also accumulated a formidable set of long-standing collaborations with above-the-line personnel. Above-the-line is a term relating to the key creative talent in the filmmaking process who also usually contribute the greatest cost to the production, namely the director, writer(s), producers and main cast. While the composer does not characteristically occupy this category, John Williams' reputation and track record positions him as one of the very elite composers working in Hollywood. His association with Spielberg began with his score for Spielberg's debut feature *The Sugarland Express* and he has scored all but two of his feature films[9] in a collaboration that has spanned the breadth of Spielberg's feature-directing career and has included some of the most popular, iconic film scores and themes ever created. The now clichéd leitmotif themes created for *Jaws*, *Close Encounters of the Third Kind* (the five bar tone), *Raiders of the Lost Ark* and *E.T.* are all popular classics and instantly recognisable. No other collaborator has so definitively and directly contributed to shaping narration in a Spielberg film, as he acknowledges '…John Williams speaks to people. John rewrites my movies musically…' (Schickel 2007).

David Koepp[10] is the only writer to have received screenwriting credit on multiple Spielberg films including the first two *Jurassic Park* films, *War of the Worlds* and *Indiana Jones and the Kingdom of the Crystal Skull*. Colin Wilson served as associate editor on *Raiders of the Lost Ark*, *Temple of Doom*, *The Last Crusade* and *Always* before being promoted to associate producer for *Jurassic Park* and subsequently as producer on *Amistad*, *The Lost World*, *War of the Worlds* and *Munich*. Walter Parkes was appointed President of Amblin Entertainment, Spielberg's production company based at Universal studios, in 1994. Together with producer partner Laurie Macdonald, Parkes assisted in the creation of the DreamWorks SKG film division and both oversaw the production of all DreamWorks features for Spielberg. Kathleen Kennedy is undoubtedly the closest and longest serving of Spielberg's producers. Beginning as his assistant on *Raiders of the Lost Ark*, she quickly rose to the position of producer or executive producer and has served in either role in almost all of Spielberg's films. Kennedy produced *E.T.*, *The Color Purple*, *Empire of the Sun*,

Always, Hook, Jurassic Park, A.I., War of the Worlds, Munich, Tintin, War Horse and *Lincoln* and received executive producer credit for many others. Kennedy's partner and fellow producer Frank Marshall also co-produced most of Spielberg's 1980s films. Also notable is Spielberg's long-term collaboration with fellow movie brat George Lucas, which began professionally with *Raiders of the Lost Ark* but stretches back to the early 1970s. Spielberg claimed in an interview in 1974:

> …I really like my contemporaries and can get more out of George Lucas, who's a good friend of mine, than I can by sitting in a screening room and screening eight Preston Sturges films. (Helpern 2000)

Hook represented the first instance of Spielberg casting stars in Dustin Hoffman and the then up-and-coming Julia Roberts who had been propelled to stardom the year before with the box-office success of *Pretty Woman* (1990). Both Richard Dreyfuss and Harrison Ford had become stars from their work on Spielberg films (with Ford receiving some additional assistance from his roles in the *Star Wars* trilogy). Spielberg had traditionally chosen to work with an ensemble of character actors but by the late 1990s he was regularly casting stars including Anthony Hopkins in *Amistad*, Tom Hanks in *Saving Private Ryan*, *Catch Me if You Can* (with Leonardo Di Caprio), *The Terminal* and *Bridge of Spies*. *Minority Report* and *War of the Worlds* feature Tom Cruise while Daniel Day-Lewis stars in *Lincoln*. That Spielberg has still applied an ensemble casting approach to some recent films (*Munich* and *War Horse*) suggests that these casting choices are driven as much by the material (story and script) as by any perceived preference in casting strategies (i.e. not being shackled by the usual necessity to cast name performers as a required prerequisite in order to guarantee financing). This echoes his use of style as driven by story requirements in a consistent classical fashion rather than for its own sake as is often the case in art-cinema. That Spielberg does not have to rely on incorporating stars as part of a feature package also illustrates his enormous power and ability to get films made exactly in the way he wants them—further evidence of his status as legitimate auteur. The large group of producers under Spielberg also facilitate the formidable development capabilities at his disposal as new projects are inexorably created and developed for him. A cursory search of *IMDB* for Spielberg's upcoming projects returns more than a dozen titles 'in development' with Spielberg attached as producer or executive producer, and as director on a further three or four features. Regardless of the longevity of these collaborations there seems little doubt as to their nature as Allan Starski, (1994) set designer for *Schindler's List*, clearly states: 'During shooting, the only person allowed to decide about everything was the director, his decision was final' (p. 79).

Practice

Spielberg as co-producer of his own films clearly permits him to retain a certain pragmatism in rationalising the cost of the more 'marginal' films—the feature projects he feels may not attract a large audience and therefore could suffer in terms of profitability. Originally perceived as a small 'personal' film by Spielberg, *E.T.* was estimated to have cost approximately 10 million dollars, the average cost for Hollywood features in the early 1980s. Similarly, *Schindler's List, Amistad, Catch Me if You Can, The Terminal, Munich, War Horse, Lincoln* and *Bridge of Spies* were all made with budgets considered average or below for their time. In contrast, *A.I. Artificial Intelligence, Minority Report, War of the Worlds* and *The BFG* were all budgeted at well over 100 million dollars and were expected to perform well. *A.I.* can be considered separately because of its link with Stanley Kubrick and the creative association of Spielberg with a 'true' auteur. This project may also have served to assist in strengthening Spielberg's own auteurist credibility—potentially an even more important consideration for Spielberg than the film's commercial success.[11]

Spielberg's ability to thrive within the Hollywood industrial system—described by Bordwell (Staiger and Thompson 1985, p. xiv) as a particular mode of film production and practice—essentially manifests itself in an ability to shrewdly manage the relationship between revenue and expenditure.

> …the first thing I realized is that the audience is the key. I've been making films through myself and for an audience, rather than for myself and the

next of kin who understand me. I guess I might be called an 'entertainment' director—or to be more crass, a 'commercial' director. I don't pretend to understand how an audience changes every two or three years—which they do—but I know what I like and I hope there are enough people out there to share that—Spielberg. (Poster 1978, p. 172)

Within this 'commercial' system, popularity and revenue are intrinsically interrelated. Spielberg consistently directs films that rarely lose money and occasionally make enormous amounts of it. While most directors face constraint and/or compromise within the system—budget limitations, creative interference and so on—Spielberg's financial success means that he is relatively unrestrained by that system. His own financial discipline permits him the freedom to shape—together with the collaborative technicians and creatives chosen by him—the kinds of films he chooses. The corollary—and irony—of this creative freedom can be seen in the controversy that surrounded the making of *Poltergeist* (1982). Busy with *E.T.*, Spielberg ceded directing duties for *Poltergeist* to the relatively inexperienced Tobe Hooper. While Hooper received directing credit, conjecture has persisted that Spielberg actually creatively controlled the film—that he effectively authored it. Buckland (2006, p. 154) claims that through the use of Barry Salt's statistical style analysis he was able to confirm that the film was directed by Hooper. Buckland's analysis is problematic on a number of levels, not least of which is his small sample size—he surveys only two of Hooper's films—and only the first 30 minutes of each film is covered, potentially giving an inaccurate reading, as Bordwell and Thompson (1985) claim of Salt's own methodology. Buckland points out that most critical commentary on the controversy favours Spielberg as the actual director in the authorial sense. Julia Philips (1991), Spielberg's co-producer on *Close Encounters of the Third Kind*, weighed in on the controversy '…we have run in to each other on the MGM lot, where he [Spielberg] is directing *Poltergeist*. He is supposed to be producing it, but Tobe Hooper, the director, it is whispered, has lost his cookies and Steven has had to step in' (p. 442). Even Pauline Kael (McBride 1997, p. 339) felt that the film was directed by Spielberg. Further, Buckland seems to disregard his cited quote by the film's producer, Frank Marshall, who described the overwhelming creative control exercised by Spielberg. He received story and co-screenwriter credit, co-produced, prepared the storyboards and 'approved' all camera angles (always the responsibility of the director), and also approved the final edit of the film with long-time editor Michael Khan. Visually, the film also contains some Spielberg 'trademarks' such as the zooming in, tracking out *Vertigo* effect also used in *Sugarland Express*, *Jaws* and *E.T.,* and the rotating room that has a cast member seemingly crawling upside-down across the ceiling—an effect used previously in *Close Encounters of the Third Kind*. In this instance, Spielberg's overwhelming 'creative' influence invokes Paisley Livingston's (2005) concept of 'coercion' where authorship cannot be attributed to someone literally forced into crafting something in a particular way and for which they are not creatively in control. The irony here is that in establishing his own freedom Spielberg appears to have recalled the kind of Hollywood 'mogul' system of control commonly exercised by studio heads during the studio era.

At the same time, with his 'commercial' films Spielberg is always mindful of the 'needs' of an audience—of constructing a narrative that maximises audience impact and affect. One often-cited example is his re-cutting of *Jaws* following favourable previews with the intention of generating even greater audience reaction (Shone 2004, p. 23). An additional, significant example relates to the trimming of a long take in *Raiders of the Lost Ark* despite Spielberg's obvious fondness for the shot as originally conceived. 'I had designed a drinking contest that takes a substantial amount of screen time. It went on for almost five minutes—which is the reason it now runs only two minutes in the movie. It didn't conform to the pacing of the rest of the picture and was really out of place. But it was the best use of the Louma Crane that I've ever experienced' (Spielberg 1981, p. 1163). In the 'traditionalist' sense, commercialism and populism undermine a filmmaker's eligibility to be considered as auteurist. For Spielberg, it is precisely these elements that permit him to operate within the Hollywood commercial industry and yet create his 'own' films as author: 'I love the idea of not being an independent filmmaker. I've liked working within the system' (Bordwell and Thompson 2008, p. 465). Bill Nichols' (1976) depiction of the auteur as struggling within the production system further distances Spielberg from consideration as traditional auteur. 'A frequent tenet of auteur criticism is that a tension exists between the artist's vision and the means at his disposal for realizing it: studio pressure, genre conventions, star demands, story requirements. These constraints are also seen as a source of strength, imposing discipline and prompting cunning subversions' (p. 306). For Spielberg, the reverse seems correct. His power and influence mean that 'studio pressure' is largely irrelevant given his capacity to configure the entire production process to his own requirements, and this is further enhanced by a self-imposed, ever present fiscal discipline.

A crucial component of this production economy is its impact on narrative form. Spielberg's strategy of directing predominantly modestly budgeted films clearly has implications for the methodology he employs in constructing his narratives. One conventional method of reducing production cost is to reduce the number of shooting days and Spielberg generally shoots quickly with fewer retakes in order to facilitate this. This also (partially) replicates the kind of practice that dominated early studio-centric Hollywood and directors like Ford, Hawks and Curtiz. Directors had tight schedules that permitted fewer shots, resulting in less coverage and therefore slower cutting rates in comparison to present practice as illustrated in Bordwell's concept of 'intensified continuity'. Ford, Hawks and Curtiz tended to shoot masters that covered all or much of a scene—often with deep space compositions—in an inherently visual and temporally efficient way that enabled tight shooting schedules to be completed on time. Significantly, Spielberg's utilisation of a shooting strategy that similarly hastens the process of filming also has stylistic and cognitive implications with respect to the manner in which his narrative is constructed. Joseph McBride (1997) points out that even on his first television directing assignment, *Eyes* (1969), Spielberg '…preferred wherever possible to stage a scene in a single flowing master shot' (p. 174)—a strategy contrary to the customary practice in television at the time. Now with an extensive body of directing work, it is clear that Spielberg applies multiple variations in his coverage[12] of scenes, ranging from single shot scenes to multiple shot and multiple, master-shot coverage. Editor Michael Kahn notes '…Steven shoots a lot of coverage. He shoots enough pieces so that he will have options when he gets into the editing room' (Duncan and Shay 1993, p. 126). His extensive experience also means that Spielberg has the confidence to alter plans at any time as long-time camera-operator Mitch Dubin observes: '...often the blocking might change; it's an organic process. Steven is always excited by new ideas, and Janusz knows the blocking is going to be all over the place' (B. B. 2006, p. 40).

This interest in new ideas appears to range across the entire production process. Rather than simply collaborate with screenwriters to create a script as is customary, for *Jurassic Park* Spielberg incorporated some of the scenes created by the storyboard artists into the screenplay, effectively reversing the normal script to storyboard production sequence (Duncan and Shay 1993, p. 149). This process also reveals the high priority accorded to visual storytelling and this is confirmed repeatedly in the sequences examined in the following chapters.

Author as Camera

Through the use of wide reverses, Spielberg actively attempts to efface evidence of authorial/filmmaker presence in a way that is consistent but more pervasive than conventional classical practice. A key component of this process that requires consideration is that relating to the role of the camera—not as its obvious function as a visual recorder but as a *presence* in and of the narration. Pudovkin (1959) considered the camera as an 'ideal, perspicuous observer' and that 'The lens of the camera is the eye of the spectator' (p. 64). This anthropomorphises the camera, giving it human-like traits, and Bordwell notes that some theorists even assigned equivalency to camera movement; panning as turning of the head or tracking as the walking or running spectator.[13] The 'ideal' or 'invisible observer' aspect incorporated the concept of the camera/spectator as being omnipresent, of always occupying the best vantage point for the scene, thus also accommodating the cinema's ability to frequently change perspective with ease. By linking the camera directly to the director the next step was to see the camera as the film's story narrator: 'Thus the invisible-witness model became classical film theory's all-purpose answer to problems involving space, authorship, point of view, and narration' (Bordwell 1985, p. 9). This privileging of the invisible observer model tended to overrate its own significance at the expense of the other elements of style: 'The invisible observer is not the *basis* of film style but only one *figure* of style' (Bordwell 1985, p. 12).

In contrast to Pudovkin's notion of the camera as presenting an unmediated view via the invisible observer, Eisenstein conceived of the camera as a device for '…transforming the profilmic event so as to maximise effect' (Bordwell 1985, p. 14). Eisenstein departs even further from the invisible observer when considering editing, arguing that the intention may often be to 'violate verisimilitude' to generate intended effects. Bordwell avers that Eisenstein considered the profilmic 'altered' even as the camera is turned on its subject: '…the profilmic event, as expressive movement or attraction, is already an expressively heightened representation of the thesis'. Bordwell (1977) also comments that from the spatial cues (and camera movement in particular), the spectator is able to '…extrapolate a dualism of filmed event and a mobile filming mechanism' (p. 23). Edward Branigan (1981, p. 60) suggests that the camera functions as a construct of the spectator to explain the 'spatial effects' viewed in the frame and 'created' by the camera including dollying, panning, tilting and so on. Branigan (2006, p. 149) in fact posits an enormous range of functions and identifications for the camera including camera as author, as impersonal subject and as a 'box' occupying a place in space. These include seven different variations relating to camera motivation and the significance this has for sustaining the 'invisibility' of technique while instead foregrounding plot and story. He also lists 15 variations in the significance of the frame itself including Eisenstein, Arnheim and Noél Burch's perception of the frame as 'an antidote to realism'. Branigan sums up his consideration of the camera by asserting that 'No genuine and exact description is proper for all occasions'.

Stephen Heath (1976, pp. 77–78) notes that the camera shares the perspective system of the photograph and to a limited extent also with the human eye. The temptation then is to perpetuate the sense of the camera as eye and therefore that it reproduces a 'qualified reality'. 'Cinema is involved with photograph and camera, its principal matter of expression that of moving photographic images…its prime achievement that of the creation of the 'impression of reality'—'neither absolutely two-dimensional nor absolutely three-dimensional, but something between'. André Bazin likewise suggested that the long take encourages the spectator to mentally process the space in the same way that they would if actually there. Christian Metz (1982) conceived of the camera as the spectator: 'I am the projector, receiving it, I am the screen; in both these figures together. I am the camera, which points and yet which records' (p. 51). Gregory Currie (1996) criticises Metz by pointing out that audiences never actually believe or even suspect that they are in the presence of '… ax murderers, world-destroying monsters, or nuclear explosions…' (p. 331).

Bordwell (1989) points to 'person-like' constructs attributable to the narrator and the camera as borne out of the auteur movement. He notes how the camera is often linked to the filmmaker, as in 'Hitchcock's camera', which also implies Hitchcock as narrator and '…suggests both the narrating presence and what it sees…' (p. 163). Bordwell extends this to a 'personification schema' that inflects the frame such that distant objects are now considered to be detached and impersonal while closer objects become involved and intimate. This draws on Andrew Sarris and his claims of authorial identification as being made possible through the work. The fragility of the 'personification schema' and even the concept of the 'invisible observer' are evident when considering Burch's (1982) observations relating to the 'rule' that the performer never acknowledge the camera's presence:

> For the spectator to receive as directed at him/her a gaze at the camera had become tantamount to the hidden voyeur's shock when his/her gaze is unmasked and returned. As a condition of being able to 'take off', to enter that 'other scene' of the film; to feel him/herself freely evolving within it, the spectator had to feel him/herself unobserved. (p. 22)

Burch's position reaffirms classical narration's suppression of the workings of style by literally emphasising the need for 'invisibility'. 'The secret of the maximisation of the diegetic process is the spectator's invulnerability'. The convention of classical practice that restrains the spectator's awareness of the camera (as a part of style) suggests that acknowledging its existence then links it to the narrator as author and in turn as filmmaker. This then undermines the desire to have narration unfold seemingly of its own accord.

Rick Altman (2008, p. 16) considers the process of a camera 'following' or choosing and framing a subject or subjects as: '...simultaneously activating both character and narrator'. Altman notes that in singling out or 'foregrounding' character or characters, this intentional action in turn draws attention to the presence of a narrator: '...someone, some thing, some system deciding who should be followed' (p. 16). Within the hierarchy of classical narration, the role related to assuming the responsibility for such decision-making, for 'deciding', rightly or wrongly where and how the camera is positioned within a scene invariably ends up being attributed to the director. As discussed earlier, Spielberg's popularity, success and resulting celebrity status has created a high degree of 'brand awareness' resulting in the perception that any film he directs must surely have been authored entirely by him. Marketing and Spielberg himself perpetuate this perception. Yet it is my contention that once the audience begin the experience of viewing a Spielberg-directed narrative, they are required to contend with specific—and unique—stylistic strategies that are designed to erase the sense of the presence of the camera. This then encourages the perception that the narration exists independently and of itself.

Notes

1. King is clearly referencing Spielberg's own experience of his parents' divorce during his childhood.
2. Spielberg as signature applies literally in the case of the *Universal Studios* series of laser discs noted in the introduction. Released in the late 1990s, they were marketed as the '*Signature Collection*' with Spielberg's signature featured prominently as part of the artwork. Spielberg's signature also appears on a recently released Blu-ray set from Universal, *Steven Spielberg Director's Collection*.
3. For example, as Raymond Bellour in *The Analysis of Film* (2000) illustrates in his prominent, shot-by-shot analyses of scenes from Hitchcock's films first published in the 1960s.
4. *Always* also under-performed at the box office. As already noted, *The BFG* is a recent big-budget production that delivered disappointing box-office returns.

5. The wide reverse is explained and examined in Chaps. 6 and 7.
6. Khan did not edit *E.T.* as he was cutting *Poltergeist* (1982), which was written and produced by Spielberg.
7. Bordwell has made a similar observation of this director.
8. Julia Philips (1991) claims that while taking publicity stills with the camera team during the production of *Close Encounters*, Spielberg refused to allow any photos to be taken of her looking through the film camera.
9. Williams did not compose *The Color Purple* or Spielberg's segment of *The Twilight Zone Movie* (1985) and he was unavailable for *Bridge of Spies* because of illness. He did compose the score for the two *Amazing Stories* episodes directed by Spielberg.
10. Melissa Mathison wrote both *E.T.* and *The BFG*.
11. *A.I.*'s box office was considered disappointing by Spielberg standards and the film was harshly criticised by some critics for supposedly distorting Kubrick's vision—criticism rejected by Spielberg.
12. Coverage refers to the camera shots used to shoot or 'cover' a scene.
13. This conception of the camera as replicating spectator perception is revisited in cognitive theory and examined in Chap. 8.

References

Altman, R. (2008). *A Theory of Narrative*. New York: Columbia University Press.
American Film Institute. (1995). *Steven Spielberg Interview* [Video File]. Retrieved from https://www.youtube.com/watch?v=UcM6sDKrX1M
Andrew, D. (1993). The Unauthorized Auteur Today. In J. Collins, H. Redner, & A. P. Collins (Eds.), *Film Theory Goes to the Movies*. London: Routledge.
B, B. (2006). The Price of Revenge. *American Cinematographer, 87*(2), 32–43.
Bazin, A. (1985). On the politique des auteurs. In J. Hiller (Ed.) & P. Graham (Trans.). *Cahiers du Cinema The 1950's Neo-Realism, Hollywood, New Wave*. Cambridge: Harvard University Press.
Bellour, R. (2000). *The Analysis of Film*. Bloomington: Indiana University Press.
Bettinson, G. (2009). Reappraising Always. *New Review of Film and Television Studies, 7*(1), 33–49.
Bordwell, D. (1977). Camera Movement and Cinematic Space. *Cine-Tracts, 1*(2). Retrieved from http://library.brown.edu/cds/cinetracts/CT02.pdf

Bordwell, D. (1979). The Art Cinema as Mode of Film Practice. *Film Criticism, 4*(1). Retrieved from Academic Search Premier.
Bordwell, D. (1985). *Narration and the Fiction Film.* London: Routledge.
Bordwell, D. (1989). *Making Meaning.* Cambridge: Harvard University Press.
Bordwell, D. (2008). *The Poetics of Cinema.* London: Routledge.
Bordwell, D. (2011). Do Filmmakers Deserve the Last Word? In D. Bordwell & K. Thompson (Eds.), *Minding Movies: Observations on the Art, Craft, and Business of Filmmaking.* Chicago: The University of Chicago Press.
Bordwell, D., & Thompson, K. (1985). Towards a Scientific Film History? *Quarterly Review of Film Studies, 10*(3), 224–237. Retrieved from Taylor & Francis Media, Cultural & Communication Studies Online Archive.
Bordwell, D., & Thompson, K. (2008). *Film Art.* New York: McGraw Hill.
Bouzereau, L. (Writer & Producer). (2004). *Saving Private Ryan: Making Saving Private Ryan* [Blu-ray supplement in S. Spielberg (Director), Saving Private Ryan]. Australia: DreamWorks.
Branigan, E. (1981). The Spectator and Film Space—Two Theories. *Screen, 22*(1). Retrieved from http://screen.oxfordjournals.org/
Branigan, E. (2006). *Projecting a Camera: Language Games in Film Theory.* New York: Routledge.
Buckland, W. (2006). *Directed by Steven Spielberg: Poetics of the Contemporary Hollywood Blockbuster.* New York: Continuum.
Burch, N. (1982). Narrative/Diegesis Thresholds, Limits. *Screen, 23*(2), 16–33. Retrieved from http://screen.oxfordjournals.org
Caldwell, J. T. (2008). *Production Culture: Industrial Reflexivity and Critical Practice in Film and Television.* Durham: Duke University Press.
Carroll, N. (1988). *Mystifying Movies: Fads and Fallacies in Contemporary Film Theory.* New York: Columbia University Press.
Currie, G. (1995). *Image and Mind: Film, Philosophy and Cognitive Science.* New York: Cambridge University Press.
Currie, G. (1996). Film, Reality, and Illusion. In D. Bordwell & N. Carroll (Eds.), *Post-Theory: Reconstructing Film Studies.* Wisconsin: University of Wisconsin Press.
Duncan, J., & Shay, D. (1993). *The Making of Jurassic Park. An Adventure 65 Million Years in the Making.* London: Boxtree.
Evans, R. (1994). *The Kid Stays in the Picture.* Glasgow: Harper Collins Publishers.
Gerstner, D. A. (2003). The Practices of Authorship. In A. Gerstner & J. Staiger (Eds.), *Authorship and Film.* New York: Routledge.

Grodal, T. (2004). Agency in Film, Filmmaking, and Reception. In T. Grodal, B. Larsen, & I. T. Laursen (Eds.), *Visual Authorship: Creativity and Intentionality in Media*. Denmark: Museum Tusculanum Press and the Authors.

Head, S. (2002). *An Interview with Steven Spielberg*. Retrieved from http://au.ign.com/articles/2002/12/17/an-interview-with-steven-spielberg?page=1

Heath, S. (1976). Narrative Space. *Screen, 17*(3). Retrieved from http://screen.oxfordjournals.org/

Helpern, D. (2000). At Sea with Steven Spielberg. In L. D. Friedman & B. Notbohm (Eds.), *Steven Spielberg Interviews*. Jackson: University Press of Mississippi.

Hogan, P. C. (2004). Auteurs and Their Brains: Cognition and Creativity in the Cinema. In T. Grodal, B. Larsen, & I. T. Laursen (Eds.), *Visual Authorship: Creativity and Intentionality in Media*. Denmark: Museum Tusculanum Press and the Authors.

Kael, P. (1994). *For Keeps: 30 Years at the Movies*. New York: Plume/Penguin Books.

Kapsis, R. (1992). *Hitchcock, The Making of a Reputation*. Chicago: University of Chicago.

King, G. (2002). *New Hollywood Cinema: An Introduction*. London: L.B. Tauris.

Listal. (2012). *Steven Spielberg's Favorite Films*. Retrieved from http://www.listal.com/list/steven-spielbergs-favorite-films

Livingston, P. (2005). *Art and Intention: A Philosophical Study*. New York: Oxford University Press.

McBride, J. (1997). *Steven Spielberg: A Biography*. New York: Simon and Schuster.

Metz, C. (1982). *The Imaginary Signifier: Psychoanalysis and the Cinema*. (C. Britton, A. Williams, B. Brewster, & A. Guzzetti, Trans.). Bloomington: Indiana University Press.

Naremore, J. (1999). Authorship. In T. Miller & R. Stam (Eds.), *A Companion to Film Theory*. Malden: Blackwell Publishing.

Neale, S. (2000). *Genre and Hollywood*. London: Routledge.

Nichols, B. (1976). Introduction. In B. Nichols (Ed.), *Movies and Methods Vol. 1*. Berkeley: University of California Press.

Phillips, J. (1991). *You'll Never Eat Lunch in This Town Again*. New York: New American Library.

Pizzello, S. (1997). Chase, Crush and Devour. *American Cinematographer, 78*(6), 38–54.

Poster, S. (1978). The Mind Behind 'Close Encounters of the Third Kind'. *American Cinematographer, 59*(2), 111–113.

Pudovkin, V. I. (1959). *Film Technique and Film Acting: The Cinema Writings of V.I. Pudovkin* (I. Montagu, Trans.). New York: Bonanza Books.

Rabinow, P. (1984). *The Foucault Reader: An Introduction to Foucault's Thought*. London: Penguin Books.

Salt, B. (2011). Reaction Time: How to Edit Movies. *New Review of Film and Television Studies, 9*(3), 341–357. Retrieved from https://doi.org/10.1080/17400309.2011.585865

Schickel, R. (Writer & Director). (2007). *Spielberg on Spielberg* [DVD documentary]. United States: Turner Classic Movies.

Shone, T. (2004). *Blockbuster*. London: Simon and Schuster.

Spielberg, S. (1981). Of Narrow Misses and Close Calls. *American Cinematographer, 62*(11), 152–203.

Staiger, J. (2000). *Perverse Spectators: The Practices of Film Reception*. New York: New York University Press.

Staiger, J. (2003). Authorship Approaches. In D. A. Gerstner & J. Staiger (Eds.), *Authorship and Film*. New York: Routledge.

Starski, A. (1994). Art Direction: From Wajda to Spielberg. In J. Boorman & W. Donohue (Eds.), *Projections 3: Film-makers on Film-Making* (pp. 69–80). England: Faber and Faber.

Tomashevsky, B. (1965). Thematics. In L. T. Lemon, M. J. Reis, & M. J. Lincoln (Trans.). *Russian Formalist Criticism: Four Essays* (pp. 61–98). London: University of Nebraska Press.

Tybjerg, C. (2004). The Makers of Movies: Authors, Subjects, Personalities, Agents? In T. Grodal, B. Larsen, & I. T. Laursen (Eds.), *Visual Authorship Creativity and Intentionality in Media* (pp. 37–66). Denmark: Museum Tusculanum Press and the authors.

Wollen, P. (1998). *Signs and Meaning in the Cinema* (4th ed.). London: British Film Institute.

Wollen, P. (2003). The Auteur Theory: Michael Curtiz and Casablanca. In D. A. Gerstner & J. Staiger (Eds.), *Authorship and Film*. New York: Routledge.

4

Continuity Editing as System

Before determining the ways Spielberg customises style, it is important to first acknowledge some of the main stylistic devices that function under the umbrella of the classical continuity system. Among these, Spielberg rigorously observes the conventions of the shot, reverse shot arrangement, subjective and point-of-view shot construction, and the multiple angle coverage of space. Yet I argue these are the very elements of the continuity system that he also uniquely modifies and that form the foundation of the wide reverse. This chapter examines these fundamental aspects of classical style within the context of conventional usage. Understanding how these devices operate conventionally will assist in comprehending the points of difference that make up the innovative aspects of Spielberg's style, which are examined in the following chapters.

Shot, Reverse Shot

Classical continuity editing relies on a set of specific 'rules'[1] that determine the construction of narrative. Temporally, the most important rule relates to the matching of action across edits. Continuous time is implied

© The Author(s) 2018
J. Mairata, *Steven Spielberg's Style by Stealth*,
https://doi.org/10.1007/978-3-319-69081-0_4

if the action of a character, characters and/or objects appears uninterrupted across a cut when the two shots occur in the same or overlapping space. While the continuity system is not the only way to construct narrative, its use and—more crucially—its ready comprehension by audiences irrespective of cultural difference has seen it dominate narrative cinema (and television) worldwide for almost a century. Salt (1992, p. 136) points out that the use of 'continuity cinema' had become common in the United States after 1914 and that American films had come to dominate Europe at about the same time. Bordwell (1996, pp. 87–107) argues that because the shot, reverse shot convention is not culturally specific and is easily understood with little or no required learning, it should be considered as a 'contingent universal'. That is, we partially comprehend the information from the arrangement of these shots at a perceptually primal level.[2]

Integral to classical continuity is the operation of the shot, reverse shot arrangement and its role in reinforcing scenographic space. Observing 'the axis-of-action' or 'the line' or 'the 180-degree rule' in shot, reverse shot patterning has traditionally been considered essential to audience comprehension of classical scenographic space. Bordwell elaborates on Bazin's comparison of the filmic spectator as retaining a similar perspective to the spectator in the theatre in the sense that both see the 'performers' from one side. In theatre this demarcation is determined by the proscenium and in classical cinema by the 180-degree line. Like the theatre, the filmic spectator can potentially view the performer from any area on this one side of the proscenium or line. Bordwell (Staiger and Thompson 1985, p. 56) notes that this comparison suffers from certain oversimplifications including the absence of the 'fourth wall' in cinema. Bazin also fails to consider the potential for the filmic perspective to cross the 180-degree line and/or enter the proscenium—as Spielberg actively does as I explain in Chap. 6.

> I go for geography. I want the audience to know not only which side the good guy is on and the bad guy is on, but which side of the screen they're in, and I want the audience to be able to edit as quickly as they want in a shot that I am loath to cut away from.—Spielberg (Windolf 2008)

At first glance, Spielberg's adherence to the rules of classical narrative seems unremarkable and largely conventional. Instances of conventional shot, reverse shot (or field, counterfield) cutting are evident in all of his films. Frames Fig. 4.1a–c (below) are taken from *Bridge of Spies* (2015). The scene begins with a close-up on Donovan that slowly tracks back to a brief over-shoulder that includes Bates before cutting to a Donovan, Bates two-shot (Fig. 4.1a) that establishes the physical positioning of the two characters in both the space and in relation to each other. This is followed by a brief over-shoulder shot of Bates (Fig. 4.1b) that prefaces a series of shot, reverse shot exchanges between the two characters.

This corresponds to the orthodox shot, reverse shot arrangement as depicted in Fig. 4.2 (below) where Fig. 4.1a matches to position I, Fig. 4.1b to position D and Fig. 4.1c to position E. The so-called line or axis-of-action is represented by the horizontal broken line that runs through the diagram. The camera positions that capture the scene are all located on one side of this line and this guarantees that the eye-line of each character will converge—they appear to be looking at each other when the two shots are cut together.

Figs. 4.1a, 4.1b, 4.1c *Bridge of Spies* (2015)

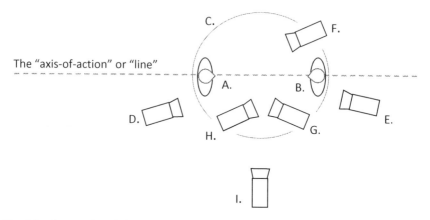

Fig. 4.2 Conventional shot, reverse shot

This is not so problematic in Fig. 4.1b–c as both characters are included in each shot, which itself aids spatial orientation. Delineating the spatial relationship between two characters becomes more complex when single close-ups are employed. Figures 4.3a and 4.3b from *Amistad* (1997) demonstrate a conventional shot, reverse shot exchange achieved via the camera positions G and H in Fig. 4.2 (above). Spatial orientation is provided in part by the direction of the gaze of each of the two characters such that the first character (Fig. 4.3a/G) is looking from left to right across the frame while the second character appears to 'answer' this with a gaze that crosses the frame from right to left (Fig. 4.3b/H). The visual effect is that the gaze/eye-lines of both appear to meet across the edit. Orientation is also almost always supplemented by previous or subsequent shot variations such as two-shots and establishing shots—as seen in the Fig. 4.1a–c example. Aberrations occur when the line is crossed. In Fig. 4.2, if the conversation between A and B is filmed on both sides of the line with A photographed by camera position F and B photographed on the other side of the line by camera position H, then the resulting footage when cut together has both characters looking right to left as in the simulation for Figs. 4.3c and 4.3d (below). They do not appear to be looking at each other. This is considered poor practice and, due to the established convention of converging or 'matching' eye-lines, may cause spectator confusion with regard to figure orientation and the relationship between the two characters. This 'crossing-the-line' is unusual in mainstream cinema and never occurs in a Spielberg film. Though rare, instances of 'crossing-the-line' and incorrect eye-lines usually occur in dialogue scenes involving multiple characters where individual eye-lines change depending to whom each character is directing their dialogue. Salt (1992) mentions Martin Scorsese and Clint Eastwood as directors who '…sometimes crossed the eye-line on purpose…' (p. 296) though he does not give specific examples. Recent studies in perceptual psychology have questioned the importance of the crossing-the-line rule in relation to its value in assisting with spatial coherence and this is considered in Chap. 8.

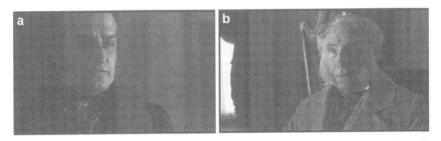

Figs. 4.3a, 4.3b

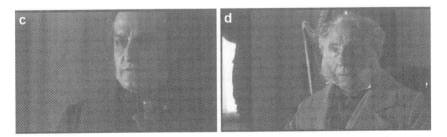

Figs. 4.3c   Simulation, 4.3d/4.3b, *Amistad* (1997)

Spielberg's preoccupation with maintaining spatial orientation is underlined by his advice to writer-director David Koepp during the preproduction for Koepp's *Premium Rush* (2012). Koepp recounts that Spielberg suggested that for action scenes involving a bicycle messenger, screen direction [or 'directional continuity' (Bordwell et al. 1985, p. 57)] should be consistent with the messenger entering one side of the screen when travelling from one side of Manhattan to the other and then applying the opposite screen direction when travelling back the other way (Roston 2013). Preserving screen direction is a traditional classical convention that has become less consistently observed since the advent of New Hollywood and intensified continuity.

The circle of action depicts the space in which profilmic activity takes place (Katz 1991, p. 231). This is labelled as C in Fig. 4.2 and in this instance encompasses the two characters (A and B). For the *Bridge of Spies* example, the three camera placements (Fig. 4.1a–c) are all positioned outside the circle of action while the two *Amistad* shots (Fig. 4.3a–b) are positioned inside the circle of action. Typically in classical narrative, scenes are constructed utilising camera placements that occupy both and in this respect Spielberg also conforms. An overuse of such single shots can lead to a degree of 'choppiness' in the editing as Bordwell (2013, p. 14) and others have observed in the films of writer/director Christopher Nolan (in *Insomnia* (2002) in particular). Alternatively, Yasujiro Ozu created a unique variation of the shot, reverse shot system that partially relied on placing the camera both inside the circle and on the 'line'.[3]

When discussing the rapid editing seen in the Bourne films, Spielberg has commented that he is reluctant to '…sacrifice geography…' (Windolf 2008) for the sake of rapid editing. Related to this is Spielberg's limited use of camera positions inside the circle. Single close-ups tend to separate the subject from its environment and/or from the other subjects present (Fig. 4.3a–d). This is in contrast to shots taken outside the circle, which usually show multiple subjects (usually characters) in the same shot and therefore assist in clarifying their relative spatial orientation (Fig. 4.1a–c). Bordwell (2006. p. 124) notes that both Kuleshov and Pudovkin identified the shot, reverse shot arrangement as incorporating 'reminders' of spatial orientation in that they repeatedly reveal the same space and objects. Each successive shot reconfirms scenographic space for the spectator using cues that include body positioning, eye-line direction and background detail.

At the same time, cinematographer Janusz Kaminski observes that 'Steven likes the actors to be as close to the camera as possible…' (Holben 2002), which implies placing the camera inside the circle to augment the tightly framed composition required. An alternative method is to employ a long focal-length (or telephoto) lens, which enables the camera to remain outside the circle. Spielberg does occasionally use this strategy although his general preference is to use wider-angle lenses (Poster 1978). Spielberg avoids the potential for spatial disconnection by employing deep space compositions that position a closer, foregrounded character with additional characters/objects in the background thus retaining spatial relativity (see Chap. 5). This manipulation of both camera and character placement (or staging/blocking) to create an alternative to the typical presentation of shot, reverse shot can be traced back to Spielberg's earliest television work. 'The one thing I refused to conform to was the television formula of close-up, two-shot, over-the-shoulders and master shot' (Poster 1978).

This is the 'formula' that has also dominated classical Hollywood cinema for decades. In tracing the development of the shot, reverse shot—or 'reverse angle' as Salt labels it—Salt (1992, p. 236) notes that the 1940s represented a consolidation period where use of the shot, reverse shot arrangement reached a peak of approximately 40 per cent of edits in a Hollywood feature film. In a further survey of 1999 releases, the average again hovers at over 40 per cent with the percentage range of the films sampled varying between 23 per cent and 70 per cent (Salt 2006, p. 334).

Variations in Shot, Reverse Shot Construction and Subjectivity

The following example from *Empire of the Sun* illustrates variation in the previous 'conventional' instances already examined. Figure 4.4a–h depicts Jim returning home to his now abandoned and ransacked home in search of his absent parents. Entering their bedroom (Fig. 4.4a), he

86   J. Mairata

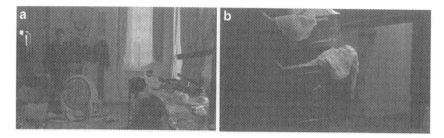

Figs. 4.4a, 4.4b

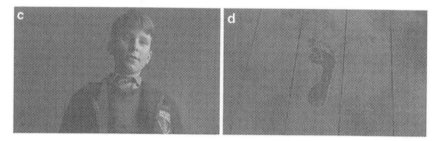

Figs. 4.4c, 4.4d

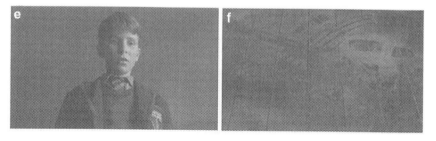

Figs. 4.4e, 4.4f

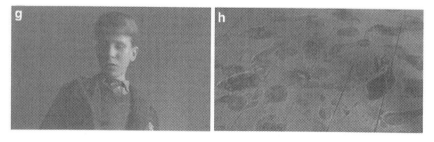

Figs. 4.4g, 4.4h   *Empire of the Sun* (1987)

notices some kind of make-up or powder-like substance spilling on to the floor. This is captured in a slow push-in shot that mimics Jim's motion and that implies his optical point-of-view (OP) (Fig. 4.4b). Following this is a series of shot, reverse shot exchanges with the camera placed inside the circle of action that visually narrate Jim's realisation that something unpleasant may have happened here. Each Jim single is followed by a close-up of the imprints left on the floor by the disturbed powder and the pattern appears to conform to Edward Branigan's (1984, p. 103) point/glance, point/object pattern typically seen in point-of-view arrangements. The shots of the powder and markings suggest subjectivity yet the shots appear tighter and lower to the floor than would be the case with shots taken from Jim's actual optical perspective. Rather than replicate OP for the floor shots, Spielberg chooses visual legibility and clarity over verisimilitude with a faithful or 'real' angle. This 'approximation' of point-of-view is not uncommon in classical narration and Spielberg applies this variation frequently. Another instance occurs in the Omaha Beach sequence examined in Chap. 6. This strategy also contributes to minimising the level of self-consciousness. Branigan (1992, p. 53) has identified a number of effects relating to the 'power' of the glance and these can all be seen operating in this scene, including: the bridging of space; the orientation to something nearby that also constructs a spatial relationship; temporal continuity with glance and object as occurring sequentially; as a link to character intention and/or reaction; and as an interaction with an object.

Each of the 'answering' reverses also contains variation in their presentation and the sequence develops in conjunction with the accompanying music by John Williams. The initial shots of Fig. 4.4c and its answer at Fig. 4.4d and again at Fig. 4.4e, f are then modified in Fig. 4.4g by Jim looking from right to left and back again, which is then answered by a pan from his shoes to the floor (Fig. 4.4h). Note that this answering pan is positioned as a reverse angle, not as an OP. The camera panning movement in the answering shot replicates Jim's head turn in the shot before. The panning movement of Fig. 4.4h implies a continuation of the shot before and at the same time clearly avoids OP by positioning the camera low on the floor in the reverse position of Fig. 4.4g. Spielberg is able to imply OP without actually applying it. This has the added advantage of again restricting the degree of self-consciousness. The final set of floor shots overwhelm Jim and he dashes across to the window and opens it, the breeze blowing away the powder and all evidence of what occurred. The patterned repetition in the shots drives the scene towards a climax and Spielberg enhances the dramatic effect by placing the camera outside the circle and behind Jim for his movement to the window. This variation in the shot, answer shot pattern serves as punctuation and underlines Jim's mental state by actually showing us *less* of him—it is his *action* of rushing to the window that enhances the telegraphing of his emotion.

The second example from *Munich* (2005) demonstrates Spielberg's general preference for shooting entire scenes as master shots and then introducing inserts as coverage during editing. As noted earlier, the traditional master shot normally covers an entire scene in a wide framing. Filmmakers may elect to only use the master or they might include additional tighter shots of significant elements. Master shots can be fixed shots or they can be moving and may begin with a tighter framing and open out to a wide or conversely begin wide and end tighter. The basic advantages of a master are: (1) it usually permits a scene to be shot more quickly as the entire scenario can be included in one shot; (2) because the framing is normally kept wide for most of the shot, this enables spectators to be constantly orientated much like an establishing shot—often also the function of a master; (3) shooting a scene in one continuous take benefits the performers by avoiding the disruption of stopping and starting that comes from shooting multiple angles and frame sizes (some of this disruption can also be alleviated by shooting multiple cameras though this can then compromise lighting detail). Classical convention usually structures scene coverage such that the scene begins with a wide establishing shot and then includes additional shots such as shot, reverse shot arrangements that may also include various frame sizes, other shots such as inserts of objects and so on—all are considered as coverage. Conversely, an entire scene may be shot using only a single shot and we can say that the coverage consisted of this one shot (Katz 1991, p. 152).

As mentioned in Chap. 2, part of Spielberg's preference for shooting masters can be traced to his tendency to shoot quickly and his replication of studio-era practice. Discussing his early television work, Spielberg explains his resistance to the television close-up and the influence of past studio practice:

What I tried to bring to TV was a lesser emphasis on the close up because the movies I learned from were really about master shots and letting the audience kind of look at the overview and kind of be their own film editor sometimes. I used to love those old movies like Orson Welles, certainly, and John Ford you know, shot wide, Howard Hawks shot wide… (Bouzereau 2001)

The contrast to Spielberg's contemporaries is particularly evident in relation to intensified continuity and Bordwell's (2006, p. 129) observation that the increased use of tighter shots has resulted in a corresponding decline in the use of masters and establishing shots.

He's very much an old-fashioned filmmaker in terms of how he tells his stories; that seems like a very tricky statement because his movies are so technologically advanced, but when you see a special effect in Steven's movies, you can experience it in a wide shot. He likes to see action play in one continuous shot rather than being interrupted by an editor's cut, and that's very old fashioned. We staged a lot of scenes in wide shots that have a lot of things happening within the frame.—Janusz Kaminsky, cinematographer. (Holben 2002)

Every shot is elaborately choreographed. He [Spielberg] always shoots them as complex masters.—Mitch Dubin, camera operator. (Thomson 2012)

Stylistically, Spielberg's shooting strategy manifests itself in his narrative in two ways: (1) the use of deep space staging and compositions and (2) the use of a master shot (or shots) to cover large segments of the staged action, which permits a reduction in the amount of cutting and use of coverage. This can include a number of variations such as matching reverse masters, long takes, wide reverses and variations of each. Dubin and Michael Kahn both note that Spielberg tends to shoot a substantial amount of coverage together with the master shots. This allows him the choice of constructing a scene along a sliding scale that ranges from the uncut master to a highly edited version or somewhere in between. The master functions as a template for Spielberg, the foundation upon which he builds the various stylistic layers and at the same time allows him to vary the visual complexity. That he uses this sliding scale means that the 'appearance' of the master is often distorted or seemingly disguised across scenes and whole films. 'Cutting up' the master (by adding in coverage) helps provide the kind of visual variation that seemingly satisfies Spielberg's claim that he is always interested in varying his style.

> I know that I have to concentrate on changing my style from film to film or often I'll be tempted to repeat techniques or approaches that have proved successful before. (Spielberg 1981)

More recently:

> I've tried to make every single movie as if it was made by a different director, because I'm very conscious of not wanting to impose a consistent style on subject matter that is not necessarily suited to that style. So I try to reinvent my own eye every time I tackle a new subject. But it's hard, because everybody has style. You can't help it. (Windolf 2008)

The scene from *Munich* (Fig. 4.5a–l) can be considered as a prototypical example of the way Spielberg deploys continuity editing within a shot, reverse shot framework in many sequences in his films. The scene incorporates multiple masters, wide reverses, a mixture of deep space and shallow staging, a combination of wide angle and long lens compositions, and 'discreet' handheld and fixed camera placement. I argue that Spielberg employs each of these devices to collectively 'energise' what is an essentially visually static but also thematically significant expository scene. He achieves this without resorting to quickened editing or overly tight compositions—characteristics of intensified continuity—and commonly seen in contemporary cinema. As is consistent with Spielberg, changes of shot are appropriately motivated and recall Hitchcock's 'camera logic'—always having the camera positioned in the right place and the right time (Bouzereau 1997). The scene runs just over three minutes and includes 27 edits, which suggests that it should contain a similar number of shots yet it comprises only 12 individual shots. Salt has pointed out that counting the number of shots in a film based on each edit can be misleading because of shot, reverse shot arrangements where the same shots are intercut and 'reused' repeatedly but are then inaccurately counted as additional shots. There are also three wide masters and one tighter master and they are

Continuity Editing as System 91

Figs. 4.5a, 4.5b

Figs. 4.5c, 4.5d

Figs. 4.5e, 4.5f

Figs. 4.5g, 4.5h

Figs. 4.5i, 4.5j

Figs. 4.5k, 4.5l   *Munich* (2005)

referred to 14 times. It seems likely that the use of three wide masters (depending on the scene, most filmmakers shoot only one) relates to the large number of characters scattered around the room (seven in all) and again underlines Spielberg's stated strategy of always prioritising the clear delineation of scenographic space. The fourth, tighter master is used to capture much of the action from the first master's perspective and would have helped to speed up the shooting process. Beginning in a tight shot that follows Avner into the room, the first master (Fig. 4.5a, d and a tighter version later in the scene) establishes the larger space. After all of the characters around Avner are introduced in a handheld pan (Fig. 4.5b–c), the first master is reused and held until Avner and the General are seated and their relative positions confirmed (Fig. 4.5d). The second master (Fig. 4.5f) is approximately 45 degrees to the right of the first and is positioned slightly higher looking down at the group. This height allows each of the characters in the room to be clearly visible—with the exception of Ephraim, whom Spielberg saves and introduces at the end the scene. The second master also facilitates the visual contrast near the end of the scene where Avner seemingly finds himself alone and that sets up the introduction of Ephraim. The third master (Fig. 4.5k and again 11 shots later) is an example of what I describe as a wide reverse in the sense that it provides a reverse vista of the space from the first master—it reveals the 'fourth wall'. The combination of these two masters alone effectively provides us with a 360-degree view of the space of the scene. The fourth, tighter master first appears at Fig. 4.5b, c, g and a further three times in the course of the scene. This shot also appears to be handheld and the relatively restrained movement contributes a sense of 'edginess' and tension in the visuals.

The alternating use of different focal length lenses is evident in the single shots of Golda Meir where the wide angle of Fig. 4.5h is contrasted to the longer lens shot at Fig. 4.5l, a return to the same wider angle two shots later and the long lens again a further two shots later. This mixture of focal lengths is consistent with Bordwell's observations for intensified continuity and the effect here is to add another layer of visual variation in the presentation of the scene. The long lens also inherently flattens the image and draws the subject—in this instance the character of Golda Meir—closer or larger in the frame thus generating emphasis. The additional layer in this case relates to plotting, with the Meir character discussing a personal matter, the death of her sister, which is followed by her making the key thematic (and motivating) point that '…family matters…' (as in family/Israel must be preserved). Yet Spielberg avoids the other stylistic tendencies consistent with intensified continuity. For a scene that consists of almost no movement and multiple characters, a restlessly moving camera and close-up reaction shots would seem mandatory within the context of contemporary Hollywood practice. Only the first establishing shot incorporates a brief tracking movement while the handheld shots are restrained in their motion. The scene includes only four medium close-ups and no close-ups. The ASL for the scene is approximately seven seconds and this is at the higher end for contemporary Hollywood. It also needs to be noted that an action scene or action film would generally involve more editing than a dialogue scene or dialogue-based drama. Nevertheless, Spielberg's resistance to close-ups, persistent use of masters and deep space compositions (Fig. 4.5g) reinforce cinematographer Kaminski's observation that Spielberg is 'old-fashioned' in his use of style. This is further evidenced in Spielberg's application of the axial cut.

'Noise': Axial Cutting as Paradox in the Classical Context

The *Munich* scene also includes three instances of axial cuts. One is a cut-in from Fig. 4.5g to Fig. 4.5h with the second at the end of the scene when Ephraim and Avner meet. The third is a cut-out from Fig. 4.5j to Fig. 4.5k. Axial cuts refer to the editing of one shot to another that occurs along the same camera axis so that the objects in the frame become larger or smaller depending on two factors: the change in distance of the camera from the subject and/or the change in lens focal length from one shot to the next. Bordwell (2001) notes that a 1926 Soviet text on editing by S. Timoshenko labels the axial cut-in as a 'concentration cut' and the axial cut-out as an 'expansion cut' (p. 16). This specific type of edit is not commonly used but does have a long history in classical style. One consequence of this choice of shooting and editing is that errors in continuity often occur. In the example from director Michael Curtiz's *The Private Lives of Elizabeth and Essex* (1939) (below), Fig. 4.6a is the final frame in a shot that has tracked parallel along with Essex (in black) and ends as he begins to emerge from behind the trumpeter, his foot on the first step. The break in continuity can clearly be seen in the cut to the next, slightly tighter shot at Fig. 4.6b where Essex is now suddenly centre frame. Another less drastic example can be seen in William Wyler's *Detective Story* (1951) where the cut-in at Fig. 4.7b reveals discontinuity in the positions of the characters' hands. Bordwell (1985, pp. 117–118) describes these instances of discontinuity across edits as 'minor deviations' or 'noise' and they represent disruptions from the smooth flow consistent with match-on-action editing. In a related context, Kristin Thompson (1986) has speculated on the nature of stylistic elements that manifest their presence beyond their intended function. In this sense they become '...counter-narrative and counter-unity'. Thompson describes this condition as cinematic 'excess'. Thompson notes Stephen Heath's claim that anything not related to the plot or story can be considered as excess. Roland Barthes mentions 'obtuse meaning' and likewise suggests that it applies to any aspect of the work that does not contribute

Continuity Editing as System 95

to narration creation or to meaning. Thompson avers that '...when motivation fails, excess begins' and suggests four ways this may occur with each relating to an instance where some aspect of style comes to the fore thus revealing the artifice.

Other variations of 'noise' also occasionally occur within the classical continuity editing system. One intentional example is the 'cheat cut' where characters—usually two facing each other—are shot at a specific distance in the wide shot but are then positioned closer together for tighter close-ups. This repositioning is usually motivated by the requirement to create a balanced composition so that there is not too much space between the characters or one character is not overly higher or lower in the frame than the other. This can be seen in the repositioning

Figs. 4.6a, 4.6b *The Private Lives of Elizabeth and Essex* (1939)

Figs. 4.7a, 4.7b *Detective Story* (1951)

Figs. 4.8a, 4.8b *Murder by the Book* (1971)

of the characters from Fig. 4.8a to Fig. 4.8b to retain compositional balance. Awkward continuity 'jumps' can also occur when the frame size from one shot to another does not change significantly or when the change of angle is less than 30 degrees—the so-called *30-degree rule*. This rule maintains that any new angle/shot on the same subject and of the same or similar frame size needs to be at least 30 degrees in difference from the first shot/angle to avoid a 'jump cut' effect (Burch 1973, p. 37). The visible disruption in continuity draws attention to the edit and therefore also to the artifice. This is a stylistic norm that has existed in classical cinema since the 1920s, though filmmakers like Jean-Luc Godard famously pioneered intentional and unmotivated instances of jump cutting during the *Nouvelle Vague*.

Directors like Tony Scott have avoided this issue by often shooting each take with two or more cameras situated on the same axis and fitted with different focal length lens. This means that the different shots from the same take can always be perfectly matched in terms of continuity. Bordwell (1985) further notes that instances of 'noise' often tend to go unnoticed by audiences and mentions Noël Carroll's belief that audiences '…postulate a coherent unity of action…' (p. 117) that prioritises an overarching comprehension of what is happening rather than a focus on minute spatial detail.[4] As the *Munich* scene demonstrates, Spielberg does employ the axial cut and variations of it. Instances of axial cutting also appear in his other films. Figures 4.9a–b, display a jarring disruption to continuity with the sudden appearance of smoke in Fig. 4.9b drawing

Continuity Editing as System 97

attention to the cut. Figure 4.9c–d is another less obvious instance where the cut-in produces a mismatch in character positioning. These 'errors' could be explained if they appeared early in Spielberg's career—such as the example from *Murder by the Book* (1971) where the awkward cut from Fig. 4.8a to Fig. 4.8b occurs because of the failure to observe the 30-degree rule and because there is not enough variation in frame size between the two shots. Yet the previous two examples are taken from *Jurassic Park* (1993), made by a now technically accomplished filmmaker with some 20 years of feature film directing experience. Even more puzzling are the more recent manifestations of awkward cutting. Figure 4.10 a–d appears in *The Kingdom of the Crystal Skull* (2008) and actually occurs in the same scene. The first instance fails to observe the 30-degree rule while the change in frame size is also problematic. The second example is a straight axial cut-in but features the character awkwardly at the edge of frame for the cut-in at Fig. 4.10d.

The paradox arises when one considers Spielberg's rigorous attention throughout his directing career to maintaining continuity regardless of

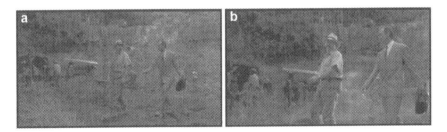

Figs. 4.9a, 4.9b

Figs. 4.9c, 4.9d   *Jurassic Park* (1993)

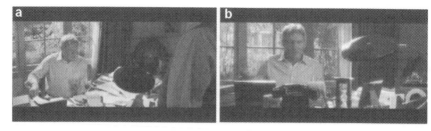

Figs. 4.10a, 4.10b

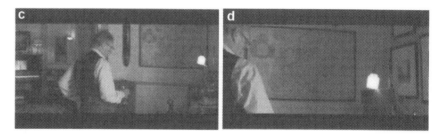

Figs. 4.10c, 4.10d   *Kingdom of the Crystal Skull* (2008)

the complexity of the scene. For Spielberg, continuity is a crucial element that must be observed at all times if the spectator is to fully 'accept' the 'world' of the narration. As classical Hollywood has always observed, discontinuity draws attention to style and must be avoided. However, as mentioned earlier, the axial cut has also enjoyed a long tradition as a legitimate editing strategy in classical Hollywood cinema. 'As with story structure, novelty is driven by an acute consciousness of recasting or reviving tradition' (Bordwell 2006, p. 174). The implication then is that Spielberg permits occasional instances of 'noise' precisely because they are part of classical tradition and that these occasional instances represent his recognition of its use in the history of Hollywood practice. It also allows him to assume complicity in the process of taking his own place in this tradition of style. This recognition of a stylistic tradition continues into the following chapter with the examination of Spielberg's revival and manipulation of multi-plane compositions and deep staging.

Notes

1. Bordwell describes these variously as 'traditional schemata' (1985, p. 57) or 'norms' (2008, p. 68).
2. I elaborate on the cognitive aspect of continuity editing in Chap. 8.
3. Ozu's system is examined in Chap. 9.
4. This has implications for understanding how spectators perceive editing and is examined in Chap. 8.

References

Bordwell, D. (1985). *Narration and the Fiction Film*. London: Routledge.
Bordwell, D. (1996). Convention, Construction and Cinematic Vision. In D. Bordwell & N. Carroll (Eds.), *Post-Theory: Reconstructing Film Studies* (pp. 87–107). Wisconsin: The University of Wisconsin Press.
Bordwell, D. (2001). Eisenstein, Socialist Realism, and the Charms of Mizanstsena. In A. Lavalley & B. P. Scherr (Eds.), *Eisenstein at 100: A Reconsideration* (pp. 13–37). New Jersey: Rutgers University Press.
Bordwell, D. (2006). *The Way Hollywood Tells It: Story and Style in Modern Movies*. Los Angeles: University of California Press.
Bordwell, D. (2008). *The Poetics of Cinema*. London: Routledge.
Bordwell, D. (2013). *Christopher Nolan: A Labyrinth of Linkages [eBook]*. Madison, Wisconsin: Irvington Way Institute Press.
Bordwell, D., & Thompson, K. (1985). Towards a Scientific Film History? *Quarterly Review of Film Studies, 10*(3), 224–237. Retrieved from Taylor & Francis Media, Cultural & Communication Studies Online Archive.
Bordwell, D., Staiger, J., & Thompson, K. (1985). *The Classical Hollywood Cinema: Film Style and Mode of Production to 1960*. New York: Routledge and Kegan Paul.
Bouzereau, L. (Writer, Director & Producer). (1997). Saboteur, A Closer Look [DVD Supplement in A. Hitchcock (Director), *Saboteur*]. Australia: Universal Pictures.
Bouzereau, L. (Writer, Director & Producer). (2001). Steven Spielberg and the Small Screen [DVD supplement in S. Spielberg (Director), *Duel*]. Australia: Universal Pictures.
Branigan, E. (1984). *Point of View in the Cinema*. Berlin: Mouton Publishers.

Branigan, E. (1992). *Narrative Comprehension and Film*. London and New York: Routledge.
Burch, N. (1973). *Theory of Film Practice*. London: Secker & Warburg.
Holben, J. (2002). Criminal Intent. *American Cinematographer, 83*(7), 34–45.
Katz, S. D. (1991). *Film Directing: Shot By Shot. Visualizing from Concept to Screen*. Michigan: Michael Wiese Productions.
Poster, S. (1978). The Mind Behind 'Close Encounters of the Third Kind'. *American Cinematographer, 59*(2), 152–203.
Roston, T. (2013, March 9). The Master Mentor. *The Sydney Morning Herald*.
Salt, B. (1992). *Film Style and Technology: History and Analysis*. London: Starword.
Salt, B. (2006). *Moving Into Pictures*. London: Starword.
Spielberg, S. (1981). Of Narrow Misses and Close Calls. *American Cinematographer, 62*(11), 1100–1103.
Thompson, K. (1986). The Concept of Cinematic Excess. In P. Rosen (Ed.), *Narrative, Apparatus, Ideology: A Film Theory Reader* (pp. 130–142). New York: Columbia University Press.
Thomson, P. (2012). Animal Instincts. *American Cinematographer, 93*(1), 48–61.
Windolf, J. (2008). Keys to the Kingdom. *Vanity Fair*. Retrieved from http://www.vanityfair.com/culture/features/2008/02/spielberg_qanda200802?currentPage=1

Film Title Editions

Curtiz, M. (Director). (1939). *The Private Lives of Elizabeth and Essex* [Motion picture, DVD (2005)]. Australia: Warner Brothers Entertainment.
Spielberg, S. (Director). (1971). *Columbo: Murder by the Book* [Television broadcast, DVD (2004)]. Australia: Universal Pictures.
Spielberg, S. (Director). (1987). *Empire of the Sun* [Motion picture, Blu-ray (2013)]. Australia: Warner Bros. Entertainment.
Spielberg, S. (Director). (1993). *Jurassic Park* [Motion picture, Blu-ray (2014)]. Australia: Universal Sony Pictures Home Entertainment.
Spielberg, S. (Director). (1997). *Amistad* [Motion picture, Blu-ray (2014)]. Australia: Paramount Pictures.
Spielberg, S. (Director). (2005). *Munich* [Motion picture, DVD (2006)]. Australia: Universal Pictures.

Spielberg, S. (Director). (2008). *Indiana Jones and the Kingdom of the Crystal Skull* [Motion picture, Blu-ray (2012)]. Australia: Lucasfilm Ltd.

Spielberg, S. (Director). (2015). Bridge of Spies [Motion picture, Blu-ray (2016)] Australia: Twentieth Century Fox Home Entertainment.

Wyler, W. (Director). (1951). *Detective Story* [Motion picture, DVD]. Australia: Payless Entertainment.

Part II

Function

5

Deep Space Composition and Staging

While the advent of anamorphic aspect ratios initially encouraged creative staging configurations that contributed to storytelling, Bordwell (2008) suggests that this skill retreated as directors reverted to less complex compositions to ensure that their narratives still remain relatively comprehensible even if screened in ratios other than those intended.

> By the end of the 1960s, most directors had no interest in articulating a scene through staging. Cutting and camera movement were enough, aided of course by close-ups of gripping performances. There emerged a generation of talented directors who loved movies, who could spin engaging yarns and elicit memorable performances, and who had an eye for anamorphic abstraction, often aided by the long lens. But they scarcely knew how to move actors around a set. (p. 324)

In losing the art of staging Bordwell (2005, p. 22) argues that current classical style has devolved into two basic staging strategies for covering and editing dialogue sequences 'walk and talk' and 'stand and deliver'. The former usually involves the camera following characters as they exchange dialogue in a way that adds a certain visual dynamism to the mise en scene. 'Stand and deliver' or 'Sit and Deliver' covers more-or-less stationery character interaction and tries to add visual energy through the tried and tested conventionality of classical continuity—an establishing wide shot, tighter singles in shot, reverse shot arrangements—not necessarily in that order and usually captured with some kind of camera movement. In this instance, it is the editing and the ability of the close-up to exploit a star's performance that makes this use of style engaging. Bordwell points out that while pre-1960s cinema also used these basic shot arrangements, it additionally often complemented them with sometimes visually elaborate deep space staging. In lamenting the disappearance of staging—and deep space staging in particular—in contemporary style, Bordwell qualifies this by singling out Spielberg as an exception, acknowledging him as '...one of the few of his cohort [including the Movie Brats] to practice more or less classical mise-en-scene' (p. 469n).

Integral to the framework of traditional, classical mise en scene is the role played by deep space composition and staging. Deep space refers to the scenographic area within the frame—the mise en scene—and suggests a degree of recessional space in the framed composition. This ranges from the most forward figure(s) back to the most distant relevant figure(s) with each figure or set of figures usually arranged in definable planes. Given the overwhelmingly anthropomorphic nature of classical cinema these figures are usually human characters. Deep focus relates to the camera lens' ability to hold the focus of figures in depth such that figure(s) nearer and further distant from the lens are all held in focus. Shorter focal length lens—or wider angle lens—tend to offer greater depth of field in contrast to longer focal length or telephoto lens. Lighting, lens quality and film stock sensitivity also contributes to the range of deep focus.[1] Staging refers to the positioning and movement of the figures in the frame—Eisenstein's 'mise-en-shot'—and includes related camera mobility. Deep staging or 'composed in depth' refers to how figures are arranged in the scenographic space and in deep space in particular. Bordwell (2005) contends that 'Because of the desire to distance cinema from its theatrical roots the study of staging in cinema has been largely ignored—critics and academics considered editing but neglected staging' (p. 8). Charles Harpole (1978, pp. 11–12) has identified three approximate 'gradients' and periods in the development of deep space composition in cinema. All of the developments inherent in these stages are relevant to the way Spielberg mobilises style. The first, or so-called primitive cinema from 1895 until around 1914, consolidated the single-plane tableau composition with lateral, front-on staging and a single layer or plane of action perpendicular to the camera. From the beginning, Harpole (1980) argues, the Lumiére brothers' early *L'arrivée d'un train en gare de La Ciotat* (1895) and the train's diagonal path through the frame helped to establish the potential for 'thinking in depth'. Noël Burch (1990, p. 172) also notes the significance of the Lumiere film in relation to depth and what he describes as the 'primitive frontality' of early French sets with their painted backdrops. He suggests that to overcome such limitations and without the benefit of Hollywood editing, French filmmakers quickly became leading innovators in deep space and staging in depth. Burch refers to this presentation of space as 'haptic', that the filmmakers could—through their cast—literally prove by touch that the space was real rather than a painted backdrop. The facilitating of deep space compositions was aided by the great quantities of light available from outdoor shooting and the use of shorter focal length lenses, which permitted a wide depth of field. Conversely, the inability of early lenses to focus on objects close to the camera resulted in an approximate four-metre distance between the camera and subject as unusable for staging. Bordwell (2008, p. 269) refers to the forward most focusable position as the 'front line' and in turn draws on the research of Barry Salt who notes a four-metre distance in early German cinema.

The relative lack of camera movement also restricted opportunities for creating depth cues. The period 1913–1919 sees staging evolving with the innovation of an added second layer of action, usually as a recessed set of characters behind the main performers. D.W. Griffith was an early American adopter of deep space composition and both Harpole and Salt (1992, p. 105) contend that in Griffith's case, the deeper level functioned largely as decoration and did not participate in the main action, which was staged largely as tableau. Salt and Ben Brewster (1990) point out that instances of deep staging—moving characters laterally deeper into the set—were already evident in French cinema as early as 1900. Bordwell (1997, p. 179) notes that deep focus and recessional staging with diagonal movement through the frame had become popular from about 1909 and by the 1920s films were exhibiting instances of up to three distinct layers of depth. In tracing the development of deep space in Swedish film of the 1910s, John Fullerton (1995) argues that cinema likely adopted deep space staging from the theatre's 'cultural establishment'. This in turn led to cinema's greater differentiation from popular cinema's traditional 'flat' scenography while the adoption of a presentation previously only seen in exclusive theatre also assisted in giving cinema wider 'cultural legitimacy'. In considering depth, Harpole cites as early examples the Odessa steps sequence in *Battleship Potemkin* (1925) and set design in German expressionism as assisting in the creation of an implied depth. Burch (1990) goes further and argues that *The Cabinet of Dr. Caligari* (1920) signals a kind of historical transition in that it fuses the 'traditional' flat, painted backdrops that characterise the tableau— albeit highly stylised in the German expressionist films—with deep space staging that always brings the actors towards the camera or in diagonals across the frame 'Thus, the same images seem to produce two historical types of representational space at once, two types which are as it were superimposed on one another' (p. 184).

American cinema and the Soviet montage had developed instances of large, off-centre foregrounds and highly recessed backgrounds, important because they '…created pictorial dynamism and emphasized the simultaneous presence of key narrative elements…' (Bordwell 1997, p. 208). This continued into the 1930s with the films of Jean Renoir while *Citizen Kane* (1942), with Orson Welles and cinematographer Greg Tolland, marked the approximate point at which deep focus across multiple planes rose to prominence as the deep space composition of choice in the United States. Eisenstein and Renoir predated Welles by several years in their use of deep focus compositions while Tolland had already used it in his work with other directors including John Ford's *The Long Voyage Home* (1940). Harpole (1980) notes that Ford had also used deep space compositions the year before for *Stagecoach* (1939) while in the same year Wyler's *Wuthering Heights* (1939) and Fleming's (and George Cukor's) *Gone With the Wind* (1939) all included instances of deep space compositions.

Why did cinema—regardless of location or nationality—evolve this form of deep space composition and staging? In discussing American two-plane depth of the 1920s and 1930s, Bordwell (1997) observes that '...off centre foregrounds set against striking depth created pictorial dynamism and emphasized the simultaneous presence of key narrative elements...' (p. 208). Lev Kuleshov (1974, p. 110) argued that the visual properties of the camera lens, represented as a pyramid on its side with the apex at the camera lens, inherently lent itself to exploring the 'three-dimensional' space that expanded with distance in front of the camera. Fullerton points out that for early Swedish cinema deep space compositions assisted in differentiating cinema from 'common' theatre while making the more complex deep space sensibility of bourgeois theatre accessible to everyone through its application and further development in popular cinema. Harpole (1978, p. 34) and Bordwell also draw on E. H. Gombrich and his examination of depth effects in painting, the adoption of linear perspective during the Renaissance and its use to create a 'realist illusion'. Noël Carroll (1988) rejects the claim of perspective as 'illusionist' and instead argues that the effect of pictorial perspective can be more accurately defined as '...engendering a strong impression of pictorial depth'. Carroll also points out that 'Albertian' or 'central' perspective is not the only way of signalling depth and that other cues include '...the comparative size of the objects portrayed, texture-density gradients, edge and overlap phenomena, the portrayal of shadows, the tendency for objects to lose detail at a distance, as well as the tendency of distant objects to turn bluish due to atmospheric impurities' (p. 127).

Another dimension of deep space as style is the role played by editing. Unlike the primitive and early European cinema where the application of editing took time to evolve and deep space existed largely of itself, Soviet montage pioneer Eisenstein also combined editing with deep space compositions. In fact, almost every Eisenstein film of the 1920s and 1930s includes sequences with compositions of objects large in the foreground and also deep in the background. Eisenstein's 'innovation' lay in his integration of deep space composition and axial cutting in a collection of 'editing-units' (shots) he called 'montage units'. Discussing axial cutting, Eisenstein commented:

...within a given editing-unit there should be a regularity in the development of the features which are taken as the basis in the determination of the unit as a whole. This means that the basic feature of the whole compositional structure should be maintained also in all its shots. The simplest means of maintaining such a unity is to shoot all the shots from the same angle, that is, not allow the camera to be changed from one side to another during the shooting of the various shots of the single unit. (Nizhny 1979, p. 77)

Remarkably, in warning against changing the camera from 'one side to another,' Eisenstein seems to be reinforcing classical continuity editing's basic law of not crossing-the-line. In this respect, and like Spielberg, Eisenstein clearly emphasises spatial orientation as an important requirement. At the same time, he pays particular attention to the storytelling possibilities of deep space staging, or *mise-en-cadre*. Discussing a sequence of shots from *Battleship Potemkin* (1925), Eisenstein (Bordwell 1993, p. 154) elaborates on the intensified effect from combining montage with *mise-en-cadre* '...the images' internal design and the microscopic patterning of the editing create a rigorous guiding of the spectator's attention'. In later writings, Eisenstein (Bordwell 2001) conceived of the deep space composition as functioning to establish space, with editing then taking over.

Eisenstein viewed deep space compositions as having three potential functions: to collect together the visual features within the frame into a 'tense unity'; to add a 'monumental effect'[2]; and to use the wide-angle lens to create '... a grotesque distortion that shakes the viewer out of his accustomed relation with things.' As Bordwell (1993, p. 150) notes, Eisenstein's application of deep space construction anticipated that of Welles and Wyler by several years. Nevertheless, by the late 1920s, American deep space compositions and continuity editing were often seamlessly integrated together into scene construction.

> In many national cinemas between 1930 and 1960 mise-en-scene was a demonstration of pacing and poise, a sustained choreography of vivid foregrounds, opposite and neatly timed background action precisely synchronized camera movements, and discreet decoupage, the whole leading the viewer gracefully and unobtrusively from one point of interest to another.

...these close foregrounds and subtle camera movements simplified or elaborated long-standing strategies of balance and decentring and recentering, blocking and revealing, aperture framing and diagonal thrusts to the foreground – in short, schemas elaborated since the very first years of cinema. (Bordwell 1997, p. 235)

The arrival of new widescreen processes such as *Cinemascope* and colour film in the early 1950s briefly compromised deep space composition and staging. The early anamorphic lenses suffered from poor depth of field while the wide framing proportions occasioned 'clothesline' or 'planimetric'[3] compositions with characters arranged in a line across the wide frame. This flat staging recalled the early tableau compositions of the 'primitive' era and it would take a few years before improving lens and film stock sensitivity permitted the reappearance of deep space compositions in the widescreen and anamorphic formats. Despite improvements in widescreen technology, classical style in the United States after 1960 also began to be influenced by the growing popularity of imported arthouse cinema and the aggressive use of long-lens compositions by directors such as Claude Lelouch, Michelangelo Antonioni and Akira Kurosawa. The seemingly less-mediated shooting style of the French New Wave, Godard's abrupt jump-cutting and its British counterpart, 'kitchen sink realism', together with the arrival of *vérité* documentary and its innovative handheld camera mobility all combined to present new stylistic possibilities for an emerging group of American filmmakers. The American New Wave or Hollywood Renaissance initially included filmmakers from television—Arthur Penn, Sidney Lumet, John Frankenheimer and later William Friedkin. They would be joined at the end of the 1960s by the mostly film school educated movie brats, themselves highly influenced by the new style of art-house cinema. Geoff King (2002, p. 47) illustrates the depth of influence of European cinema on the emerging American filmmakers noting that both Godard and Truffaut had been offered directing duties on *Bonnie and Clyde* (1967).[4]

It was in this climate of stylistic change that Spielberg commenced his own filmmaking career. Despite initially being confined to the highly structured, creatively restrictive environment of television production, Spielberg quickly established his preference for the type of deep space compositions common before the 1960s. Even *Amblin'* (1968), Spielberg's 25-minute short film, shot in 35 mm and his first 'professional' narrative, exhibits many instances of deep space compositions. I have divided his use of deep space compositions into seven broad categories and include two subcategories notable for their instances of rare deviations from a deep space sensibility. The five main categories are: two-plane compositions with aggressive foregrounds, two-plane staging, two-plane staging with camera movement, three-plane composition and staging, and long takes in deep space. The sixth section consists of the two subcategories, these being inverted deep focus, and planimetric as aberration. The final, seventh section considers deep space across multiple shots within a scene. Instances of variation in all of the following categories do occur in the sense that a two-plane deep focus composition may evolve into three planes or a long take may incorporate elements of deep space for only part of its duration. I have avoided inter-category variation in the interests of presenting each category as an illustrative stylistic template that demonstrates how Spielberg specifically mobilises and manipulates deep space in both shot composition and scene construction.

> I'd love to see directors not shoot so many close-ups. I'd love to see directors start trusting the audience to be the film editor with their eyes, the way you are sometimes with a stage play, where the audience selects who they would choose to look at while a scene is being played, with two characters, four characters, six characters. There's so much cutting and so many close-ups being shot today I think directly as an influence from television. …And as a result, it's too easy for filmmakers. It's very easy to put somebody up against a wall and shoot a close-up, and they say the words and you go on to the next shot…I'd like to see some staging come back.—Spielberg (Ebert and Siskel 1991, p. 72)

Two-Plane Composition

Figures 5.1a–b, 5.2a, 5.3a, 5.4a, 5.5a and 5.6a demonstrate instances of two-plane, deep space compositions ranging from 1969 to 2002 and recall the kind of deep space foreground, background composition common from the 1920s. *Eyes* (1969) is an episode of the *Night Gallery* television series and Spielberg's first professional television directing assignment. Figure 5.1a shows a deep space composition and staging arrangement that continues through the scene with the background character moving left to right and the foreground character compensating by moving from right to left thus maintaining the deep space composition. Figure 5.1b is composed with an aggressive foreground that occupies almost two-thirds of the frame, almost squeezing out the rear character. Spielberg biographer Joseph McBride (1997, p. 176) notes that there was some reshooting of the episode without Spielberg's involvement, reputedly because of problems relating to the cutting of some scenes. The reshooting appears to have been minor and does not cast doubt on authorial responsibility for the episode. The appearance of two- and three-plane deep space compositions in a manner consistent with Spielberg's following work reinforces this conclusion. Though heavy handed in its overemphasis of foregrounding, the composition clearly reveals Spielberg's early and already well-formed preference for deep space arrangements. Only Figs. 5.5 and 5.6 do not employ deep focus and in the latter the selective focus on Agatha in the foreground both directs the viewer's attention and emphasises her performance. As Bordwell (1997) has noted, the spectator's attention often gravitates to elements in the frame that are in focus—one of a number of methods that the filmmaker employs to direct the viewer to specific areas of the frame.

Figs. 5.1a, 5.1b *Eyes* (1969)

Fig. 5.2a *Murder by the Book* (1971)

Fig. 5.3a *Duel* (1971)

Fig. 5.4a *The Sugarland Express* (1974)

Fig. 5.5a *Raiders of the Lost Ark* (1981)

Fig. 5.6a *Minority Report* (2002)

Two-Plane Staging

These examples use two-plane composition and add significant movement within the frame. Figure 5.7a–b is another early example (1971) that demonstrates Spielberg's confidence with deep space staging as both characters alternate foreground and background places during the course of the shot. Figure 5.8a–b uses a long lens to compress the distance between the fishermen and approaching aircraft, further heightening the spatial tension between the two objects. Figure 5.9a–c employs actor staging—rather than camera movement or editing—to dramatically vary Indi's position in a single shot from distant background to extreme close-up. In each of these instances, movement is toward the camera and recalls the weight Eisenstein places on this strategy '…bringing the action forward can intensify the action, building towards a dramatic and emotional climax' (Bordwell 2001). In Fig. 5.7a–b the movement forward and backward energises the scenographic space and creates a kind of visual variation while simultaneously balancing the narrative significance of both characters. Figures 5.8a–b and 5.9a–c take advantage of an initially deep space and then use it to emphasise the object moving through that space—aircraft and Indi—with staging that 'intensifies' the action. Both could also be seen to heighten emotion in the 'Eisensteinian' context though Fig. 5.9c also clearly draws on the extrinsic classical convention of close-up as punctuation.

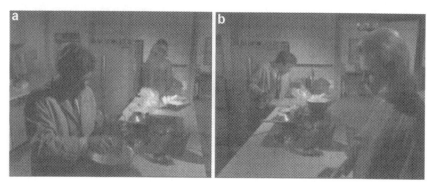

Figs. 5.7a, 5.7b *Murder by the Book* (1971)

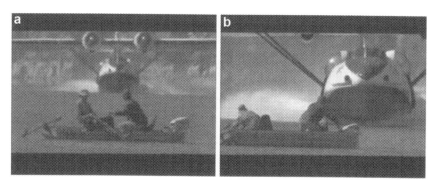

Figs. 5.8a, 5.8b *Always* (1989)

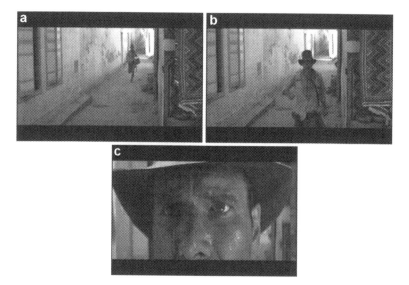

Figs. 5.9a, 5.9b, 5.9c *Raiders of the Lost Ark* (1981)

Two-Plane Staging with Camera Movement

This third variation in the two-plane realm is the least commonly deployed by Spielberg yet his use of it lacks none of the visual flair of his other staging choices. Figure 5.10a–d is another early example with the camera tracking back and zooming out from the Mercedes car as it proceeds along the street. This demonstrates Spielberg's highly developed visual sense with the shot elaborately linking the two main causal agents in the episode. The driver of the Mercedes, Ken is planning to murder Martin, the typist in the office. The camera continues to both track back and zoom out until the office space with Martin typing is revealed. The harsh lighting and strong cast shadows evident in the office space (Fig. 5.10d) betray the technical difficulties that would have arisen from trying to expose for both a bright, daylight exterior and the contrasting, darker office interior in the same shot. While the shot may have been innovative by 1970s TV standards, Salt (1992, p. 163) notes that Erich von Stroheim's 1920s films included shots that were often exposed for both interior and daylight exteriors simultaneously, the high light levels in turn permitting deep focus.

Figs. 5.10a, 5.10b

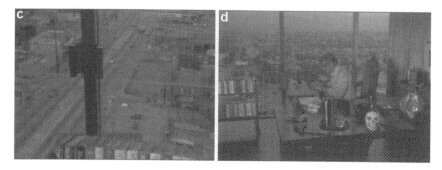

Figs. 5.10c, 5.10d *Murder by the Book* (1971)

This use of a zoom is rare for Spielberg and other than for the 'Vertigo effect' track out, zoom in of Fig. 5.11a–b, zooms are largely avoided. The scarce use of zooms is consistent with Hollywood practice up until the late 1960s where zoom shots were applied minimally and almost always unobtrusively. Robert Altman changed this with an extensive use of zoom shots in many of his features and variations on this visual style were adopted by others including Stuart Rosenberg for *Cool Hand Luke* (1968) and Stanley Kubrick for *Barry Lyndon* (1975). The prominent use of the zoom lens was another by-product of the *verite* or *direct cinema* documentary form/style that incorporated zoom shots together with handheld cameras to create a sense of immediacy and the impression of a less mediated, more 'truthful' depiction.

First used by Alfred Hitchcock and cinematographer Robert Burks to suggest the effect of vertigo on protagonist Scottie in *Vertigo* (1958), the distinctive visual distortion created by tracking the camera away from the subject while simultaneously zooming into it has been frequently copied by filmmakers and is now considered a cliché. Spielberg does repeat this effect in *The Sugarland Express* (1974), *Jaws* (1975) and again in both *E.T.* (1982) and the Spielberg written and produced *Poltergeist* (1982). In each instance, Spielberg uses the shot as punctuation. In *Jaws* it signals Brody's realisation that a shark attack is in progress. In Fig. 5.11a–b it reveals the protagonists as exposed—literally—to the waiting police sharpshooters. The deep space composition here ties together the protagonists and their fate while the

Deep Space Composition and Staging   119

unusual visual effect underlines this with its unsettling sense that something is visually and thematically not quite right. Figure 5.12a–b employs a counter track that moves the camera from right to left around the seated Al as the aircraft approaches. As with both previous examples, the deft movement spatially and geographically ties together the two main subjects in the same shot without recourse to editing. They effectively function as establishing shots yet manage to avoid the blandness of the traditional wide establishing shot by replacing it with a visually evolving dynamic between relevant subjects and their place in the scenographic space.

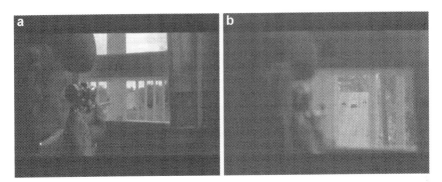

Figs. 5.11a, 5.11b   *The Sugarland Express* (1974)

Figs. 5.12a, 5.12b   *Always* (1989)

Three-Plane Composition and Staging

Also from *Eyes*, Fig. 5.13a presents a three-plane composition that mimics the kind of deep focus staging seen in *Citizen Kane* (1941) (Fig. 5.14a), itself predated by the tri-plane deep focus compositions from Eisenstein's lost *Bezhin Meadow* (1937) (Fig. 5.17a). The ungainliness of this early effort at deep focus staging does nevertheless reveal an early determination on Spielberg's part to favour deep space composition, regardless of its appropriateness. Placing Dr Heatherton (Fig. 5.13a) nearest the camera seems forced and unmotivated—he has nothing to do there, while his speech is to the other two characters behind him, further emphasising the awkwardness of his placement. In this instance, Spielberg prioritises staging and style over causal logic and motivation in a reversal of classical practice that he subsequently resolves in his later work. Television's inherent requirement for tighter framings and more close-ups to counter the screen's small dimensions proves no impediment to Spielberg's choice of deep space compositions and his determination to reject TV's tight framing convention. Figure 5.15a also depicts a highly stylised deep space composition consistent with a young filmmaker still calibrating his sense of configuring deep space. In this case the tri-plane composition is pretentiously expressed through the dryer window, which has no significance in the narrative and likely distracts.

Fig. 5.13a *Eyes* (1969)

Fig. 5.14a *Citizen Kane* (1941)

Fig. 5.15a *Duel* (1971)

All of the compositions demonstrate Spielberg's preference for the kind of diagonal, 'recessive space' perspective that both Harpole and Bordwell (2005, p. 167) attribute to Heinrich Wolfflin and that link directly to the original 'thinking in depth' conception Harpole associates with the Lumiere brothers mentioned earlier. This is particularly evident in Figs. 5.20a, 5.23a and 5.29a where characters are arranged in a receding, diagonal line that emphasises the deep space composition. Yet Spielberg is equally adept at presenting the three planes in multiple variations, with each according emphasis to different parts of the frame. The 'scattered' compositions of Figs. 5.18a, 5.25a, 5.27a and to a lesser extent Figs. 5.19a and 5.24a encourage viewers to, in Spielberg's words '…be the film editor with their eyes…' and recalls André Bazin's (1967, p. 36) own claim that deep space allows the viewer to choose what to look at in the frame rather than have the decision made for us by editing. Bazin believed that editing functioned as a 'telling' while deep space staging produced a more desirable, more realistically implied 'recording'. Charles Barr (1963, pp. 4–24) perpetuated this perception when considering deep space in *Cinemascope*, arguing that Eisenstein's montage was 'crude' and resulted in 'force feeding' of the audience rather than permitting them to explore the frame for meaning. 'Our responses are not "signposted" by successive close-ups—foot tripping over tail, result, various re-actions. No single reading of the scene is imposed. One could put it another way: the scene, as directed, is at once more subtle and more authentic'.

Within the deep space paradigm Spielberg does employ strategies to cue audience attention. Objects large in the frame tend to capture our attention first, and given the anthropomorphic nature of space in classical cinema,[5] this is particularly the case with human figures and faces. The centre of the frame is also always a powerful cue as are degrees of light and dark while the importance of focus in directing attention has already been mentioned. Spielberg adroitly applies all of these cues in various combinations within deep space. Figure 5.16a positions the sadistic Albert as a diminutive figure in the background as he watches Celie in labour, yet his placement in the centre of the frame—complete with torch light—enhances his significance, suggesting an unrelenting presence and a sense of menace. Likewise, Fig. 5.19a excludes Pete from the foreground group of the 'living' but his placement near the centre background reinforces the sense of a benevolent presence. Figure 5.18a uses light to rebalance different figure sizes with the prominent Indi backlit and silhouetted while the distant figures of Elsa and Walter are compensated with bright lighting that lifts them from the background. In Fig. 5.21a, the Jewish labour camp internee reacts as she hears she is to be executed and Spielberg reinforces the starkness of her centred close-up with the SS officer who has decided her fate visible behind her. The source of the problem—the incorrectly laid building foundation—is also clearly visible behind him. The notion of a frame within a frame is applied in Fig. 5.24a as the foregrounded arresting device, a 'Halo' (a kind of cranial handcuff), frames its intended victim in a visual association that reinforces the narrative significance of both elements as well as the narrative merging of foreground and background. Spielberg's adherence to the classical norm of frontality—of characters always facing or favouring the camera—is readily visible in these instances. His ability to prioritise the face is evident in the staging for Fig. 5.26a where each character carefully occupies a defined and unobstructed area within an evolving deep space configuration (Bordwell 1997, p. 171).

Fig. 5.16a *The Color Purple* (1985)

Fig. 5.17a *Bezhin Meadow* (1935)

Fig. 5.18a *The Last Crusade* (1989)

Fig. 5.19a *Always* (1989)

Fig. 5.20a *Hook* (1981)

Fig. 5.21a *Schindler's List* (1993)

Fig. 5.22a *Saving Private Ryan* (1998)

Deep Space Composition and Staging 125

Fig. 5.23a *Amistad* (1997)

Figs. 5.24a, 5.24b *Minority Report* (2002)

Fig. 5.25a *Catch Me if You Can* (2002)

Fig. 5.26a *The Terminal* (2004)

Fig. 5.27a *Munich* (2005)

Fig. 5.28a *Lincoln* (2012)

Fig. 5.29a *Bridge of Spies* (2015)

Long Takes in Deep Space

As a filmmaker who prefers to shoot lengthy masters, and seems critical of too much editing, Spielberg actually employs the long take only infrequently in his own films. For Carroll (2008, p. 116) the long take—or 'sequence shot'—is defined by successive changes in framing within the course of the one shot. In the interests of clearly signalling shots that are significantly above the ASL, I define a long take as a shot that runs for more than 60 seconds. Spielberg films with one long take include: *Duel*,

1941, The Last Crusade, The Lost World, Catch Me if You Can, War of the Worlds, Tintin and *War Horse. Close Encounters, Schindler's List* and *A. I.* have two; *The Color Purple, Always, Minority Report, The Terminal* and *Bridge of Spies* have three. The made-for-television *The Mission* (1985) has four, and *Raiders of the Lost Ark* and *Lincoln* have five. *The Sugarland Express, Jaws* and *Saving Private Ryan* each have six long takes. *Munich* is notable for the large number of extended shots that run for less than 60 seconds but that are still substantially over the ASL. As I will explain shortly, Spielberg often shoots an extended take as a mobile master that he then later breaks up with coverage such as inserts and/or reverses. Traditionally working hand in hand with deep space compositions, the long take also affords a continuous temporality and the opportunity to explore space through staging without the imposition of cutting.

Figure 5.30a–g is one of the celebrated long takes in *Jaws* (1975) and runs for 165 seconds. This shot displays a range of staging characteristics that combines early anamorphic widescreen staging with 1940s deep space composition. Beginning with a highly unusual—for Spielberg—planimetric arrangement, he establishes a hierarchy of narrative significance with a framing that places the resistant mayor in the centre and Hooper (left) and Brody either side. As Hooper and Brody argue with the mayor, they change their relative positions and the three slowly move to the right, the camera tracking along with them. Spielberg is able to seamlessly motivate the camera track as a response to Hooper and Brody's movement—itself causally motivated by their frustration at the mayor's stubbornness. The constant reconfiguring of the 'clothesline' formation with the actors repeatedly repositioning themselves also adds variation to what would otherwise be a visually static arrangement. Midway through the shot the characters arrive in front of the defaced Amity Island billboard and the flat composition changes to deep space/focus as Hooper moves away and into the middle ground near the billboard. This change to a multi-plane configuration is predicated by the crowd that appears from Fig. 5.30c and helps the composition to transition smoothly from flat to deep space with the billboard. The altered 'message' on the billboard is emphasised directly by Hooper's movement toward it and his referencing of the defacement but Brody's movement away to Hooper (Fig. 5.30e) further opens up the view of the billboard underscoring what Hooper has just pointed out (the added shark fin). The staging also reinforces the point of the scene by briefly holding on Hooper and Brody with the shark fin clearly visible at 'water level' once the mayor has exited the frame (Fig. 5.30g).[6] The scene continues with a cut to a two-shot of Brody and the mayor yet the sense of a complete narrative structure within the long take is clearly evident. Beginning with their arrival and the ensuing argument, the composition at the end of the scene concludes the narrative information by visually emphasising what Brody and Hooper have been arguing all along—that there is a shark prowling in the waters off Amity.

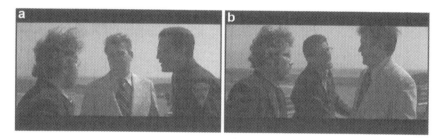

Figs. 5.30a, 5.30b

Figs. 5.30c, 5.30d

Deep Space Composition and Staging 129

Figs. 5.30e, 5.30f, 5.30g *Jaws* (1975)

Figure 5.31a–h is a three-shot[7] scene that runs for 96 seconds. The scene begins with a typical establishing shot (Fig. 5.31a) as Marcus arrives outside Indi's home and the long take begins with Indi receiving Marcus at the front door. In deciding to capture almost all of the action in one shot, a wide angle lens is used and the distortion in the horizontal planes can be seen in the lit, background display shelving (Figs. 5.31b and 5.31e) and the way they appear to bend down on the left and right. The bending lamp at Fig. 5.31c also displays the distortion caused by the short focal length lens. These 'imperfections' represent part of the visual compromise that results from choosing to cover all of the staging in a confined space without any additional shots. Spielberg nuances the coverage with five specific camera movements. The first brings Marcus and Indi from the door to the centre of the room (Fig. 5.31b). When Indi moves to the left and begins packing, the camera pans and tracks in to a two shot with Marcus seated on the couch arm, his face well lit—creating a deep focus composition with Indi and the lamp in the foreground (Fig. 5.31c). As Marcus warns Indi of the unknown danger awaiting him, the camera slowly tracks in (Fig. 5.31d), isolating Marcus in what Bordwell (2006, p. 144) describes generically as '…ominous dollies up to faces…'—a camera movement that gained popularity in the 1960s. Often used to great effect by Spielberg,[8] the slow track-in functions as a kind of drawn out close-up with the tightening frame also suggesting increased intensity and tension—particularly when accompanied by 'ominous' music as it is here. The camera's fourth movement involves a track back as Indi crosses the frame and returns from his desk with the revolver.

The choice of long take over cutting also results in compromises beyond the visual distortion caused by the short lens. This time, Spielberg foregoes frontality by choosing to stick with the single shot master that favours Marcus. As such, his warning to Indi (Fig. 5.31d) is not matched by a reverse close-up and Spielberg is instead forced to play Indi's reaction as he walks across the room to his desk (Fig. 5.31e). Similarly, Fig. 5.30e sacrifices a frontal two-shot of Brody and Hooper as Brody tries to convince Hooper to continue and their interaction is instead played at a compromised distance and angle. A similar issue occurs with the following example where Paula is buried deep in the background space for much of the shot (Fig. 5.32c–f). Yet Spielberg realises the limits of the long take and the importance of prioritising narrative clarity over style. Figure 5.30g is followed by a tighter shot of the mayor and Brody as he continues to try persuasion, while Fig. 5.31g interrupts the long take with an insert close-up of the revolver. Rather than leave the shot unbroken as many directors would, Spielberg readily introduces cutting where required. As with the *Jaws* example, this long take functions as a complete entity with beginning, middle and end in the form of the packed suitcase that also simultaneously propels the narrative smoothly forward into the next scene.

The Kingdom of the Crystal Skull (2008) includes a similar scene with Marcus' successor meeting Indi at his home. Also a 'two-hander' (involving two characters), the scene likewise begins with a conventional establishing shot of Indi's home and then cuts to the interior space. The similarity continues with both characters initially walking and talking together, followed by one sitting and the other continuing to move about the space. In this instance it is Indi who sits and the Dean who continues to move. The other major distinction is that the scene lacks deep space staging, uses a longer lens and is covered with 11 separate shots in a style more consistent with contemporary classical practice—and intensified continuity.

Deep Space Composition and Staging 131

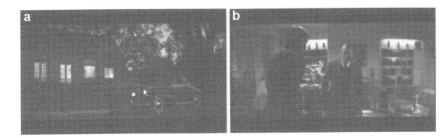

Figs. 5.31a, 5.31b

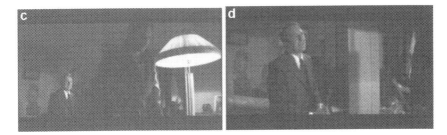

Figs. 5.31c, 5.31d

Figs. 5.31e, 5.31f

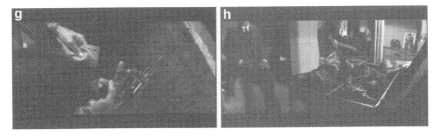

Figs. 5.31g, 5.31h *Raiders of the Lost Ark* (1981)

Fast forwarding some 20 years after *Raiders* to *Catch Me if You Can* (2002), it is possible to see the same staging and deep space strategies at work in the 147-second-long take that appears early in the film. Initially placing Frank and Jack in the foreground and Paula deep in the set (Fig. 5.32c), Spielberg (and cinematographer Kaminski) compensates for her distant presence by bathing her in light—a strategy seen previously in Figs. 5.18a and 5.31c. Staging Paula so that she remains deep in the set until Jack exits also reinforces the plot revelation relating to Frank's discovery of their illicit affair (Jack and Paula's) and their discomfort at having been found out is underlined by this separation. As with the *Raiders* master (Fig. 5.31b–f), here Spielberg makes use of all of the available scenographic space. This can be seen in the lateral entry of the characters from the left (Fig. 5.32a), the foregrounding of Frank and Jack until the latter's exit (Fig. 5.32e), the small track-in to establish Frank as the new foreground (Fig. 5.32f) and Paula as traversing between background and foreground (Fig. 5.32g). As with the previous two examples the depiction of space is strictly theatrical-like in its ignoring of the 'fourth wall' or the space occupied by and behind the camera. This is worth noting because in the following three chapters I explore how Spielberg applies an aggressive set of strategies that constantly acknowledge and reveal this fourth side.

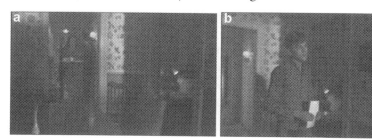

Figs. 5.32a, 5.32b

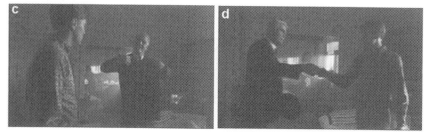

Figs. 5.32c, 5.32d

Deep Space Composition and Staging

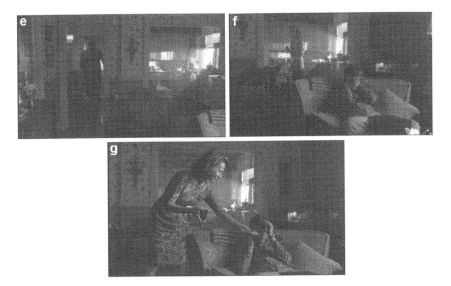

Figs. 5.32e, 5.32f, 5.32g *Catch Me if You Can* (2002)

Inverted Deep Focus: Narrow Depth of Field

In contrast to the deep focus and deep space arrangements of the previous compositions, these examples highlight Spielberg's versatility in constructing a narrative using a highly restricted range of focus depth. Figure 5.33a shows the air-traffic controller nearest to camera in focus while the controller directly behind him, only a few inches further away, is clearly soft. This shot is used to mark the point of high dramatic tension in the sequence as the apparent UFO is heard to pass by the reporting aircraft while the controllers gather in a group to listen in. During all of this, Spielberg enhances the intensity by having the camera slowly track back, revealing another controller who speaks as the focus shifts to him (Fig. 5.33b) and then on to the fourth controller who also speaks on cue once he appears in focus right of frame (Fig. 5.33c). As the shot continues to track back the original controller gradually becomes increasingly defocused though he continues speaking. The selective focus of each new controller briefly prioritises his presence in the frame until the camera movement stops with the deep space, shallow focus composition at Fig. 5.33c. This shot is followed by a cutaway of other controllers in the room noticing the unfolding drama. Figure 5.33d begins with the same composition as Fig. 5.33c but now the camera reverses its direction and tracks slowly back in towards the original controller until he is again in focus—the movement creating another instance of an 'ominous dolly' and functions to further escalate dramatic intensity. Figure 5.33e follows another cutaway of the controller's radar screen and the tightly packed composition, selective focus and the centring of the original controller all emphasise his importance as the focal point. He functions as the vehicle and mouthpiece for communicating the experience of the pilots on the radio and literally the narrative itself. Essentially a static scene with almost no character movement, the role of style in generating dramatic tension is easily overlooked. In true Bazin-like fashion, the change in focus and camera movement simulates editing, directing the viewer where to look and how to feel, but with a subtlety that likely goes unnoticed by most viewers. As Spielberg notes, manipulating a deep space composition actually contributes to a reduced sense of authorial presence:

> It makes the audience feel that subconsciously someone is not manipulating what they're watching, someone is not intruding upon what they're watching by having a big finger pointing, 'Look at this, look at this now, look, look over here, look over here, look, look, look.'—Spielberg (Ebert and Siskel 1991, p. 75)

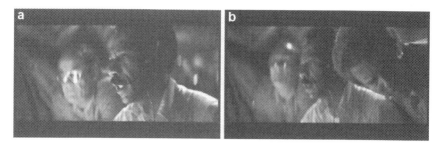

Figs. 5.33a, 5.33b

Deep Space Composition and Staging   135

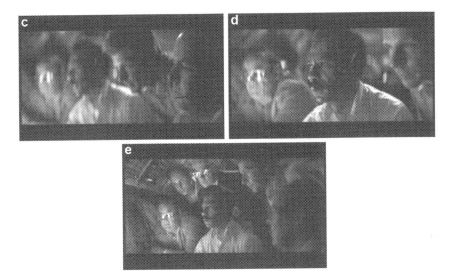

Figs. 5.33c, 5.33d, 5.33e *Close Encounters of the Third Kind* (1977)

Planimetric Composition as Aberration

The Kingdom of the Crystal Skull (2008) includes the only instance of a planimetric shot composition in a Spielberg film (Fig. 5.34a–b). The planimetric-like composition was previously alluded to as present in the long take from *Jaws* (Fig. 5.30a–b). Yet, in *Jaws* the lateral staging appears only briefly as the shot begins in depth with the three characters walking up to the frame, composes itself as a brief lateral arrangement and changes to the deep space composition as discussed. With the *Crystal Skull* example Spielberg is unable to resist a multi-plane composition and has the aircraft pass by in a foreground wipe revealing Indi and Mutt standing in a planimetric, tableau-like row facing the camera. The billowing dust that masks the shot (Fig. 5.34b) replaces the departed aircraft as a foreground layer and also softens the harshness of the staged artificiality of the characters as clearly arranged for camera. This composition is a curious conception for a Spielberg film and it is telling of Spielberg's stylistic priorities that he has deployed this arrangement only this once. One of the major 'problems' in relation to Spielberg's style with a composition like this (Fig. 5.34c enlargement) is that it recalls the kind of staged composition commonly seen in portraiture. Wes Anderson often incorporates this planimetric arrangement in his films as stylistic device as Fig. 5.35a demonstrates. Anderson occasionally combines this frontal, planimetric arrangement within a deep space composition as Fig. 5.35b illustrates. Bordwell (1997, p.261) has also described these compositions as 'mug shot' framing and the absurdity, oddness and high degree of self-consciousness of the staging by Anderson suggests that stylistic 'invisibility' is not the intention. Bordwell (2005, p. 167) notes that the planimetric composition began to reappear (following on from the tableau of 'primitive' cinema and Buster Keaton's occasional use in the 1920s) in the 1960s and links this to the increased use of long lenses and their inherent characteristic of compressing image fields/layers within a reduced depth of field.

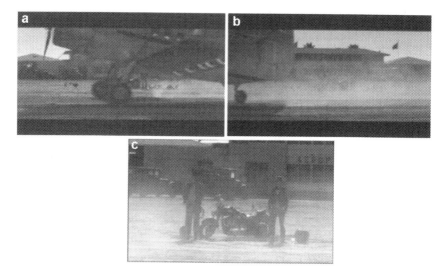

Figs. 5.34a, 5.34b, 5.34c (enlargement of 5.34b)

Deep Space Composition and Staging 137

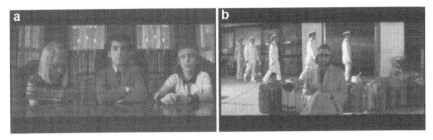

Figs. 5.35a, 5.35b *The Royal Tenenbaums* (2001)

Considered potentially also as a reaction/variation to deep space compositions, the planimetric staging was initially championed by directors like Godard who likely appreciated the sense of staged artificiality and its seeming 'challenge' to the traditional 'transparency' of classical style. Filmmakers such as director/actor Pierre Étaix also applied such flat compositions in the service of humour—much as Anderson does. Along with Godard and others, Bordwell cites Angelopoulos for his use of planimetric compositions in both lateral and recessional configurations and Takeshi Kitano for his planimetric compositions and 'compass point editing' (the significance of this in relation to Spielberg is examined in Chap. 9). He also notes its adoption in the United States in the 1990s by independent filmmakers like Anderson.

Bordwell has suggested a number of functions accorded the planimetric composition by different filmmakers. Yet, these kinds of compositions suggest a high degree of self-consciousness—that the cast is posing for the viewer—and this overt, even acknowledged level of artificiality recalls the foregrounding of style over narration most often associated with non-classical forms of cinema and art-cinema in particular. Lending prominence to style is highly antithetical to Spielberg's conventional, classical subordination of style to narrative. That Spielberg flirts only briefly with this type of composition and at the same time 'softens' it by enfolding it within a deep space composition further points to a certain discomfort in its deployment and signals that its sensibility is incompatible with his own. This is significant because the shot does seem ill-placed (as opposed to an Anderson film where it would instantly blend) and this incongruity again highlights Spielberg's prioritising of shot and scene construction as narrative seeming to exist independently of any maker. William Link (McBride 1997), co-producer of Spielberg's *Columbo* (1971a) episodes, observed an early resistance from Spielberg to 'flat' compositions: 'He would avoid dead on shots. He would come at you with interesting, different angles' (p. 190).

Deep Space Construction Across Multiple Shots in a Scene

This scene (Fig. 5.36a–l) consists of 22 shots in a sustained presentation of deep focus compositions in three planes from multiple perspectives[9] within the framework of classical continuity editing. The scene also demonstrates Spielberg's fusing of more recent classical decoupage—Bordwell's intensified continuity—with the traditional classical aesthetic of deep focus composition and staging. The combination also recalls Bazin's 'narrational dialectic' (Bordwell's expression) as applied by Bazin (Bordwell 1997, p. 62) to Welles for his combining of deep space compositions and montage. Figure 5.36a pans from left to right following the portable toilet as it passes on a trailer, the shot coming to rest on Clovis and Lou Jean as they crouch behind the police car (Fig. 5.36b). The shot establishes the point of the scene—that a toilet *has* been organised for Lou Jean—and reveals them now waiting outside the police car. The shot visually answers the problem created in the final shot of the previous scene where Lou Jean declares that she needs to 'pee'. It's also another example of Spielberg's skill in unobtrusively deploying cause and effect with the smooth transition from one scene to the next. The use of a long lens also gives the narrative energy as the toilet rushes past and provides a jolting contrast to the static car interior of the previous shot.[10] Recalling the recent practice of cutting from a long lens shot to a wide angle, the second shot (Fig. 5.36c) presents a wider, tri-plane deep space composition that still manages to include the portable toilet passing in the far distance, centre of frame (glimpsed above Officer Maxwell's hat). Figure 5.36d–e continues the visual theme of the toilet by continuing to centre it in the distance while the camera tracks back simultaneously following it and the two police officers until the toilet reaches the police car in the middle of the field, the

Deep Space Composition and Staging 139

two officers now foregrounded either side. This shot also establishes the scenographic space, orientating the subjects in the frame—the police, the fugitives and the toilet—in relation to each other. Figure 5.36f is also significant because it reveals a portion of scenographic space not seen again but that contributes to creating a 360-degree vista. This constructing of a complete space is an integral function of the wide reverse examined in the following chapter. Figure 5.36f is another contrastingly long lens, deep space composition and this is again juxtaposed with the return to the wide-angle deep space of Fig. 5.36g–h. This shot begins with Lou Jean running towards camera (Fig. 5.36g) and then running back to the car while Clovis replaces her in an aggressive foreground (Fig. 5.36h) that effectively functions as a master and is returned to repeatedly, making up five of the 22 shots in the scene. This foreground composition of Clovis in Fig. 5.36h and its reverse at Fig. 5.36k allows the frame to capture his face in close-up without compromising our view of the surrounding space or diminishing its significance and supports Spielberg's claim (quoted earlier) about providing the viewer with choice in where in the frame we should look. Bordwell (1997. p. 59) quotes William Wyler making a similar comment in that deep space and the long take lets the viewer '…do his own cutting' while Bazin also argued that the deep space composition permits the simultaneous presentation of wide shot and close-up. In a variation of Bazin and Spielberg's own 'deep space editing', the movement of characters from background to foreground and back again invokes Eisenstein's (Nizhny 1979, p. 138) later conception of 'hidden editing', and the idea that character movement in depth switches viewer attention to parts of the frame.

Figs. 5.36a, 5.36b

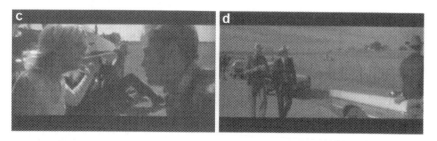

Figs. 5.36c, 5.36d

Figs. 5.36e, 5.36f

Figs. 5.36g, 5.36h

Figs. 5.36i, 5.36j

Deep Space Composition and Staging 141

Figs. 5.36k, 5.36l *The Sugarland Express* (1974)

This kind of foreground composition directly contradicts Béla Balász's (2004) assertion that: 'Even if we had just seen the owner of the face in a long shot, when we look into the eyes in a close-up, we no longer think of that wide space, because the expression and significance of the face has no relation to space and no connection with it' (p. 316). One can assume that Balász refers to the 'conventional' sense of the close-up in which the face consumes most or the entire frame. In this case though, it is not just the face that negates our notion of space but the fact that the framing denies our view of the scenographic space. In discussing Dreyer's early films, and *The Parson's Widow* (1920) in particular, Bordwell (1981, p. 41) conceives of a 'dialectic of tableau and face' where the static, 'painterly' even clinical scenographic space is contrasted with the '…intense narrative activity…' of the human face in close-up.

Note the police car and officers from Figs. 5.36d and 5.36e in the background of Fig. 5.36g. This pattern of including portions from a previous shot in the subsequent shot continues throughout the scene. This repetition of objects across shots creates an in-built spatial redundancy that permits Spielberg to exercise a high degree of omnipresence and dramatically change camera positions, shot direction and frame size from shot to shot without risking viewer disorientation. Figure 5.36i continues this contrast with a wide shot of the trailer driver exiting the truck and the contrast continues in Fig. 5.36j with a striking deep focus arrangement of the parked police cars. From Fig. 5.36h to 5.36k the camera travels in a full 180-degree arc. Reinforcing this redundancy is Spielberg's care in respecting classical convention with regard to continuity editing and despite the seemingly ubiquitous camera positions, no camera placement other than Fig. 5.36f strays beyond the 180-degree

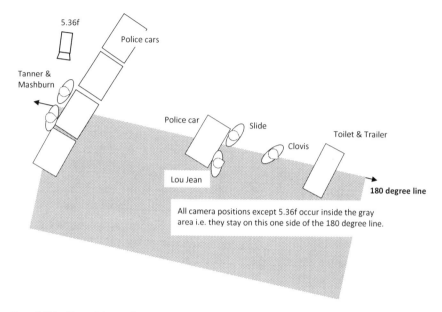

Fig. 5.37 Portable toilet sequence. Overhead view, *The Sugarland Express* (1974)

axis known as 'the line-of-action' (Fig. 5.37, below). Even the detailed attention to figure continuity across shots can be seen in the still departing truck glimpsed in the far distance later in the scene and the retreating policeman who had been hiding in the toilet also visible in the background. This seemingly 'incidental' observing of continuity also has implications for notions of a less mediated or more 'real' unfolding of events in the sense that regardless of where the camera is pointing, the scene continues to unfold both on-screen and off. Bazin (1974) observed a similar effect in Renoir's deep space compositions, claiming that onscreen and off-screen space seemed to exist simultaneously.

> …the mise-en-scene cannot limit itself to what is represented on the screen. The rest of the scene, while effectively hidden, should not cease to exist. The action is not bounded by the screen, but merely passes through it. And a person who enters the camera's field of vision is coming from other areas of the action, and not from some limbo, some imaginary 'backstage.' Likewise, the camera should be able to spin suddenly without picking up any holes or dead spots in the action. (p. 89)

In addition to the outwardly ad-hoc revealing of space, Alfred Hitchcock (Truffaut 1983, p. 114) argues for the effectiveness of contrasting object sizes '…smallest to biggest, furthest to nearest…' as a useful device for generating dramatic impact. Just as Spielberg contrasts the tight foregrounding of Clovis with the wide field and back again, Hitchcock (1995) explains:

> The size of image is a very important consideration. To spring a surprise, like when Paul Newman in *Torn Curtain* goes out to the farm, I have a little tiny figure crossing the field and when he arrives there, it goes *voom!* to the big head. That's a change in image size, which is very vital. (p. 308)

The foregrounded Clovis is interrupted by the wide of Fig. 5.36i, which is then contrasted with a return to Clovis large in the frame. At Fig. 5.36l, another wide of the departing truck, this shot also bookended by Clovis large in the frame. Spielberg uses a striking, extreme wide shot once more across the roof of a police car and again the shot is preceded and followed by Clovis in close-up.

Then there is the role of scenographic space itself. Ross Exo Adams (2011) observes '…hierarchy and play between figure and ground, or character and backdrop…' in his analysis of Godard's use of space in *Contempt* (1963). He argues that through the diminution of character size in certain shots, space becomes a dominant element that threatens to 'absorb' the characters.

> …the background suddenly seems to project its depth forward, engulfing both the characters and foreground into a single 'fixed' composition: the figure ground relationship becomes confounded leaving an enriched space of both figure and ground. Here, the importance of the individual characters is challenged by their momentary subjugation to the strangely composed visual setting they find themselves in.

Adams isolates four variations of spatial manipulation deployed by Godard in *Contempt* that he argues enables space to compete directly with the characters in the frame. He does not venture to explain why Godard pursues this strategy other than to suggest the potential motive of satire in relation to subverting classical convention. He describes the first as 'scale shift' where shooting characters at a distance results in the background competing or seeming to overwhelm them. The second is 'de-centering' where the characters are 'sidelined' at the edge of frame or depicted through a '...severely composed symmetry...' that foregrounds space over the character. The third involves the 'imposition of symmetry' where characters merge into the décor because of its symmetrical similarity to the human form. Adams cites the example in one scene of a statue and how it mimics the character's positioning thus overwhelming or at least distracting the viewer from the human form. The final variation is 'absorption' and relates to the character becoming consumed by the background. Here Adams suggests that the background somehow thrusts forward—the example here being of a large, indoor tree fern that obscures the character.

Spielberg employs a similar strategy of alternating spatial prominence. Besides creating energy, the long lens of Fig. 5.36b flattens Clovis and Lou Jean against the police car and the background, as if they are overwhelmed by the situation. This is immediately contrasted by the next shot, Fig. 5.36c where the wide angle has them literally 'pop out' of the background into an aggressive foreground—the implication here being that they are working to re-establish their ascendancy. This regaining of the initiative continues with Clovis' depiction in aggressive foregrounds. Yet the sense of police 'authority' reappears at intervals through the scene with long lens reminders of their presence as embedded in space: Fig. 5.36f and the 'barrier' of police cars in the background; Fig. 5.36j and the 'barrier' now seen in a reverse shot; the police officers reluctantly holstering their guns in a subsequent long lens composition. As well as underpinning the perceived degree of control as exercised by the characters, the interaction with space also underlines the scene's narrative structure. As with the long takes, the scene exhibits Spielberg's preference for beginnings, middles and an ending within the scene. This scene begins with Clovis and Lou Jean disorientated, shows them re-establish control through the scene and then finally has them achieve their goal—the scene literally closing along with the toilet door. As one scene ends another seamlessly begins and Spielberg again demonstrates a smooth transition into the next scene with the closing toilet door followed by Baby Langston opening the door to begin the next scene. When one considers that the majority of the staging of the scene is inherently static and recalls Bordwell's 'stand and deliver' classification, the deep focus compositions, contrasting shot sizes and omnipresent camera all simultaneously work to disguise the fixed nature of the staging and impart a sense of an event unfolding freely, seemingly without authorship.

Analysis of Spielberg's deep space compositions reveals the crucial role played by scenographic space in contributing to narrative construction. To claim that space is like a character in his films would be an exaggeration, although it is not far from the truth as the consistent fusion of facial close-ups and space attest (Figs. 5.5a, 5.6a, 5.9c, 5.21a, 5.24b, 5.26a, 5.33a and 5.36h—this shot tightens considerably on Clovis later in the scene). Two related components are clearly manifested in his deep focus compositions and staging. The first involves the promotion of scenographic space as functioning in concert with anthropomorphic requirements—the depiction of human figures and their actions—such that one supports and informs the other. In this respect, the dual depiction of faces and space results in each being considered in the context of its proximity with the other. Rather than isolate the face from space as is traditionally practiced in the close-up, the deep space compositions serve to add to the information available 'in' the face by reinforcing by association the setting as integral to that face. The second component of the space/face duality is that it constantly reminds the viewer that the events are happening in a 'complete' space such that this space is not broken or excluded by the conventional close-up's tendency to 'extract' the face from scenographic space. A third element relates to how space is used to assist in generating narrative emphasis by alternately foregrounding it or pushing it back in relation to the characters and how this underlines their power within a situation. While Spielberg facilitates an aggressive role for space, he never allows it to exceed the classical norm of space as subservient to narrative logic. Yet Spielberg goes further in his manipulation of scenographic space and the next three chapters examine how he integrates deep space with the classical shot, reverse shot convention.

Notes

1. Spielberg is one of only a few Hollywood directors still shooting with film.
2. This refers to 'monumentalism', the visual act of making something appear grand, spectacular or impressive. This included anything officially sanctioned by the Communist Party and was usually related to Soviet political achievement or proletariat 'power' and heroism.
3. Bordwell borrows this term from Heinrich Wölfflin's use as denoting a single object plane parallel to the background.
4. King even suggests that the film as directed by Arthur Penn features a shot inspired by the Odessa steps sequence from *Battleship Potemkin* (1925).
5. Bordwell (1981) notes that in classical cinema scenographic space is judged/comprehended in terms of its relation to the human body (p. 37).
6. Bordwell (1997, p. 254) discusses the deep focus aspect of this shot and how the staging and placement of the shark's fin emphasises Hooper's comments about the shark's size.
7. Strictly speaking, it is a two shot scene with the long take and the insert making up the two shots but in this instance I count an edit as a change to another shot.
8. *Munich*, *Lincoln* and *Bridge of Spies* are notable for the high number of scenes that include shots that push-in to characters.
9. Of the 22 shots only four are not deep focus compositions and of these three are close-ups.
10. Generating humour is also a clear intention of the toilet passing by.

References

Adams, R. E. (2011). Foreground, Background, Drama: The Cinematic Space of Le Mepris. *Critical Quarterly, 53*(1), 14–28. Retrieved from Academic Search Premier.

Bazin, A. (1974). *Jean Renoir*. W. W. Halsey II & W. H. Simon (Trans.). London: W. H. Allen.

Balasz, B. (2004). The Close-up. In L. Braudy & M. Cohen (Eds.), *Film Theory and Criticism* (6th ed.). New York: Oxford University Press.

Barr, C. (1963). Cinemascope Before and After. *Film Quarterly, 16*(4).

Bazin, A. (1967). *What Is Cinema? Volume 1.* H. Gray (Trans.). Berkeley and Los Angeles: University of California Press.
Bordwell, D. (1981). *The Films of Carl-Theodor Dreyer.* Los Angeles: University of California Press.
Bordwell, D. (1993). *The Cinema of Eisenstein.* Cambridge: Harvard University Press.
Bordwell, D. (1997). *On the History of Film Style.* Cambridge, MA/London: Harvard University Press.
Bordwell, D. (2001). Eisenstein, Socialist Realism, and the Charms of Mizanstsena. In A. Lavalley & B. P. Scherr (Eds.), *Eisenstein at 100: A Reconsideration* (pp. 13–37). New Jersey: Rutgers University Press.
Bordwell, D. (2005). *Figures Traced in Light: On Cinematic Staging.* Los Angeles: University of California Press.
Bordwell, D. (2006). *The Way Hollywood Tells It: Story and Style in Modern Movies.* Los Angeles: University of California Press.
Bordwell, D. (2008). *The Poetics of Cinema.* London: Routledge.
Brewster, B. (1990). Deep Staging in French Films 1900–1914. In T. Elsaesser & T. Barker (Eds.), *Early Cinema, Space, Frame, Narration* (pp. 45–55). London: British Film Institute.
Burch, N. (1990). *Life to Those Shadows.* B. Brewter, (Ed. & Trans.). Berkeley and Los Angeles: University of California Press.
Carroll, N. (1988). *Mystifying Movies: Fads and Fallacies in Contemporary Film Theory.* New York: Columbia University Press.
Carroll, N. (2008). *The Philosophy of Motion Pictures.* Singapore: Blackwell Publishing Ltd.
Ebert, R., & Siskel, G. (1991). *The Future of the Movies.* Kansas City: Andrews & McMeel.
Fullerton, J. (1995). Contextualizing the Innovation of Deep Staging in Swedish Films. In K. Dibbets & B. Hogenkamp (Eds.), *Film and the First World War* (pp. 86–96). Amsterdam: Amsterdam University Press.
Harpole, C. H. (1978). *Gradients of Depth in the Cinema Image.* New York: Arno Press.
Harpole, C. H. (1980). Ideological and Technological Determinism in Deep-Space Cinema Images: Issues in Ideology, Technological History, and Aesthetics. *Film Quarterly,* 33(3), (pp. 11–22). Retrieved from http://www.jstor.org/stable/1212186
Hitchcock, A. (1995). *Hitchcock on Hitchcock: Selected Writings and Interviews.* S. Gottlieb (Ed.). Berkeley and Los Angeles: University of California Press.

King, G. (2002). *New Hollywood Cinema: An Introduction*. London: L.B. Tauris.
Kuleshov, L. (1974). The Art of the Cinema. In R. Levaco (Ed. & Trans.). *Kuleshov on Film*. Los Angeles: University of California Press.
McBride, J. (1997). *Steven Spielberg: A Biography*. New York: Simon and Schuster.
Nizhny, V. (1979). *Lessons with Eisenstein*. I. Montagu & J. Leyda. (Eds. & Trans.). New York: Da Capo Press.
Salt, B. (1992). *Film Style and Technology: History and Analysis*. London: Starword.
Truffaut, F. (1983). *Hitchcock Truffaut*. New York: Simon & Schuster, Inc.

Film Title Editions

Anderson, W. (Director). (2001). *The Royal Tenenbaums* [Motion picture, DVD (2002)]. United States: The Criterion Collection.
Eisenstein, S. (Director). (1935–37). *Bezhin Meadow* [Motion picture, DVD (1997)]. United States: Image Entertainment.
Spielberg, S. (Director). (1968). Night Gallery: *Eyes* [Television broadcast, DVD (2009)]. Australia: Universal Studios.
Spielberg, S. (Director). (1971). *Columbo: Murder by the Book* [Television broadcast, DVD (2004)]. Australia: Universal Pictures.
Spielberg, S. (Director). (1971). *Duel* [Motion picture, Blu-ray (2014)]. Australia: Universal Sony Pictures Home Entertainment.
Spielberg, S. (Director). (1974). *The Sugarland Express* [Motion picture, Blu-ray (2014)]. Australia: Universal Sony Pictures Home Entertainment.
Spielberg, S. (Director). (1975). *Jaws* [Motion picture, Blu-ray (2014)]. Austraila: Universal Sony Pictures Home Entertainment.
Spielberg, S. (Director). (1977). *Close Encounters of the Third Kind* [Motion picture, Blu-ray (2007)]. United States: Sony Pictures Home Entertainment.
Spielberg, S. (Director). (1981). *Indiana Jones and the Raiders of the Lost Ark* [Motion picture, Blu-ray (2012)]. Australia: Lucasfilm Ltd.
Spielberg, S. (Director). (1984). *Indiana Jones and the Temple of Doom* [Motion picture, Blu-ray (2012)]. Australia: Lucasfilm Ltd.
Spielberg, S. (Director). (1985). *The Color Purple* [Motion picture, DVD (2003)]. United States: Warner Home Video.
Spielberg, S. (Director). (1985). *Amazing Stories: The Mission* [Television broadcast, DVD (2009)]. Australia: Universal Studios.

Spielberg, S. (Director). (1989). *Indiana Jones and the Last Crusade* [Motion picture, Blu-ray (2012)]. Australia: Lucasfilm Ltd.
Spielberg, S. (Director). (1989). *Always* [Motion picture, Blu-ray (2014)]. Australia: Universal Sony Pictures Home Entertainment.
Spielberg, S. (Director). (1991). *Hook* [Motion picture, DVD (2000)]. Australia: Columbia TriStar Home Video.
Spielberg, S. (Director). (1993). *Schindler's List* [Motion picture, Blu-ray (2013)]. Australia: Universal Sony Pictures Home Entertainment.
Spielberg, S. (Director). (1997). *Amistad* [Motion picture, Blu-ray (2014)]. Australia: Paramount Pictures.
Spielberg, S. (Director). (1997). *The Lost World: Jurassic Park* [Motion picture, Blu-ray (2014)]. Australia: Universal Sony Pictures Home Entertainment.
Spielberg, S. (Director). (1998). *Saving Private Ryan* [Motion picture, Blu-ray (2010)]. Australia: Paramount Pictures.
Spielberg, S. (Director). (2002). *Minority Report* [Motion picture, Blu-ray (2010)]. United Kingdom: 20th Century Fox.
Spielberg, S. (Director). (2002). *Catch Me if You Can* [Motion picture, Blu-ray (2012)]. Australia: Paramount Pictures.
Spielberg, S. (Director). (2004). *The Terminal* [Motion picture, Blu-ray (2014)]. Australia: Paramount Pictures.
Spielberg, S. (Director). (2005). *Munich* [Motion picture, DVD (2006)]. Australia: Universal Pictures.
Spielberg, S. (Director). (2008). *Indiana Jones and the Kingdom of the Crystal Skull* [Motion picture, Blu-ray (2012)]. Australia: Lucasfilm Ltd.
Spielberg, S. (Director). (2012). *Lincoln* [Motion picture, Blu-ray (2013)] Australia: Twentieth Century Fox Home Entertainment.
Spielberg, S. (Director). (2015). *Bridge of Spies* [Motion picture, Blu-ray (2016)] Australia: Twentieth Century Fox Home Entertainment.
Welles, O. (Director). (1941). *Citizen Kane* [Motion picture, Blu-ray (2011)]. United States: Warner Home Video.

6

Space and the Wide Reverse Strategy

At this point I have examined how Spielberg utilises the conventions and norms of the classical continuity system including 'rediscovering' deep space compositions and staging and how he uses both to construct narration. At the same time, I have also noted Spielberg's reluctance to employ the conventional shot, reverse shot configuration with the kind of frequency that is characteristic of classical Hollywood narration. Instead, it is my contention that Spielberg uniquely modifies the shot, reverse shot to create an emphatically cinematic[1] system that constructs a kind of 'panoramic' scenographic space. I call this the wide reverse and it has wide ranging implications for how his narration is created and perceived.

Kristin Thompson (1999) contends that the shot, reverse shot arrangement in its classical configuration is so effective at anchoring narrative legibility that it functions as a kind of perceptual foundation upon which filmmakers are able to introduce potentially more extreme stylistic strategies. As Bordwell notes: 'The most striking stylistic changes in film history often don't stem from absolute innovation but rather from a recasting of received devices' (2008, p. 27). The wide reverse features camera placements that occupy positions on or adjacent to the axis-of-action for a

© The Author(s) 2018
J. Mairata, *Steven Spielberg's Style by Stealth*,
https://doi.org/10.1007/978-3-319-69081-0_6

scene. These positions are represented in Fig. 6.1 (below) with camera positions G and H. These illustrate that the wide reverse exists as a modification or 'recasting' of the shot, reverse shot, represented in the conventional sense by positions D and E. In traditional usage, any camera placement in or on the circle of action and on the axis-of-action/line functions to cue subjectivity, most often perceived as implying character optical point-of-view (OP). This sense of subjectivity is removed when the camera is placed well outside the action such that it captures a wide vista of space that includes any potential agent for OP. Negating subjectivity also results in the wide reverse as suggestive of a low degree of self-consciousness. At the same time, and like the shot, reverse shot, the wide reverse similarly avoids spatial confusion by overlapping the presence of objects from one shot to the next, which assists in orientating the spectator. The chief characteristic of the wide reverse is that it always involves a change of angle of 180 degrees. In this respect it can be considered a 'true' reverse in contrast to the shot, reverse shot where the cameras are usually positioned at oblique angles (D and E) to the subject and therefore do not comprehensively reveal the reverse space or field of each other.

Spielberg activates a number of variations within the framework of wide reverses relating to camera placement and reverse shot combinations although all involve 180-degree reversals and many also incorporate deep

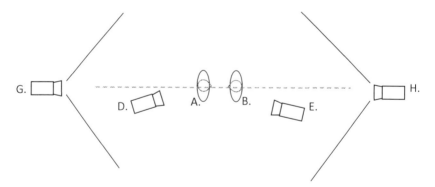

Fig. 6.1   Wide reverse coverage

space compositions. This is consistent with Bordwell's (2005) contention that '…filmmakers have a cumulative schema-based conception of stylistic continuity and change…' (p. 252). Part of this cumulative process involves 'replication'—copying conventional practice and 'revision'—applying change and adaptation to that convention. Bordwell adds 'reject' as a third aspect of the stylistic schema relating to the evolving nature of classical style. Bordwell is also referencing E. H. Gombrich's (1977) conception of the artist as readily involved in the modification and evolution of style '…a reliance on the schema can block the path to effective portrayal unless it is accompanied by a constant willingness to correct and revise' (p. 145).

The wide reverse is essentially an amalgamation of this process of reconfiguring conventional practice and may in part explain why this system has tended to go unnoticed as a unique stylistic device within the classical paradigm and in Spielberg's work. I have separated the range of wide reverses into type A, which are examined in this chapter, and type B, which take up the following chapter. Type A reverses can be further divided into two categories: Complex Spatial Configuration Reverses, and Simple Spatial Configuration Reverses. The first category refers to the repeated (even aggressive) application of wide reverses within a scene or sequence and involves one or a combination of the construction of a complex scenographic space, high frequency editing and the manipulation of multiple featured subjects/objects. The second category considers the placement of the wide reverse in a less complex, more contained fashion, in brief scenes made up of a limited number of shots. Four examples from the first category and four from the second are examined to illustrate how the wide reverse is deployed in the scene, how it contributes to narrative creation and the fundamental implications its use has for spectator comprehension.

This arrangement of the wide reverse can be seen operating repeatedly in sequences in many of Spielberg's films beginning with his early television work and continuing right through to his recent work as director. Furthermore, this formal strategy is often activated during causally significant scenes and/or sequences with the intention of emphasising their importance. One example of this is in the concept I label as *cine-tableau*, which is examined later in this chapter.

Type A Wide Reverses

Complex Spatial Configuration Reverses: Four Examples

1. Roy Neary's Close Encounter

Taken from *Close Encounters of the Third Kind* (1977), this scene depicts the protagonist undergoing a life-changing experience that causally motivates him (and the audience) through the rest of the film as he searches—often seemingly irrationally—for an explanation for his close encounter and the resulting embedded 'vision' of Devil's Tower. The sequence runs for almost four minutes and includes 47 edits. It begins with a traditional establishing shot as the pick-up truck stops at the railway crossing (Fig. 6.2a—below). This is reversed by almost 180 degrees with the camera now over Neary's right shoulder in a tighter shot looking forward (Fig. 6.2b). Another 180-degree reverse reveals the lights approaching in the background over Neary's right shoulder (Fig. 6.2c). Next, the shift is 90 degrees to Neary in profile (Fig. 6.2d) but this is followed with another almost 180-degree reverse, which is actually two shots—a tighter shot of approximately only 11 frames (less than half a second, Fig. 6.2e) followed by a wider framed shot (Fig. 6.2f) although both appear to be on the same axis.

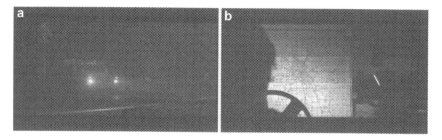

Figs. 6.2a, 6.2b

Space and the Wide Reverse Strategy   155

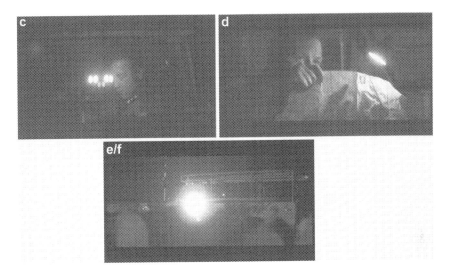

Figs. 6.2c, 6.2d, 6.2e/f *Close Encounters of the Third Kind* (1977)

With these first five shots, and succession of reverses, Spielberg constructs a 360-degree scenographic space that reveals the area in which the rest of the scene unfolds (Fig. 6.3, below). Despite such extreme, repeated changes in angle, these initial shots do not disorientate the spectator, partly because Spielberg is careful to provide graphic, overlapping 'markers' or elements of each shot that function as a smooth 'hinge'[2] transition into the following shot. These include: Neary, the steering wheel (Fig. 6.2b); Neary again and the similar approaching lights from the previous scene (Fig. 6.2c); Neary with the map (Fig. 6.2d); the deep space composition that includes the letterboxes (foreground); the truck (middle distance); the railway crossing sign (background) (Fig. 6.2e/f)—all of which assist in reinforcing and confirming spatial logic. Diegetic sound also contributes to orientation as Roy can be heard mumbling to himself (he says he is lost—expository information that clearly reinforces and motivates his behaviour and contextualises the location).

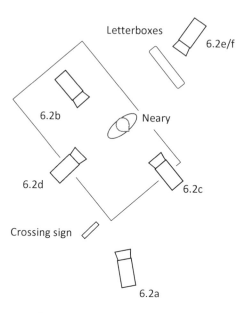

Fig. 6.3 Roy Neary's close encounter—overhead view—initial shot reverses, *Close Encounters of the Third Kind* (1977)

In keeping with the generally interchangeable nature of classical style, the scene could seemingly function if the series of reverses were omitted. Interchangeable here is used in the sense that almost any classical scene can conceivably be shot and constructed in multiple ways. As Bordwell (2006) points out, Hollywood utilises '…flexible but bounded variation…' (p. 14). A certain range of stylistic strategies is available to the filmmaker but this range is confined to the norms and historically developed and accepted conventions of the classical system. Another filmmaker might begin with the establishing shot (Fig. 6.2a) and then cut straight to the profile of the Neary character realising that something is amiss (Fig. 6.2d). One immediate casualty of this trimming would be the 360-degree creation of scenographic space. Another would be the loss of the shot showing the lights rising vertically behind an unknowing Neary (Fig. 6.2c). Part of the reason the rising lights deception works so effectively is because it is so smoothly integrated into the reverse structure. In typical classical fashion, and recalling Bazin's concept of 'objective reality', it is almost as if the shot has caught the event occurring rather than the event as carefully contrived. The storytelling capacity inherent in this shot is another instance of Spielberg's skill at communicating narration purely visually. Set up or 'primed' in the previous scene where the lights approaching from the rear are seen to belong to a car, we are encouraged, or lured, into assuming that the subsequent set of approaching lights also belong to a car. That the lights begin to rise vertically immediately forces us—as Branigan and Bordwell would suggest—to hurriedly revise our hypothesis. Another component of the effectiveness of this shot is that the audience briefly knows more than the character. We see the lights rise and sense that something is not 'normal' while Neary remains unaware. It is Spielberg applying one of Hitchcock's most famous techniques for generating tension and suspense.

Warren Buckland and Thomas Elsaesser (2002, p. 88) suggests the multiple reverses as merely an example of 'commentary,' of the camera anticipating the action and of style dictating content. While establishing a complete space is one of the most significant functions of the multiple reverses, they also fulfil additional tasks. These five shots, placed on the outside of the circle of action looking in, confirm and reconfirm Neary (literally) as the anthropomorphic centre of the constructed space, thus emphasising the character's significance in the scene and also continuously remind us of his prominence in the narrative. The duration of each of the reverses also performs an important editing function. Figure 6.2a runs for 11 seconds, Fig. 6.2b for four seconds, Fig. 6.2c for 20 seconds, Fig. 6.2d for 14 seconds, Fig. 6.2e for 11 frames and Fig. 6.2f for three seconds. The first four shots unfold at a leisurely pace—the calm before the upheaval. The brevity of Fig. 6.2e and Fig. 6.2f reflects Neary's growing agitation and the cutting rate accelerates appreciably as the close encounter event commences with shot durations reduced to one and two seconds per shot. The end of the close encounter sees the shot length return to prior levels. Editing therefore makes use of the reverses to assist with the cutting pace of the scene. The reverses and the energetic cutting also disguise the static nature of a scene featuring the protagonist simply sitting in his stationary truck. The reverses also give the impression of a complete space. Yet the degree of space revealed is carefully calibrated to exclude the space above the frame to maximise the significance of this area of off-screen space as occupied by the alien presence. Even within individual shots, Spielberg carefully directs spectator attention as in Fig. 6.2d, where the lowered map creates an aperture framing that neatly reveals and emphasises Neary's eyes—the most expressive and emotionally communicative element in the frame. This action also suggests Bordwell's (2001) conception of Eisenstein's *mise-en-geste* as a '…scenically contextualised physical action…' (p. 145). Neary's reaction portrays his sudden realisation that there is something wrong with his surroundings. This acknowledgment effectively inserts him into the space and this in turn initiates the close encounter event that follows.

The most significant function of the reverses lies in the arrangement and interaction of the shots themselves. Crucially, the pattern of 180-degree reversals means that each subsequent shot reveals the space previously occupied by the camera in the shot but then also 'anticipates' the subsequent camera placement. Figure 6.2b reveals the space occupied by the camera in Fig. 6.2a while also revealing the space that will be occupied by the camera in Fig. 6.2c. Likewise, Fig. 6.2c now also shows the space taken by the camera in Fig. 6.2b. The process is reset with the 90-degree shift to Fig. 6.2d, which includes the space that the camera occupies in Fig. 6.2e/f, while this shot reveals the camera position from Fig. 6.2d. The significance of this methodical showing and 'revising' can be further explained when considered in relation to components of Jean Pierre Oudart's conception of the suture.

Reconfiguring the Suture

Oudart (1977, pp. 35–43) contends that in the classical shot, reverse shot system, the initial shot is one field while the reverse shot, the 'fourth side', contains an 'absence' or 'the absent one'. Once the reverse shot is revealed and a character appears, the absent one becomes the field of the imaginary. This replacing of the absent one '…erases the absence or the empty field, and sutures the cinematic discourse by enveloping it in a new dimension, the Imaginary: the fourth side, a pure field of absence, becomes the imaginary field of the film and the field of its imaginary'. Daniel Dayan (1974) repeats this connection to language and makes explicit the Marxist link 'When shot two replaces shot one, the absent-one is transferred from the level of enunciation to the level of fiction. As a result of this, the code effectively disappears and the ideological effect of the film is thereby secured. The code, which produces an imaginary, ideological effect, is hidden by the message. Unable to see the workings of the code, the spectator is at its mercy' (p. 30).

Most contentious is the connection with Lacanian psychoanalysis and Oudart's claim of a process contained within the spectator's unconscious in perceiving the shot, reverse shot. Beginning with a perception of the first shot as a 'fantasmatic reality' (Allen 1995, p. 34), this quickly changes to a troubling 'lack' as the spectator becomes aware of the frame and the absence emanating from the 'fourth side'. Stephen Heath (1976) emphasises the 'negation' aspect where revealing one side to the spectator means that the other side is then withheld and applies this to classical narration as a whole with the narration as an on-going process of 'this but not that' (p. 107). Noël Carroll (1996, p. 415) attacks Oudart's unconscious experience hypothesis in perceiving the shot, reverse shot by noting that editing is processed in the conscious or pre-conscious—not unconscious. Carroll (1988) also questions Oudart's claim of a '...dialectic of delight or dejection...' in experiencing the shot, reverse shot simply by noting that he himself has never sensed this process. 'If a formulation is all explanation and proposes little or no evidence, then we have good reason to reject it. But the suturing theories we have reviewed are exactly of this sort...' (p. 188).

Of interest is Dayan's (1974) articulation of a 'revising' process.

> The suture is always chronologically posterior to the corresponding shot; i.e., when we finally know what the other field was, the filmic field is no longer on the screen. The meaning of a shot is given retrospectively; it does not meet the shot on the screen, but only in the memory of the spectator. The process of reading the film (perceiving its meaning) is therefore a retroactive one, wherein the present modifies the past. (p. 31)

Dayan interprets this as a device for preserving the dominant ideology, a kind of covert way of manipulating meaning. Kaja Silverman (1986) makes a similar observation of the suture and editing where each shot informs and modifies the signification of both prior and subsequent shots. 'The cut guarantees that both the preceding and the subsequent shots will function as structuring absences to the present shot. These absences make possible a signifying ensemble, convert one shot into a signifier of the next one, and the signified of the preceding one' (p. 222).

Yet the existence of a stylistic device that is capable of 'retrospectively' modifying a shot's value does offer potential as a persuasive cognitive tool. My conception of 'reconfiguring' the suture involves jettisoning both the (largely discredited) ideological and psychoanalytical components and then reconsidering it in terms of its function as a stylistic, perceptual dynamic relating to the shot, reverse shot arrangement. If we consider the suture purely in terms of its stylistic function then the issue with Oudart's conception is that it applies only to dialogue scenes and only—according to Bordwell (1985, p. 111)—when the camera is positioned at oblique angles to the subject (as in camera positions D and E, Fig. 6.1). When this is considered together with Salt's observation that the shot, reverse shot constitutes, on average, approximately 40 per cent of the shots in a classical feature, then the application of the suture can be quite restricted.

The advantage of the stripped down, wide reverse version of suture is that it can potentially be applied to any scene at any time—unlike Oudart's highly specific requirements for the shot, reverse shot version. Crucially, Oudart states that 'the absent one', the 'fourth side', can be identified with the narrator or author. Bordwell (1985) then makes the next logical step:

> Shot/reverse-shot cutting plays down narration by creating the sense that no scenographic space remains unaccounted for. If shot 2 shows that something is 'on the other side' of shot 1, there is no place for the narrator to hide. (p. 111)

Edward Branigan (1992) interprets Bordwell:

> ...when space is reversed we do not see a camera, sets, or technicians but only more diegetic space which seemingly is part of a consistent and unified group of spaces with no disturbing (causal) outside influences (e.g., by an 'author'). (p. 44)

In filling in the gaps created by 'the other', Spielberg's system of reverses operates to suppress authorial presence by repeatedly 'reminding' the spectator through this process of 'revising' previous and subsequent shots that there is no camera (and related crew) where one should be—or should have been. The implication then is that the narration exists of itself, thus again invoking Bazin's notion of the narration as occurring autonomously. This effect is further intensified in some of the following instances of reverse use where Spielberg also incorporates deep space compositions into the wide reverse device.

2. Second Shark Attack

This elaborate set-piece sequence from *Jaws* (1975) marks the plot's transition into the second act as Brody witnesses the attack that both confirms the shark's presence and also ensures his range of knowledge now matches that of the audience. It also foregrounds his personal involvement with the attacks as the victim's mother later holds him responsible for not having closed the beaches earlier. This greater personal involvement 'raises the stakes' and functions to clearly define his goal (kill the shark), which in turn drives the narrative forward until the film's resolution. The sequence can be divided into three sections—pre-attack, attack and post-attack, again reflecting a beginning, middle and end structure. Each section deploys its own distinct set of wide reverses with variation specific to that section. Camera placement for all three sections is predominantly inside the circle of action looking out, which assists in creating a sense of being immersed in the middle of the action, and this is emphasised by the staging of foregrounded action.

The first tracking shot (Fig. 6.4a–c) introduces the key characters—the 'raft boy' (victim, Alex Kintner), his mother (who features at the end of the scene) and the protagonist Brody. This first shot also establishes a wide view of one side of the beach. Shot two (6.4d) is a 90-degree shift and potentially Brody's optical point of view (OP) showing the water. Shot three (Fig. 6.4e) is a tight 180-degree reverse and shot four reverses again by 180 degrees showing the dog entering the water. Shot five (Fig. 6.4g) is a 90-degree shift that reinforces the mother's presence (and therefore her significance) as her son passes her in the foreground. The next four shots (Fig. 6.4h–k) repeat characters already seen and all face the ocean. Shot ten (Fig. 6.4l) is a 90-degree angle change and reveals the only side of the beach not previously seen. *The first ten shots of the scene methodically compile for us a 360 degree view of the space in which the action of the scene will take place.*

Figs. 6.4a, 6.4b

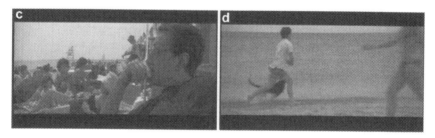

Figs. 6.4c, 6.4d

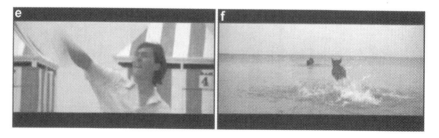

Figs. 6.4e, 6.4f

Space and the Wide Reverse Strategy 163

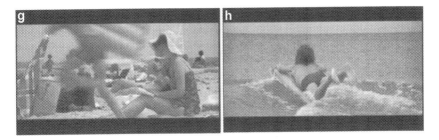

Figs. 6.4g, 6.4h

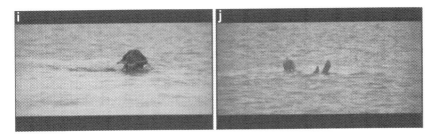

Figs. 6.4i, 6.4j

Figs. 6.4k, 6.4l *Jaws* (1975)

The next part of the sequence functions to cement Brody's involvement in the narrative. A series of shot, reverse shots suggest Brody's OP although the varying focal lengths mitigate against this. This is another example of Spielberg freely mixing different focal lengths—even when the shots are seemingly motivated by character OP and therefore should all employ the same perspective.

This scene is celebrated for its use of characters passing in the foreground to create a wipe transition effect from the point/glance to the point/object and back again. The wipe paradoxically draws attention to the edit by establishing a pattern of expected reverse fields but the expectation also reduces the disruptive aspect of the cut itself by focusing attention on the foreground action—on the movement rather than the cut. '…the cuts are seemingly hidden by a "wipe" effect of foreground characters passing in front of camera. The result is both documentary realism and flaunting of technique, while increasing tension by blocking the spectator's view and, implicitly, Brody's' (Morris 2007, p. 60).

Having already established the relevant space, the successive 180-degree reverses function to build tension and empathy for the protagonist as Spielberg draws out spectator expectation. With the camera positioned inside the circle, Spielberg utilises foregrounded action with people passing close to the frame to create the wipe transitions that suggest a crowded beach but that also smooths the shot change. This is particularly evident with the reframing transitions of Brody where the wipe effect softens the double axial cut-ins to Brody in close-up. The deep space, profile shots of Brody serve multiple functions including: a visual respite from the constant reversing, a widening of the frame to accommodate the inclusion of new characters, and as a conduit to character empathy—much in the same way as the angle at Fig. 6.2d and the close-up of Neary is repeatedly referred to during the close encounter scene.

Spielberg again generates the narrative almost exclusively through visuals. The dialogue is largely irrelevant and functions to distract the protagonist, while simultaneously intensifying the tension. Having established the narrative space and multiple characters—including Brody's own children—this later part consolidates Brody's significance as protagonist by orientating all of the action around his perspective and reactions. Another important characteristic relating to Spielberg's use of wide reverses is the constant linking between characters and scenographic space. Examples of this linking can be seen in the use of a dioptre to permit an extreme deep focus composition that links both the water and the businessman speaking to Brody. This linking also has implications for temporality by perpetuating a sense that this is all happening continuously and simultaneously, thus reinforcing the similar sensibility as generated by the wide reverses. The scene transitions into the next phase with six brief shots (one shot is only one frame, the others are each approximately half a second in duration) of the children splashing and this is then contrasted with 'calm' shots of the boy calling for the now missing dog. At this point, the narrative momentarily again privileges the audience with greater knowledge than Brody—the missing dog, the stick in the water, and this greater knowledge carries on into the attack section.

This awareness translates into the reveal of underwater space and this extended shot, accompanied by John Williams' now iconic shark attack leitmotif, suggests that we are privy to the shark's point of view. The attack is revealed through multiple perspectives including that of the shark, those on the beach and nearby swimmers. Spielberg uses the elaborate *Vertigo* track in, zoom out shot to signal Brody's realisation of the attack and then includes two sets of reverses. Again, different focal lengths are used with a relatively wider angle preceded and followed by longer lens shots that compress the action and make the fleeing crowd seem larger and more chaotic.

3. Omaha Beach Landing

This sequence from *Saving Private Ryan* (1998) uses the wide reverse strategy initially to create a spatial 'anchor' that orientates the spectator amid the unfolding chaos. This begins with the first, somewhat indistinct wide shot of the beach taken from the rear of the landing craft (Fig. 6.5a—although there are 18 shots before this of the soldiers travelling in the landing craft). This is tightly reversed in shot two (Fig. 6.5b) and then a wide elevated tracking shot (Fig. 6.5c) from the German bunker that reveals the origin and placement of the firing machine gun. Figure 6.5d is a reverse long lens view of the bunker and reinforces its spatial positioning in relation to the foregrounded soldiers on the landing craft. Spielberg reiterates this positioning and the importance of the bunker by including it in the next two shorter lens shots—one from the right side of the landing craft (Fig. 6.5e) and the next from the left side (Fig. 6.5f). If we consider the position of these two shots as a de facto master perspective and then reverse this with the wide machine gun shots (Fig. 6.5c—and repeated twice more in the scene), we can construct a line of axis between the two perspectives—much like the imaginary line drawn between two characters facing each other and commonly used in shooting dialogue (the axis of action or line). This becomes the line that the character's eye-lines and camera placements do not cross for the remainder of this sequence (except for two instances I will explore later and excluding the underwater shots where the spatial orientation is arbitrary). All of the action that takes place for this sequence on the beach therefore occurs looking either towards the bunker from the beach, from the beach to the bunker or along the beach to the left (from the landing American soldiers' perspective). Except for two brief shots, the right side of the beach is never revealed. The wide reverses are also causally significant because they establish the source of the carnage and therefore simultaneously identify the goal for the soldiers and the spectator—to knock out the bunker. The delineation of scenographic space and the nature of the character's goal orientation are both confirmed in the first seven shots of a sequence that includes some 77 shots.

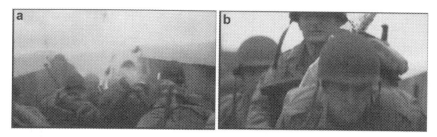

Figs. 6.5a, 6.5b

Figs. 6.5c, 6.5d

Figs. 6.5e, 6.5f *Saving Private Ryan* (1998)

The wide reverses continue their orientating role by appearing at regular intervals during the sequence. There are only two instances where shots appear to 'cross the line' and show an area on the 'other side'. The first is cued by Captain Miller (the protagonist)—his eye-line shifts from left to right and then crosses the line so that the shot ends with his eye-line now right to left. This cues the next tight shot of the soldier catching fire and the cut to the wide shot of the soldiers being engulfed by flames. It is implied from the ordering of the shots and the protagonist's eye-line that these shots represent the protagonist's OP (and this is seemingly confirmed by his reaction shot where he is still looking right to left), yet one can ask which shot is actually from his OP as one is a tight shot and the other wide? If we apply the criterion of the focal length that most closely approximates what the human eye sees, said to be a lens of about 50 mm, then it is the second shot that is the closer match. Regardless of which is the more accurate representation of OP, this example is a further instance of the 'malleability' of OP in the classical context. Branigan (1984, p. 81) describes this kind of variation as 'deviant POV' or 'dynamic perception' and it is not uncommon in classical cinema. The abiding element in these variants is that the shot perspective remains faithful to the character's sightline.

If one compares the pattern of spatial use in this sequence to that operating in the examined second shark attack from *Jaws* (1975), a film made more than 20 years earlier, the similarities relating to the structuring of the coverage is significant. One obvious point is that the location for both sequences is the same (a beach) and that this would encourage deploying similar strategies for spatial arrangement and staging. Despite this, the high degree of similarity is compelling. The *Jaws* sequence also anchors the depiction of scenographic space between the activity in the water and the 180 degree reverse of Brody sitting on the beach watching, much like the landing craft and the machine gun bunker in *Ryan*. The *Jaws* sequence similarly uses 90-degree variations with Brody in the foreground and one side of the beach visible in the distance. Both sequences also largely orientate the depiction of events around the eye-line of their protagonists so that the spectator sees what the character sees either as a subjective reverse or in a wider, objective shot.

Regardless of *Ryan's* seemingly more ambitious staging and elaborate visuals (and sound effects) courtesy of visual effects (including the 'shaky-cam', bullet trails, bullet impacts and muted colour palette), the similarities between the two sequences in terms of the fundamental construction of scenographic space and its role in orientating the spectator further illustrate Spielberg's continued application of the wide reverse strategy. It also underlines the level of intentionality applied to manipulating space and its significance in creating a more coherent and immersive narrative experience for the spectator.

4. Indiana Jones Escapes

The opening action sequence from *Raiders of the Lost Ark* (1981) that ends with the protagonist escaping by seaplane is essentially infused throughout with wide 180-degree reverse shot combinations that create—or give the impression of creating—a 360-degree scenographic space. The sequence can be loosely divided into three scenes: (1) discovering the idol and fleeing the chamber, (2) outrunning the giant boulder and (3) escaping the pursuing Hovitos Indians.

A. Discovering the Idol and Fleeing the Chamber

In contrast to the previous examples, Spielberg delays the reveal of the entire chamber and this is likely due to a preference for prolonging the mystery and 'atmosphere' of this location. Instead, the golden idol is quickly established in the first wide reverse/OP (Fig. 6.6c) and the character goal and purpose of the scene are immediately confirmed for the audience. Table 6.1 (below) shows the application of wide reverses (in red) as evenly distributed at the beginning, middle and end of the scene. (The oblique shots in blue indicate reverses that are not quite 180 degrees.) The reverse variation in this instance consists of reversing from a tight composition to a wide reverse and back to the tight framing, though the changes of angle still preserve a full 180 degrees. The alternating tight (shot 3), wide (shot 4), tight (shot 5), wide (shot 6) reverses offer limited

Space and the Wide Reverse Strategy

detail in terms of revealing scenographic space yet still effectively expose the previous and subsequent camera positions. Another variation of the wide framing at shot 24 and the tight shot of shot 25 illustrates Spielberg's use of the tight, wide juxtaposition as contributing to dramatic tension—as also seen in the *Jaws* example. The failure to successfully substitute the idol for sand is signalled by the use of a wide reverse (shot 29) and this continues with the reverse from shot 32 to shot 34 as Indi rushes into and then away from the camera. The contrasting shot reverses also complement the interaction between Indi and Satipo (the assistant). The 'internal' crosscutting from one to the other adds to the visual dynamic and Satipo's emotional reactions both emphasise the significance of Indi's actions and 'humanise' his essentially stoic performance. Internal in this sense refers to crosscutting within the one space of a scene in contrast to the more customary practice of using crosscutting to link action occurring in two different spaces. The inserts of Satipo also permit variations in the pacing of the editing by providing another character that can be referred to when and if shots need to be tightened or lengthened.

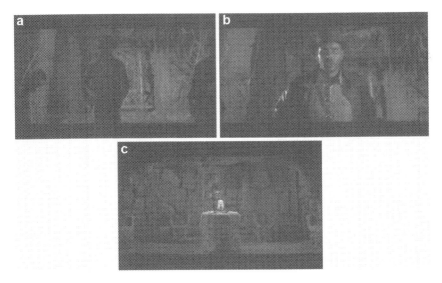

Figs. 6.6a, 6.6b, 6.6c   *Raiders of the Lost Ark* (1981)

Table 6.1 Golden idol chamber—coverage and angles *Raiders of the Lost Ark* (1981)

Shot	Description	Angle – from previous shot
1 (6.6a-b)	Indi arrives in chamber	Wide push-in to Indi
2 (6.6c)	Golden statue (long lens)	Wide 180 reverse (Long lens)
3	Indi looking	180 reverse
4	Indi and Satipo (helper) looking	Wide 180 reverse (wide angle)
5	Indi restrains Satipo	180 reverse
6	Indi, Satipo probe floor	Wide 180 reverse (wide angle)
7	Over shoulder looking down at floor	Overhead
8	MCU Satipo watches	Oblique
9	Over shoulder Indi presses floor	Overhead (same as 161)
10	Dart fires from wall	Oblique mid
11	Dart embeds in log	Oblique reverse
12	Over shoulder with statue in background	Wide (same as 160)
13	Indi's shoe as he steps	Insert - tracking
14	Wall from where dart fired	Insert - tracking
15	Indi advances – stumbles	Wide – from behind Indi
16	Satipo reacts	180 reverse
17	Indi advances	Wide 180 reverse
18	Statue	Mid shot – tracking in
19	Indi's shoe as he steps	Insert – tracking
20	Indi arrives at statue	Track in to mid
21	Satipo reacts	Track in
22	Indi considers statue	Loose mid
23	Tight on statue/ sifting sand in foreground	Oblique reverse
24	Indi prepares to take statue	Extreme Wide oblique reverse
25	Indi about to take statue	Loose mid
26	Mid Satipo reacts	Insert
27	Indi takes statue	Loose mid
28	Mid Satipo reacts	Insert
29	Indi turns to exit – rumbling begins	Loose mid
30	Satipo reacts	Insert
31	Indi reacts	Loose mid
32	Indi runs	Wide 180 reverse
33	Indi runs	Analytical cut in
34	Indi runs	Wide 180 reverse
35	Darts firing from wall	Tight on wall - tracking
36	Indi runs	Full shot - tracking
37	Darts firing from opposite wall	Oblique reverse, tracking
38	Indi runs through frame and exits	Frontal tight to camera

B. Outrunning the Giant Boulder

Figure 6.7a shows Indi turning to favour camera in response to an off-screen sound with his eye-line suggesting the sound originates from somewhere behind and above the camera. Figure 6.7b confirms the source of the sound (the boulder), by revealing this space as a 180-degree reverse while Fig. 6.7c and 6.7d are each again wide reverses that establish a 360-degree space and repeatedly reveal the camera positions in the previous shot. The following four shots that complete the scene are all size variations taken from the axis of Fig. 6.7d with Indi running toward camera, the boulder close behind. Reversing these remaining shots would prove visually pointless as the boulder would obscure anything behind it. The repeated positioning of the shots of Indi running towards camera imply that he is running to the safety of the audience or to the safety of the other side—and the significance of this in relation to spectator identification and/or affect is examined in Chap. 8.

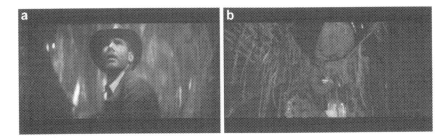

Figs. 6.7a, 6.7b

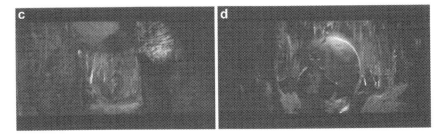

Figs. 6.7c, 6.7d   *Raiders of the Lost Ark* (1981)

C. Escaping the Pursuing Hovitos

Following a brief dialogue sequence that introduces Indi's nemesis, the remaining part of the sequence involves two intercut lines of action—Indi running from the Hovitos and Gus waiting at the seaplane. The crosscutting between the two locations recalls the earlier similar cutting pattern between Indi and Satipo. Indi, the Hovitos and Gus are quickly introduced in the first two shots while the first three shots involve wide compositions (Fig. 6.8a–c) and establish the respective spaces. These first three shots are also 180-degree reverses. Shots five (Fig. 6.8e) and six (Fig. 6.8f) seem to continue this reversal but are in fact both facing in approximately the same direction—the sense of a continuing reversal arises largely from the two lines of action and the initially different spaces. From shot seven all of the remaining shots until shot 15 involve reversals as the pursued and pursuer pattern is maintained. Throughout, Spielberg mixes high camera positioning with low, long lens with wide, a tracking shot with deep space compositions and another moving shot that suggests OP.

Figs. 6.8a, 6.8b

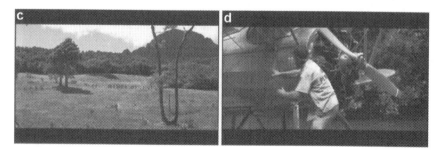

Figs. 6.8c, 6.8d

Space and the Wide Reverse Strategy 173

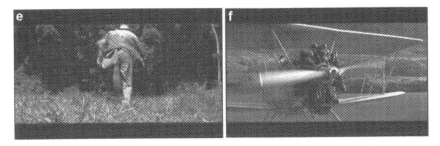

Figs. 6.8e, 6.8f   *Raiders of the Lost Ark* (1981)

The three scenes seamlessly integrate wide reverses and variations for generating scenographic space into the classical crosscutting pattern that Spielberg utilises for the chamber and seaplane scenes in particular. A sense of spectator engagement is also maintained by again staging Indi such that he is often running toward the camera. Related is Eisenstein's concept of the action as '…flowing around the camera…' and the significance of this is considered in greater detail in the following chapter.

Simple Spatial Configuration Reverses: Four Examples

1. The Car Ferry

In contrast to the aggressive editing seen in the complex group examples, this sequence from *Jaws* (1975) consists of only six shots yet Spielberg still manages to generate a 360-degree view of the location. This is achieved through a combination of a revolving platform (the ferry), deep space composition and a wide reverse. Warren Buckland (2006) has noted the visual ingenuity of the constantly changing background that is generated as the ferry rotates to dock with the opposite bank, together with the use of deep space compositions. He also mentions Spielberg's strategy of staging the actors so that they simulate analytical cutting by having them slowly approach the camera's position (Fig. 6.9a–c). Yet Buckland fails to register the significance of the next and final shot of the sequence (Fig. 6.9d). This shot only runs for approximately four seconds and in it the Mayor can be heard calling to the ferry operator: 'Okay, you can take us back now'. Figure 6.9d is a 180-degree reverse (Fig. 6.10, below) and shows the Mayor and Brody standing in their final positions from Fig. 6.9c implying that the cut to Fig. 6.9d is temporally continuous and observes classical continuity—also further underlined by the Mayor's dialogue. Figure 6.9d clearly reveals the space occupied by the camera (and crew) for the shooting of Fig. 6.9a–c. Figure 6.9e is a production still taken during the shooting of the barge scene (shot at the Chappaquiddick Ferry) and illustrates the large amount of equipment and crew required to shoot the angle at Fig. 6.9a–c. Shooting the reverse at Fig. 6.9d would have necessitated clearing all trace of this assuming that the long take (Fig. 6.9a–c) was shot first as would have been likely. As with most of the other examples of wide reverses, the need to remove all trace of cast and crew from the previous shot and the time-consuming nature of this process again underline the high degree of importance Spielberg accords the wide reverse.

Figs. 6.9a, 6.9b

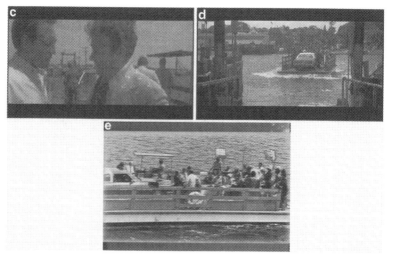

Figs. 6.9c, 6.9d, 6.9e   Production still *Jaws* (1975)

Space and the Wide Reverse Strategy   175

From the perspective of syuzhet information, Fig. 6.9d is redundant—it does not really contribute any plot information and the scene could easily have concluded at the end of Fig. 6.9c after the mayor has made his point. Figure 6.9d is really about showing 'the other side'. It is foregrounding space, further emphasising the importance of revealing this 'fourth wall', and completing a 360-degree space that simultaneously reveals the space occupied by the camera and crew. While the action depicted in Fig. 6.9d may not be causally important, the scene itself is. The Mayor's refusal to close the beaches essentially propels the plot

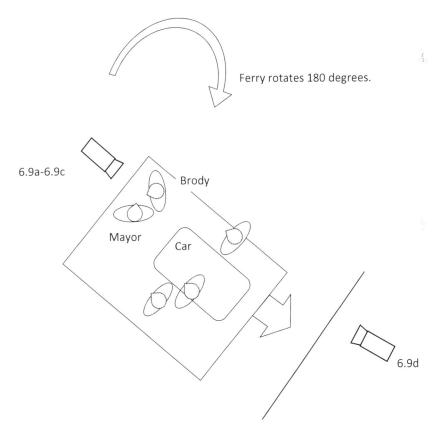

Fig. 6.10 Ferry scene—overhead view—wide reverse, *Jaws* (1975)

forward as his decision precipitates the subsequent shark attack in the next scene, which is in turn blamed on Brody by the victim's mother. As mentioned earlier, this further consolidates Brody's integration into the plot as protagonist by making his involvement not just professional, but also personal.

2. Airfield Attack

Taken from *Empire of the Sun* (1985), this brief but visually spectacular sequence is unique (for Spielberg) in its attempt to depict a character's hallucination or vision—in this case it is that of the protagonist, Jim. I have included this example because while I argue that Spielberg uses the wide reverse system to create a more convincing scenographic space, he activates it here to create the fantastic.[3] Yet it's a fantasy that appears 'real' to Jim so the highly subjective nature of some shots still functions within classical convention in two ways: at the level of style they are motivated by the character's body movement and eye-line as OP—something that he sees, and at the level of characterisation and fabula development. Jim's psychological condition as a prisoner of war suffering from malnutrition and exhaustion is a causal factor that realistically motivates his fantasy (together with an earlier 'planted' character trait and behaviour that revolves around an enthusiasm for the P51 Mustang fighter).

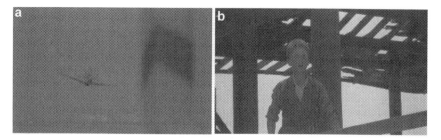

Figs. 6.11a, 6.11b

Space and the Wide Reverse Strategy 177

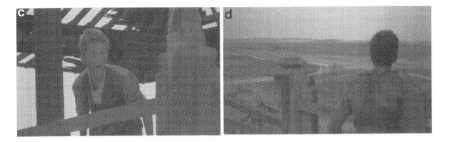

Figs. 6.11c, 6.11d

Figs. 6.11e, 6.11f *Empire of the Sun* (1987)

Jim's view of the American fighter attack on the airfield serves as the centrepiece section of the sequence. The shot, reverse shot pattern begins with him running along a rooftop terrace and this is reversed with Jim now in the foreground and the aircraft strafing the airfield in the middle distance. Jim's changing eye-line (he looks to his left) cues the next reverse (Fig. 6.11a), which is ostensibly his OP as the fighter approaches in slow motion. Figure 6.11b–c reverses again back to a similar or same set-up as the two previous shots. Figure 6.11d–f is a wide reverse tracking shot showing the fighter passing by with Jim in the foreground. This shot is remarkable for both its composition and virtuosity—the camera counter tracking at what must have been a very high speed to capture the passing fighter while the composition represents an elaborate, further instance of Spielberg's preference for three layers of depth with Jim, the fighter and the camp buildings demarcating specific layers. Movement is also significant as a factor in generating a dynamic space as the subject's movement (the aircraft) through the frame combines with the camera's tracking, which creates the 'monocular movement parallax' effect—a sense of depth as the perspective relation between the objects changes because of the movement. This shot is also aberrant in the sense that the shots before and after are part of a conventional classical OP construction (point/glance, point/object, reaction and so on) yet Fig. 6.11d is a wide taken from behind Jim so is inconsistent with this convention. Again, this is another example of Spielberg prioritising the wide reverse strategy— Figure 6.11d reveals the space or the fourth side of Fig. 6.11b–c. Figure 6.11d is reversed again in the next shot, signalling a return to classical subjectivity with the shot movement and Jim's eye-line implying this is the fighter pilot's point-of-view. The next shot compliments this with a reverse suggesting not only Jim's OP but also his fantasy manifesting itself as the pilot seemingly acknowledges him with a wave. Shots Fig. 6.11a and 6.11d and the subsequent reverse all depict the fighter in slow motion and this functions on two levels: to punctuate and emphasise Jim's fantasy and, at a more basic technical level, capture and draw out the depiction of an object passing by at great speed. This is followed by a reverse close-up reaction of Jim that is in turn followed by another reverse that signals for the spectator a return to normalcy as the fighter speeds past—the return to objectivity inferred by the now normal speed of the fighter, that the pilot is not actually waving to Jim, and the return of diegetic sound.

Spielberg constructs for the spectator this brief subjective insight into the protagonist's experience entirely visually and entirely within the bounds of textbook classical convention. The 'normal' narrative flow is interrupted by first Jim's eye-line, which in turn motivates the reverse subjective OP shot of the fighter approaching in slow motion. This is reversed with the protagonist still looking, which cues the wide reverse of the fighter passing by. Spielberg smoothly establishes the subjective pattern with Jim as the privileged centre of it and at the same time deploys wide reverses within the framework of the conventional point-of-view exchange.

3. Death Notification

From *Saving Private Ryan* (1998) this brief, seven-shot scene provides fabula information entirely visually and entirely by utilising wide reverses beginning with the foregrounded army car and the distant farmhouse (Fig. 6.12a). The constant reversing is tempered by the use of reflections, which are the only two shots to feature a frontal view of Mrs Ryan. Note that the army car can be seen through the window in the distance in Fig. 6.12b and again through the window in the final shot as Mrs Ryan exits the front door. The camera tracks with her until the shot ends in a typical, three-layered deep space composition with the photo of the four brothers lit prominently in the foreground. Like many of the other examples, this scene also appears at a point where the story transitions into the next act—this scene capping the first act with a visually emotive elaboration of the film's main premise.

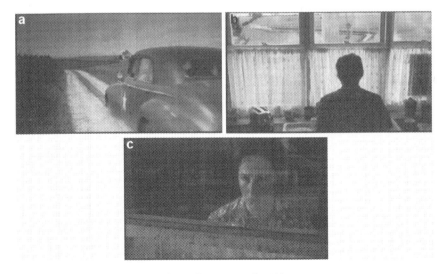

Figs. 6.12a, 6.12b. 6.12c *Saving Private Ryan* (1998)

4. Establishing the Arrival Hall

Taken from the opening scene of *The Terminal* (2004), the methodical construction of space recalls that used for Neary's close encounter and contrasts with the double 360-degree tracking shot Spielberg employs later in the film to construct scenographic space for the main location (the transit terminal) where most of the action takes place (examined in Chap. 7). The opening establishing wide-tracking shot (Fig. 6.13a) is reversed with a brief, contrasting tight shot (Fig. 6.13b), which then cuts to a similar but wider angle (Fig. 6.13c) that tracks from right to left (reversing the motion in the first shot). The overhead shot (Fig. 6.13d) is followed by the long lens frontal view (Fig. 6.13e) of passengers arriving and this is more or less reversed in the following high position shot (Fig. 6.13f) as they pass below (this shot appears to be a continuation of Fig. 6.13e). Figure 6.13a is so wide that it effectively reveals three of the four walls (approximately 270 degrees) while Fig. 6.13b and 6.13c reveal the fourth side and the camera space from Fig. 6.13a. The shots following Fig. 6.13f consist of singles and close-ups of customs officers, passengers and inserts. The 22nd shot of the scene (Fig. 6.13g) presents yet another wide perspective of the space constructed in the first six shots but also functions transitionally to introduce and establish a new scenographic space as well as two of the principal cast. While the protagonist is introduced in this first terminal space the narrative quickly shifts to the next office location and this initial terminal area is not seen again.

Figs. 6.13a, 6.13b

Space and the Wide Reverse Strategy   181

Figs. 6.13c, 6.13d

Figs. 6.13e, 6.13f, 6.13g   *The Terminal* (2004)

Eisenstein's 'Zones of Action'

Bordwell (1985) has observed that classical cinema usually establishes space before narration and in Chap. 3, I noted Eisenstein's similar belief that space be specifically considered and planned for prior to the shooting of a scene. The above eight examples illustrate how wide reverses—in quickly establishing complete scenographic spaces—in turn allow for the demarcation and emphasis of specific, key areas or 'zones of action' within the determined space. Spectator awareness of the total space of the scene therefore allows for an understanding of the physical relativity and thematic significance of any one specific space to any other space in that complete area. For example, the *Jaws* beach scene identifies Brody sitting on the beach as one zone and the water as another. The scene functions around the interaction between these two spaces—beach as safe, water as unsafe. Similarly, the chamber scene from *Raiders of the Lost Ark* specifies Indi with the gold idol as one zone while the helper, Satipo, occupies the other. That he remains near the entrance to the chamber allows us to understand where he is in relation to Indi as well as the entire area of the chamber and, as mentioned, permits variation in the editing by crosscutting from one area to the other. The simple spatial configuration reverses also highlight specific areas of the scenographic space. The arrival of the army car at the Ryan home in *Saving Private Ryan* functions by initially establishing two spaces at extreme ends of the depicted scenographic space and then resolves the scene by bringing the action in each space together. The army car establishes one zone (Fig. 6.12a), Mrs Ryan the other (Fig. 6.12b), and she is positioned at the other extreme edge of the scenographic space. The tension and drama of the scene are generated by the army car gradually traversing the space until it occupies Mrs Ryan's space and the scene is resolved.

A measure of Spielberg's ability to disguise or submerge wide reverses within conventional decoupage can be appreciated when considering the comments of some theorists. Edward Branigan (1976) contrasts Yasijuro Ozu's construction of a 360-degree scenographic space with his claim that Hollywood is seemingly restricted to a range of 180 degrees, based as it is on the classical continuity system's traditional axis of action 'There is also a sense of depth and completeness not found in classical Hollywood films: Ozu reveals all the walls of a room and not just three' (p. 97). Discussing classical cinema and examining the first scene from *Jaws* as an example of classical continuity editing, Stephen Heath (1976) comments 'The 180 degree line that the camera is forbidden to cross answers exactly to the 180 degree line of the screen behind which the spectator cannot and must not go...' (p. 88). Both Branigan and Heath equate the 180-degree rule to the screen as the proscenium, which cannot be breached, yet the numerous instances of wide reverses and of the 360-degree vistas created in *Jaws* contradict this claim. Fellow directors seem more aware of Spielberg's strategy. Also discussing *Jaws*, Pauline Kael (1975) relates a conversation with an 'older director' who observed of Spielberg, 'He must never have seen a play; he's the first of us who doesn't think in terms of the proscenium arch. With him, there's nothing but the camera lens' (p. 136). If we recall Raymond Durgnat's (1968, p. 15) long-held assertion that the shot, reverse shot system 'strait-jackets' Hollywood style, then revealing a number of additional functions of the wide reverse—based as it is on the shot, reverse shot—further demonstrates its versatility and wide ranging impact on style and narration.

Style by Stealth: Additional Stylistic Implications of Wide Reverses

I have detected four additional stylistic functions over and above those already examined:

1. Negating Kuleshov's Optical Pyramid
As discussed in Chap. 5, Lev Kuleshov observed that the camera's vision was highly restricted near the lens but that this opened out to create what he described as a simulation of three dimensional space. This near-lens restriction in turn placed strict limits on the staging of action close to the camera due to the issues this would have with the masking of background elements. The wide reverse removes the narrowness of the view near the camera's lens by revealing this area in the reversed shot as illustrated in Fig. 6.1 (above) where reverses G and H reveal each other's space adjacent to the camera's lens (as well as to the camera itself). The wide reverse effectively contributes both senses of depth and volume to the scenographic space—both highly desired attributes within classical representations of space.

2. Revival of Foregrounding
Relating to the restrictions inherent in the optical pyramid, Bordwell (1997, p. 208) discusses the rise of two-plane compositions in the 1920s where a large foreground object and recessed background would then be reversed in editing with the background object now dramatically thrust forward. Salt notes even earlier manifestations of this in his discussion of

'scene reverses', which I consider in Chap. 9. *Saving Private Ryan* exhibits multiple instances beginning with the initial beach landing where the foregrounded machine gun (Fig. 6.5c) is reversed so that the soldiers scrambling to disembark become foregrounded—the bunker housing the machine gun now clearly visible in the distant background (Fig. 6.5d—long lens; Fig. 6.5e and 6.5f—wider angle).

3. Constructing Whole Objects

Branigan (2006, p. 167) maintains that in viewing objects photographed by the camera—he uses the example of a tree—the spectator constructs multi-dimensional views of that tree based on prior knowledge. It is as if it is '…seen through many possible angles…' This is also another 'by-product' of the wide reverse process. We are given a complimentary, reverse perspective of key objects—whether they be Neary sitting in his truck, Jim watching from the rooftop, Indi fleeing the pursuing Indians or the T-Rex emerging through the broken fencing (examined in Chap. 7). In each instance, the reverse perspective produces another view of mise en scene and all elements in the frame and thus assists in the creation of a more 'complete' or 'solid' object(s) and does so seemingly without subjugating narration in favour of style.

4. Invoking the Theatrical Tableau as Cine-tableau

I have indicated that Spielberg tends to apply the wide reverse during narratively significant scenes and moments so that they assist in emphasising the importance of the depicted event. Ben Brewster and Lea Jacobs (1997, pp. 41–48) have examined how early cinema adopted the device of the tableau from theatre where it functioned to '…arrest the flow of the narrative so as to produce a heightened sense of its significance'. The definition of tableau needs to be clarified in this context. Studies in cinema tend to apply the term to the static, wide-shot compositions of early cinema. Brewster and Jacobs—and Arthur Pougin before them—use the same term to describe the moment in a theatre performance where—typically—characters halt the performance to variously break into a brief musical interlude, present some kind of symbolic depiction (e.g. god versus the devil) or even simply have the cast freeze in a fixed position for some seconds. This tableau moment usually occurred at the end of an act but could also appear at other times during the performance and its main purpose was to present a '...summary of a situation, allegorical commentary, punctuation of important narrative moments'. Brewster and Jacobs have traced the continued use of this device into early cinema where it quickly became complemented by camera movement, the close-up or cutting to a new scene—stylistic elements that came to entirely supplant the theatrical form of the tableau.

Eisenstein was also aware of the potential of the reverse shot for producing emphasis and punctuation

> ...if we shoot a shot from an opposite angle, changing the camera set-up by 180 degrees, the resultant shot would upset the unity of the general action if it were given simply as a regular part of it. But suppose we wish to accentuate, to underline, the snatching up of the table-cloth, then we might give a shot from the reverse camera-angle, from the diametrically opposed angle, with the camera turned by 180 degrees. (Nizhny 1979, p. 80)

Eisenstein seems in this instance to suggest the reverse as a tighter composition that contributes to creating impact. Spielberg applies this in: the cut from the wide in the Neary close encounter to the tight over-shoulder of Neary examining the map (Fig. 6.2b); multiple instances in the wide views of the truck and contrasting reversed close-ups of Mann in *Duel*; inverted instances as OP in Indi's glance to the wide of the idol and the two-shot of Brody and the Mayor reverse to the wide of the ferry (Fig. 6.9d). I also note and examine other instances of this 'impact reverse' as I label it, in scenes by Michael Mann and Carl Theodore Dreyer in Chap. 9.

If we conceive of the theatrical tableau as a process where the action briefly freezes, suspending and thus punctuating a moment, the wide reverse can be seen to essentially fulfil this function. In *Raiders of the Lost Ark*, Indi's momentary pause as he looks over his shoulder at the off-screen sound (Fig. 6.7a) itself perpetuates and underlines the reverse that reveals him—still briefly in the same pose—but now with the boulder advancing towards him in the background (Fig. 6.7b). While the second shot reveals the state of affairs, the first *cut* to the reverse functions as punctuation, setting up the danger that is realised by the reverse. Similarly, the ferry scene reverse (Fig. 6.9d) from *Jaws* momentarily captures the characters in the same position from Fig. 6.9c, the repetition simulating a 'freeze' that underlines the significance of what has just occurred. Remarkably, and in contrast to the original theatre tableau, Spielberg's wide reverses seamlessly integrate narrative punctuation without drawing attention to the device.

Each of the eight examples deploys the wide reverse strategy in a structurally consistent way creating mostly 360-degree scenographic perspectives that suggest a 'complete' world of the scene. Spielberg orchestrates this while operating within the classical paradigm and by utilising a modified adaptation of the shot, reverse shot convention that permits the operation of style within the classical continuity editing framework. Unlike the traditional shot, reverse shot that is almost exclusively reserved for dialogue passages, the wide reverse is not restricted by this requirement and can potentially be activated at any point or time in the narration. This further allows the continued prioritisation of syuzhet requirements while also preserving the 'invisibility' of the role of style. The principal associated effect is in the construction of a narration seemingly of itself and without authorship and this further reinforces the perception of the scene as complete and existing as a self-perpetuating event. This process continues with some inherent modification in the type B variations examined in the following chapter.

Notes

1. Unlike many devices in cinema, the wide reverse is not influenced by theatre, painting or literature.
2. Bordwell (1988, p. 113) uses this term to describe Yasujiro Ozu's 90 degree transitions and how parts of the set are visually repeated as an overlap to assist with spatial orientation.
3. More specifically, the scene reveals Jim's imagination as a seemingly 'real' event – the pilot waving from his cockpit. This is not to be confused with Spielberg's many fantastic worlds. Even in these, character perception is always depicted as 'realistic' not imagined. One recent exception is the brief dream sequence at the beginning of *Lincoln* though the visuals are

treated to suggest difference and Lincoln can be heard in voiceover describing the scene as a dream. Glimpses of imagined events can also be seen in *Duel* when Mann imagines confronting the truck drivers and Avner imagines the recently deceased Robert appearing as a reflection in the store window in *Munich*.

References

Allen, R. (1995). *Projecting Illusion: Film Spectatorship and the Impression of Reality*. New York: Cambridge University Press.
Bordwell, D. (1985). *Narration and the Fiction Film*. London: Routledge.
Bordwell, D. (1988). *Ozu and the Poetics of Cinema*. Princeton: Princeton University Press.
Bordwell, D. (1997). *On the History of Film Style*. Cambridge, MA/London: Harvard University Press.
Bordwell, D. (2001). Eisenstein, Socialist Realism, and the Charms of Mizanstsena. In A. Lavalley & B. P. Scherr (Eds.), *Eisenstein at 100: A Reconsideration* (pp. 13–37). New Brunswick: Rutgers University Press.
Bordwell, D. (2005). *Figures Traced in Light: On Cinematic Staging*. Los Angeles: University of California Press.
Bordwell, D. (2006). *The Way Hollywood Tells It: Story and Style in Modern Movies*. Los Angeles: University of California Press.
Bordwell, D. (2008). *The Poetics of Cinema*. London: Routledge.
Branigan, E. (1976). The Space of Equinox Flower. *Screen, 17*(2), 74–105. Retrieved from http://screen.oxfordjournals.org/
Branigan, E. (1984). *Point of View in the Cinema*. Berlin: Mouton Publishers.
Branigan, E. (1992). *Narrative Comprehension and Film*. London/New York: Routledge.
Branigan, E. (2006). *Projecting a Camera: Language Games in Film Theory*. New York: Routledge.
Brewster, B., & Jacobs, L. (1997). *Theatre to Cinema: Stage Pictorialism and the Early Feature Film*. New York: Oxford University Press.
Buckland, W. (2006). *Directed by Steven Spielberg: Poetics of the Contemporary Hollywood Blockbuster*. New York: Continuum.
Buckland, W., & Elsaesser, T. (2002). *Studying Contemporary American Film. A Guide to Movie Analysis*. London: Bloomsbury Academic.
Carroll, N. (1988). *Mystifying Movies: Fads and Fallacies in Contemporary Film Theory*. New York: Columbia University Press.

Carroll, N. (1996). *Theorizing the Moving Image*. Cambridge: Cambridge University Press.
Dayan, D. (1974). The Tutor-Code of Classical Cinema. *Film Quarterly, 28*(1), 22–31. Retrieved from http://www.jstor.org/stable/1211439
Durgnat, R. (1968). Ebb and Flow, Images of the Mind – Part Two. *Films and Filming, 14*(11), 12–15.
Gombrich, E. H. (1977). *Art and Illusion: A Study in the Psychology of Pictorial Representation* (5th ed.). London: Phaidon Press Limited.
Heath, S. (1976). Narrative Space. *Screen, 17*(3), 68–112. Retrieved from http://screen.oxfordjournals.org/
Kael, P. (1975). The Current Cinema Notes on Evolving Heroes, Morals, Audiences. *The New Yorker, 54*, 136–143.
Morris, N. (2007). *The Cinema of Steven Spielberg Empire of Light*. London: Wallflower Press.
Nizhny, V. (1979). *Lessons with Eisenstein* (I. Montagu & J. Leyda, Eds. & Trans.). New York: Da Capo Press.
Oudart, J. P. (1977). Cinema and Suture. *Screen, 18*(4), 35–47. Retrieved from http://screen.oxfordjournals.org/
Silverman, K. (1986). Suture. In P. Rosen (Ed.), *Narrative, Apparatus, Ideology: A Film Theory Reader*. New York: Columbia University Press.
Thompson, K. (1999). *Storytelling in the New Hollywood: Understanding Classical Narrative Technique*. Cambridge: Harvard University Press.

Film Title Editions

Spielberg, S. (Director). (1975). *Jaws* [Motion picture, Blu-ray (2014)]. Australia: Universal Sony Pictures Home Entertainment.
Spielberg, S. (Director). (1977). *Close Encounters of the Third Kind* [Motion picture, Blu-ray (2007)]. United States: Sony Pictures Home Entertainment.
Spielberg, S. (Director). (1981). *Indiana Jones and the Raiders of the Lost Ark* [Motion picture, Blu-ray (2012)]. Australia: Lucasfilm Ltd.
Spielberg, S. (Director). (1987). *Empire of the Sun* [Motion picture, Blu-ray (2013)]. Australia: Warner Bros. Entertainment.
Spielberg, S. (Director). (1998). *Saving Private Ryan* [Motion picture, Blu-ray (2010)]. Australia: Paramount Pictures.
Spielberg, S. (Director). (2004). *The Terminal* [Motion picture, Blu-ray (2014)]. Australia: Paramount Pictures.

7

The Wide Reverse and Extended Variation

Some directors actively cultivate a 'personal' style through the repeated use of specific devices—such as Wes Anderson and his frequent application of planimetric compositions. However, Spielberg claims that he always applies variation to his style.

> I think every movie I've made after Indiana Jones, I've tried to make every single movie as if it was made by a different director, because I'm very conscious of not wanting to impose a consistent style on subject matter that is not necessarily suited to that style. So I try to re-invent my own eye every time I tackle a new subject. (Windolf 2008)

While Spielberg may claim to vary his style from film to film, he consistently operates within the parameters of classical style with its varied but finite range of options. Any potential instances of overt style are consistently avoided by incorporating a high degree of compositional and realistic motivation into each event. One might ask why Spielberg does not use wide reverses more frequently or even in all of his scenes given its inherent value. Bordwell notes that in terms of classical style, repetition tends to diminish effectiveness. If a filmmaker shoots most of a film in

© The Author(s) 2018
J. Mairata, *Steven Spielberg's Style by Stealth*,
https://doi.org/10.1007/978-3-319-69081-0_7

close-up then its function as a device for signalling emphasis or punctuation is likely to be compromised. Spielberg has commented on the use of the close-up '…when Hawks and Ford went in for the close-up it was to tell a story, to drum home a point and they used the close-up as a powerful tool of narrative storytelling' (Bouzereau 2001). Spielberg is also known for frequently revising shooting plans while on the set and one can assume that in certain circumstances, the wide reverse might not be appropriate and/or other strategies might function equally successfully. Yet Spielberg does apply the wide-reverse strategy across many of his films. I have already noted that because the wide reverse is likely developed from stylistic conventions like the shot, reverse shot and deep space, its existence as specific device tends to go unnoticed.

This is further accentuated by Spielberg's application of multiple variations and I have identified and grouped them here as Type B wide reverses. These still fulfil many of the functions of the Type A reverses (Chap. 6) including prioritising the construction of a panoramic sense of scenographic space and revealing camera positions. These variations can be divided into two cinematographic based categories: *Single Reverses* and *Single-Shot Reverses*. The single reverses consist of a shot that depicts a specific space (shot 1), with this shot then followed by a reverse shot (shot 2) that usually depicts a 180-degree reverse perspective of the first shot and that simultaneously reveals both the space occupied by the camera in shot one as well as the space 'behind the camera'. This arrangement also again functions in reverse with shot 1 'anticipating' the space to be used by the camera for shot 2, which validates the sense of an 'absent' camera. With this shot, reverse shot arrangement, each shot reveals the space that the camera *will* occupy or *has* occupied. Unlike the multiple shot reverses discussed in the previous chapter, these single reverse 'pairings' tend toward brevity in terms of screen time and as such suggest a more surreptitious influence on spectator perception.

The single-shot reverses usually involve a tracking camera movement that exposes the space occupied by the camera in the later part of the shot. The space revealed 'simulates' a shot 2 reverse but does so with an uninterrupted (no cutting) tracking motion that ends with the camera having also panned through 180 degrees. These shots are potentially, cognitively paradoxical in that while the reverse movement of the camera and revealing of space occupied by the camera earlier in the shot suggests an absent camera, the often elaborate camera movement tends to foreground style. This drawing of attention to the artifice implies an authorial presence, contradicting the sense of an absent camera/author. Unlike the single reverses that still preserve all of the inherent additional effects noted in the previous chapter, the single-shot reverses do not resolve the optical pyramid or create the cine-tableau.

Type B Wide-Reverse Variations

The following ten instances are taken from nine of Spielberg's features. The final example is a 'series' of single reverses in the *Tyrannosaurus rex* set-piece sequence from *Jurassic Park*. I have included this to demonstrate how Spielberg distributes the single reverse across the sequence, embedding individual instances at significant moments within a part of the scene so that they effectively punctuate those moments.

Single Reverses: Ten Examples

1. Murder by the Book

Spielberg's early work on the television series *Columbo* represents an approximate midpoint in his television career output that began with *Eyes* (1969) and ended with the television feature *Savage* (1973).[1] The *Columbo* episode *Murder by the Book* exhibits two examples of single, wide-reverse shot arrangements. The example examined here (Fig. 7.1a–c) includes an insert shot of a revolver (with its obvious 'priming' or foregrounding function). The wide reverse is clearly evident as Spielberg reverses the high, tilting down angle of car and car park (Fig. 7.1a) with the low, tilting up, deep space composition (Fig. 7.1c) that reveals the building—and camera space of the first shot—in the background of the reverse. All of this is largely cloaked by the significant amount of narrative information conveyed in the shots, including the introduction and revealing of the antagonist as he exits the car. His reveal is given dramatic emphasis through the build-up provided by the earlier intercut shots of the car travelling along the road (Fig. 5.10a) and then entering the building car park. The shots also establish the office building and location of the first two scenes while the gun reveal encourages the spectator to speculate/hypothesise with regard to its significance.

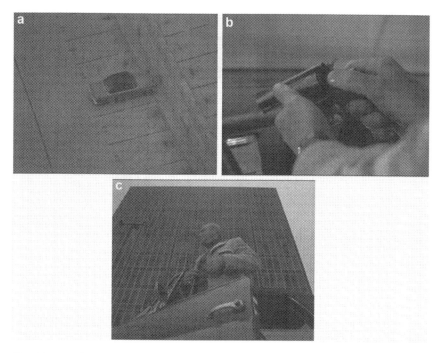

Figs. 7.1a, 7.1b, 7.1c *Murder by the Book* (1971)

The reverses also visually connect two separate spaces, the travelling car and the office interior as established and intercut in the opening scenes, by fluidly linking the two spaces (as reverses). They further reinforce Spielberg's early rejection of the artificiality of studio-based shooting by clearly revealing that these are 'real' spaces, not studio sets. The constant sound of typing that continues as non-diegetic audio over the shots of the moving car also works to connect the two spaces. The audio effect itself recalls a similar manipulation of sound (footsteps) across different spaces (and temporality) in John Boorman's *Point Blank* (1967).

2. Duel

Within months of completing *Murder by the Book*, Spielberg would direct *Duel* (1971), which features a range of single reverses, single-shot reverses and a complex, multi-shot wide-reverse sequence. Spielberg employs a single reverse variation in a sequence where Mann tries to identify the truck driver from a group of men sitting at a diner counter. The first shot tracks (Fig. 7.2a–b) along the row of seated diners with the watching Mann glimpsed between diners in the background. The second shot (Fig. 7.2c) is a tighter, long lens composition that emphasises Mann's discomfort and efficiently includes the truck in a deep space composition that complements the spatial arrangement of the previous shot as well as that of the next. The third shot (Fig. 7.2d) is a wider-angle reverse zoom that initially reveals all the diners as well as the space occupied by the camera in the previous two shots. This exchange of reverse shots occurs well into the sequence and reinforces my contention that part of its function is to covertly reaffirm the sense of a narrative without a narrator—particularly as the tracking and zooming camera betrays an overt display of style that is once again masked by the busy nature of the narrative elements. The slow moving tracking shot underlines the tension while the subsequent zoom personifies Mann's growing unease. This use of the zoom was common in the late 1960s and early 1970s in Hollywood and its application here is likely a reflection of its use as fashionable at the time.

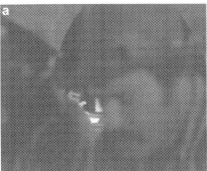 

Figs. 7.2a, 7.2b

Figs. 7.2c, 7.2d   *Duel* (1971)

Duel features multiple examples of wide reverses that reveal camera positions during the chase sequences in particular. However, I have chosen to disqualify them as legitimate examples as they essentially function in a similar way to conventional, shot, reverse shot dialogue scenes. This applies in the sense that car-truck-car-truck reverses appear repeatedly because of the plot contrivance that positions the car and truck as characters in an adversarial relationship. Buckland (2006, pp. 78–79) charts the multiple angle variations used in shooting Mann driving the car and notes the '…almost 360 degree…' view achieved inside the vehicle. I would add that this 360-degree view also exists to depict space *outside* the vehicle using wide reverses. This not only serves to orientate the audience with regard to where the car and truck exist in relation to each other but also to add more visual variation in the coverage and further enliven a potentially, visually bland depiction of a character who spends much of the film within the confines of a car. The multiple angles used to film the car interior and car to truck shots also reflect Spielberg's strategy of taking full advantage of the 360-degree coverage possible with location shooting. This is in contrast to the otherwise highly restrictive camera placement and accompanying spatial compromises that the then commonly used (particularly for television), studio based, rear-projection photography process would have imposed.

3. The Sugarland Express

Sugarland Express (1974) also involves numerous sustained sequences shot in and around cars. This long lens reverse (Figs.7.3a and 7.3b) simultaneously reveals camera positions and facilitates striking, deep space compositions that visually emphasise and dramatise the situation the characters find themselves in.

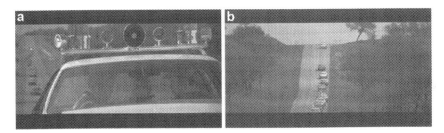

Figs. 7.3a, 7.3b *The Sugarland Express* (1974)

This is almost immediately contrasted visually with a wide-angle reverse that also includes (Fig. 7.4a) the rear-view mirror reflection of Captain Tanner and is itself a reverse contained within the same shot, the frame in this instance divided into two horizontal segments—the upper one looking back at the Captain, the lower looking forward at the three in the leading car. This use of a reflected image is an early example of a 'reflected reverse' examined in more detail later in this chapter. Together with the reflected reverse, the reverse proper pattern is completed with the wide-angle reverse (Fig. 7.4b) taken from the front of the lead car looking back at the following car that again reveals the camera space occupied in the previous shot. Narratively, the reflected reverse accentuates this moment as the first direct contact between Tanner and Lou Jean, marking the first point at which Tanner's tacit understanding of Lou Jean's situation manifests itself. His acknowledgment of her gesture suggests his character as sympathetic—a crucial element that assists in generating audience engagement with this character.[2]

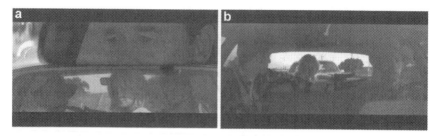

Figs. 7.4a, 7.4b   *The Sugarland Express* (1974)

4 & 5. Jaws

In *Jaws* (1975), Spielberg employs another single reverse variation by having the camera track in through the shark's jaws (Fig. 7.5a–b) depicting the departing boat 'Orca' with main cast as they head out to sea to hunt the shark. This is then reversed with a deep space composition from the boat looking back at the dock (Fig. 7.5c). Together with the obvious nature of the threat as indicated by the framed jaws, Spielberg adds the slow 'ominous' track-in to emphasise the waiting danger as well as underline the plot's switch into the final act and the inevitable showdown that awaits. The extreme change in camera placement also underlines the omnipresent nature of Spielberg's coverage.

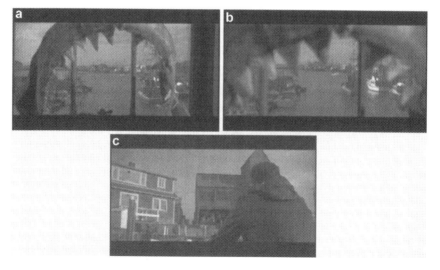

Figs. 7.5a, 7.5b, 7.5c   *Jaws* (1975)

The wide reverses in Fig. 7.6a–c additionally deliver a visual variation from the deck level shots as seen in the third act up to this point. The high camera position and reversal emphasises the three characters and their isolation at sea. These visually dramatic reversals and the not insignificant time that would have been consumed in capturing Fig. 7.6b—with a camera and operator perched high in the mast above Quint—provides further evidence of Spielberg's prioritising of the wide-reverse strategy. This recalls the ferry reverse (Fig. 6.9c–d), the previous example with the Orca heading out to sea and the time-consuming requirement that this action be repeated with and without camera and crew on board. The visual variation continues later with an extended sequence taking place underwater, which ensures that Spielberg has created and accounted for scenographic space at water level, above the water and underwater.

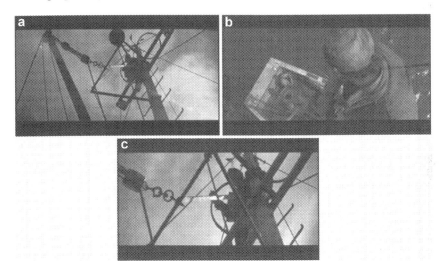

Figs. 7.6a, 7.6b, 7.6c *Jaws* (1975)

6. Close Encounters of the Third Kind

The India scene from *Close Encounters of the Third Kind* includes this visually dramatic wide reverse (Fig. 7.7a–b) with the hands abruptly thrusting and fingers pointing upwards—the holy man from Fig. 7.7a clearly visible in the distance in the reverse, his arms still raised. Another dynamic example of camera as omnipresent, the foregrounded holy man and distant crowd is visually contrasted in the reverse with the now foregrounded crowd. The staging and composition recall Hitchcock's '…smallest to biggest, furthest to nearest…' dynamic size contrast discussed in Chap. 5, which is designed to generate impact. The reverse also invokes the concept of the 'signifying sum' with the two shots only suggesting meaning when considered together. Spielberg immerses the audience in the action, keeping us over the holy man's shoulder as he addresses the crowd and then immediately with the crowd as they respond. The sudden raising of the pointing hands and the accompanying loud verbal exclamation from the crowd punctuates the moment both visually and aurally, and succinctly explains the point of the scene. Spielberg has commented that this scene is significant for the '…central plot twist…' (Combs 1978, pp. 111–113), so the wide reverse also functions to visually emphasise and dramatise the narrative point of the scene—that a close encounter has occurred here. Spielberg adds another stylistic element in the transition to the new space for the next scene by matching the figure movement of Fig. 7.7b—the vertical motion of the hands—with people standing and applauding in the initial shots of the new scene (Fig. 7.7c) carrying forward the energy and momentum of the climax in Fig. 7.7b into this scene. This also smooths over the transition to a new location with the cut 'disguised' by the matching movement in the shots before and after the cut.

Figs. 7.7a, 7.7b, 7.7c *Close Encounters of the Third Kind* (1977)

7. Raiders of the Lost Ark

In Fig. 7.8a–c from *Raiders of the Lost Ark*, a single wide reverse is used to establish the presence of the German submarine and the protagonist's awareness of it by visually linking them together in Fig. 7.8b (and also by the Captain's expository dialogue). The variation in the presentation of this reverse begins with Fig. 7.8a, which is itself a reverse pan that follows Indi entering the bridge and ends with him looking at the submarine. Figure 7.8b is an axial cut that uses a wider angle lens than the previous shot and the framing as shown here lasts for barely a second as the camera pans with Indi as he exits the bridge in an action that reverses that of the previous shot. The change in focal length from Fig. 7.8a to Fig. 7.8b functions to allow Fig. 7.8b to clearly orientate the submarine with a balanced composition that is then faithfully reversed in the next shot (Fig. 7.8c). On this occasion, it is the brevity of the composition in Fig. 7.8b together with the energy in the staging that has Indi rushing into the shot and then almost immediately rushing out again that 'cloaks' the operation of the wide reverse. In contrast, Figure 7.8c runs for almost five seconds, is remarkably static after the movement of the previous shots and also functions to again confirm the 'real' location nature of the scenography. After a brief interlude of comedic romance, the reverse and extended duration of Fig. 7.8c also punctuates the narrative by indicating that the main plot is now being re-engaged.

Figs. 7.8a, 7.8b, 7.8c *Raiders of the Lost Ark* (1981)

8. 1941

Invoking a sense of 'self-allusion', the shots in Fig. 7.9a–f from *1941* (1979) play out the punch line to Spielberg's parody of the opening sequence from his own *Jaws* (1975) that depicts the first shark attack. In the *1941* version, the swimmer becomes stranded atop the periscope of a surfacing Japanese submarine and is discovered by a lone submarine sailor. Shots Figs. 7.9a–b and 7.9d are framed below the sailor from inside the submarine looking up at the stranded swimmer. These are intercut as reverses with Fig. 7.9c and 7.9e but the wide reverse finally appears at Fig. 7.9f following a brief interior submarine shot. All of the previous examples examined function in part to emphasise the sense of a 'real' space as opposed to the artificiality of studio sets. The subject matter and tone of *1941* means that creating a sense of a real space is in this instance coloured by genre convention that permits a flexibility in what needs to be expressed narratively and how it is achieved. In effect, 'realness' is to be avoided at all costs. The film makes extensive use of 'artificial' spaces including studio interiors, studio-based (back lot) streets, water tank shooting and elaborate miniature sequences to a degree not previously seen in a Spielberg film. As such, the wide reverse is modified and is presented as a tight composition that suggests both subjectivity and a relatively high degree of self-consciousness. The sailor's point of view is more approximate than actual in Fig. 7.9a–b and 7.9d. Branigan (1975) describes this type of shot somewhat confusingly as a 'reverse angle' in terms of its relation to the conventional point-of-view shot in which the camera view directly simulates that of the observer. He points out that one advantage of this view '…is that it is a more stable articulation since we view the direct spatial relation of subject and object' (p. 59). This desire to constantly orientate the spectator is consistent with Spielberg's overall methodology that seeks to also link character perspective with the spectator's scenographic comprehension. This is an additional, significant aspect of the wide reverse and is examined in Chap. 8.

The self-consciousness manifests itself in the design of Fig. 7.9a and the way the swimmer is slowly revealed by the sailor lifting his head to gaze at her perched above him—the humour (or intended humour) generated through the specific placement of the camera and the resulting perspective that permits the reveal. In this instance, authorial invisibility is sacrificed in the interest of narrative requirements with the reveal in Fig. 7.9a–b compromising the sense of a greater objectivity as seen in the other wide reverses.

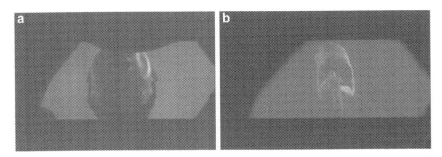

Figs. 7.9a, 7.9b

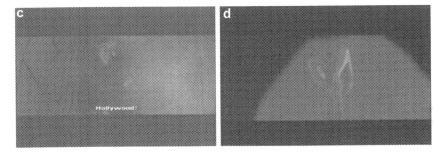

Figs. 7.9c, 7.9d

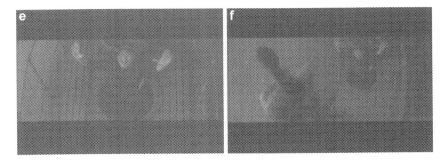

Figs. 7.9e, 7.9f *1941* (1979)

9. Schindler's List

I detected only three instances of wide reverses in *Schindler's List* (1993) and this may be in part due to Spielberg's preference for a more so-called documentary or *verite*-inspired style. The use of black and white stock and much handheld camera work reinforces the intention to replicate or recall the kind of seemingly unmediated footage captured by newsreel cameras during the Second World War. Yet Spielberg often juxtaposes the 'raw' street footage with interior scenes and sequences that display his preference for deep space compositions and elaborate staging that contradicts any sense of immediacy or the sense of a 'real'. This is further underlined by the repeated use of high contrast lighting—usually with a backlit, key light—that silhouettes and sculptures the characters, often producing striking, even beautiful images (Fig. 7.10f) rather than the 'gritty realism' of the exterior visuals.

Figure 7.10a–e is most notable for the way it uses reverses to shift character identification away from the protagonist (Schindler) to a minor character (Regina Perlman). One shot (Fig. 7.10a, 7.10c and 7.10e) serves as a single master with the reverses (Fig. 7.10b and 7.10d) cut into it. The choice and order of the reverses also seem unusual. The first reverse (Fig. 7.10b) is a wide angle that approximately reproduces the point of view of someone standing at the top of the stairs looking down. Yet Schindler only appears at the top of the stairs in Fig. 7.10c and the following reverse (Fig. 7.10d) recreates a similar point-of-view perspective but uses a longer lens for a tighter framing that privileges Regina's expression. As such, all five shots prioritise Regina and her place in the mise en scene. The master emphasises her position in the frame with a deep space composition (particularly so when Schindler appears at the top of the stairs, in the far background) and orientates the stairwell and Schindler essentially from her perspective. Figure 7.10d is the tightest shot in the set and so again emphasises Regina while even the wide reverse at Fig. 7.10b—in the absence of a point/glance shot of Schindler—suggests isolation and vulnerability. Having Schindler always far away in the background literally underscores his remoteness. As with the other instances, the reverses complete a 360-degree view of the space and both reveal and anticipate camera placement.

The Wide Reverse and Extended Variation   203

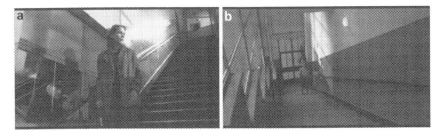

Figs. 7.10a, 7.10b

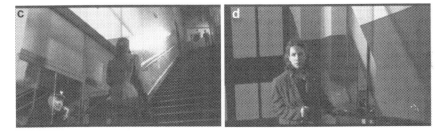

Figs. 7.10c, 7.10d

Figs. 7.10e, 7.10f   *Schindler's List* (1993)

10. A–E. Jurassic Park

Jurassic Park (1993) includes a number of elaborate visual sequences that featured the then cutting-edge application of digital animation in the creation of seemingly life-like dinosaurs. The set-piece sequence—both in terms of spectacle and narrative development—involves the reveal of the *Tyrannosaurus rex* (*T. rex*) and its function in terrorising the cast and separating the children and Grant from the others. This also establishes an additional, separate line of action as the children and Grant make their way to safety. The sequence begins approximately one hour into the film and runs for nine minutes, beginning with the *T. rex* breaching the fence, terrorising the children in the SUV and consuming Gennaro, and concludes with the *T. rex* pushing the SUV over the embankment. Within these nine minutes, Spielberg activates six separate instances of reverses with each incorporating some kind of stylistic variation such that each presents its shot, reverse shot pattern in a unique way. One scene depicts the *T. rex* attacking the two children through the roof of their SUV. Spielberg shoots this almost entirely as optical point-of-view (OP) (including that from the *T. rex*) and I have omitted it from consideration here because the repeated reverses categorise it as a complex instance (I consider its use of OP in Chap. 8). The remaining five examples that follow all incorporate OP or Branigan's 'reverse field'. While the sequence should be considered as complex in terms of its cutting, coverage and integration of computer generated images, I argue that the depiction of space remains relatively straightforward and explain why this is the case in each instance.

(A)

The first shot combination represents another variation of the 'traditional' shot, reverse shot arrangement. In this instance, Spielberg modifies OP editing in a scene that announces the *T. rex* as an approaching but off-screen presence. The reverse exchange is motivated by Tim's gaze (Fig. 7.11a), or 'point/glance' (Branigan 1984, p. 103), and this is answered by Fig. 7.11b–c in a conventional, point-of-view construction. Tim's initial look appears to be almost right at the camera—it is a similar space to that occupied by the camera and so also instigates the process of revealing camera space that occurs in the reverse or 'point/object' shot (Fig. 7.11b–c). This shot commences the shot, reverse shot pattern proper and is characterised by a slow ('ominous') track-in to the plastic cups—until Fig. 7.11c. This is reversed by Fig. 7.11d–e, which also repeats the slow push-in motion toward Tim while keeping the plastic cups in the lower, foreground area of the frame. Rather than arrange the point-of-view sequence conventionally and repeat the point/glance shot (Fig. 7.11a) as a reaction, Spielberg widens the frame in a variation of Branigan's 'closed POV' and instead includes both Tim and object (plastic cups), which Branigan (1975) argues results in: 'an over determination' that encourages '…a high degree of narrative stability… [and] serves to re-establish time and space and what we've seen' (p. 60).

What at first appears a routine application of OP shot construction actually generates much more through Spielberg's refinement of point-of-view, shot, reverse shot editing, a moving camera and diegetic sound. Narratively, and in terms of the conception of the scene, the low frequency sound and vibrating water aurally and visually implies an object of great size approaching, further enhanced by keeping the object off screen, thus highlighting the space outside the vehicle. A sense of touch or feel can be added by those cinemas or home theatre systems capable of reproducing the low frequency vibration. By presenting this as a shot, reverse shot arrangement, Spielberg distils these sensory elements (vibration as visual, sound and feel) and minimises authorial presence with a set of stylistic choices that literally distract and overwhelm the spectator, creating a more immersive, more complete narration that is defined by spectator anticipation. The point-of-view, reverse combination is further enhanced by the slow, matching track-in movements that engage spectator with character and connote uneasiness, as *Jurassic* cinematographer Dean Cundey notes: 'He brings the audience right into a character's face, so they can see what's in his or her eyes. It's a way of developing empathy' (Fisher 1993). Considered in the context of the narrative they service, the staging of these two shots vividly initiates and develops the build-up that leads to the introduction of the *T. rex*.

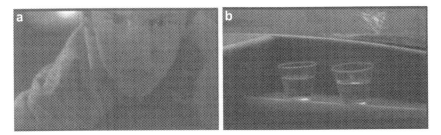

Figs. 7.11a, 711b

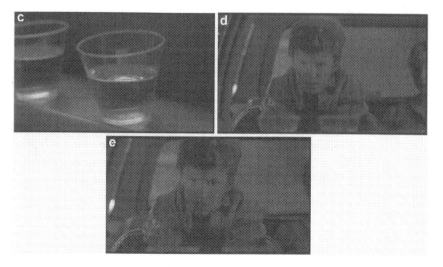

Figs. 7.11c, 7.11d, 7.11e *Jurassic Park* (1993)

(B)

The first full body view of the *T. rex* occurs with a wide or re-establishing shot at Fig. 7.12a that functions to orientate the *T. rex* relative to the vehicles. This shot also reveals the scale of the dinosaur in relation to the vehicles—as Spielberg points out 'I like to use wide frames to create suspense—shots where the characters are small and vulnerable in the frame, surrounded by the environment' (Pizzello 1997). Figure 7.12b is a close-up reaction shot of Malcolm and Grant and is followed by the reverse (Fig. 7.12c), taken from the rear of their vehicle looking forward at the passing *T. rex*. Like the previous example (Fig. 7.11a–e), Spielberg again integrates the shot, reverse shot arrangement within a point-of-view structure. The point/glance shot (Fig. 7.12b) is followed by the point/object shot as a reverse shot with both subject and object contained in the frame (Fig. 7.12c).

Warren Buckland (1999) has argued that the digital technology used to create the dinosaurs in Jurassic Park and its sequels '…conceals the symbolic mechanisms from the spectator more seamlessly than optical technology…' This leads to a more 'real' perception of the dinosaurs because of the way it '…layers, combines and merges the digital and the analogue into a single coherent image, resulting in a unified diegetic space'. In arguing for the superiority of the digital domain where the filmmaker has 'full control over each pixel'—in contrast to traditional optical effects, which lack 'sophistication'—Buckland seems to suggest that all 'pre-digital' effects films lacked convincing special effects. Paul Sellors (2000) challenges Buckland by arguing that the optical effects in films such as *The Last Laugh* (1924), *King Kong* (1933), *2001: A Space Odyssey* (1968), *Star Wars* (1976) and many others were every bit as convincing in terms of their realisation of a 'unified diegetic space' for audiences in the time of their making. Buckland further undermines his own logic by pointing out that the digital effects in the sequel to *Jurassic Park*, *The Lost World: Jurassic Park* (1997) are more complex because of advances in technology, thus implying that for the earlier *Jurassic Park*, the filmmakers clearly did *not* have: 'full control over each pixel'. He also seems to ignore that a substantial amount of the dinosaur elements in *Jurassic Park* were literally part of the diegetic/profilmic space because they were realised as live-action 'animatronic' machines that physically existed as parts of dinosaurs, including use of a mechanical *T. rex* head for the tighter shots in the sequence.

While the development of digital technology and its integration into the profilmic does play a role in suggesting a more convincing diegesis, the contribution of the wide reverse is again overlooked. Figure 7.12c is also the reverse of the wide Fig. 7.12a while the repetition of the presence of the *T. rex* in Fig. 7.12c and the evident temporal continuity between the shots assists in encouraging the perception that the *T. rex* is part of the profilmic, and therefore as 'real' as the human characters. The reverse (Fig. 7.12c) also recalls Branigan's 'many possible angles' as examined in Chap. 6. This is also then further reinforced by the point/object nature of Fig. 7.12c that allows the audience to see what both Malcolm and Grant see—the passing *T. rex*—more or less perceptually as they see it. Because we seemingly see what they are seeing this then underlines the logic that the *T. rex* exists as legitimately as the other profilmic elements in the frame.

Shot on Stage 16 at the Warner Bros Studios in Los Angeles (Duncan and Shay 1993), the illusion of the action as taking place in a 'real' space (as opposed to the artificiality of a studio) is reinforced by an earlier day scene in the film at the 'actual' location in Hawaii, which establishes that location as a real space. Simulating an outdoor location space on a soundstage is a common, highly skilled practice with a long tradition in Hollywood cinema. Spielberg has utilised this strategy in many of his films, despite his initial preference in the early 1970s for filming in exterior locations.[3] In this instance, the wide establishing shot of the *T. rex* (Fig. 7.12a) also recalls the location space established in the earlier day scene while the reverse (Fig. 7.12c) fuses together not only the dinosaur but also the space and together with the point-of-view arrangement, powerfully suggests that the characters and *T. rex* inhabit the same 'real' scenographic space.

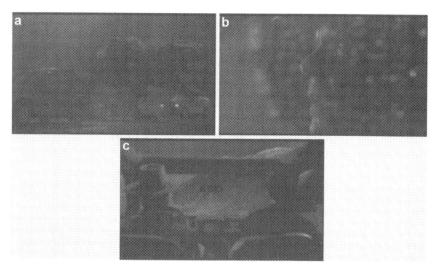

Figs. 7.12a, 7.12b, 7.12c *Jurassic Park* (1993)

(C)

The fourth[4] instance of reverses employs two, shot, reverse shot arrangements with Fig. 7.13a anchoring each of the two reverses and in fact appears to be the same shot as Fig. 7.13c with the two reverses cut into it. Figure 7.13b is the first reverse and includes Grant in the foreground to assist with orientating spatial relations between him and the *T. rex* while the long lens compresses the distance between them heightening the sense of danger and Grant's vulnerability. The long lens 'effect' also functions to integrate the digital dinosaur into the proflimic by replicating the visual compression inherent in long lens compositions. The second reverse (Fig. 7.13d) uses a shorter lens and a wider composition to clearly show the movement of the *T. rex* as it follows the flare. It is curious given the great attention and time that would have been taken in shooting the two different reverses of the *T. rex* (even before including the extensive animation requirements) that Spielberg does not use a tighter shot of Grant to better capture his reaction in Fig. 7.13c.

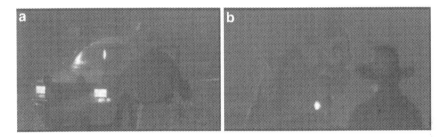

Figs. 7.13a, 7.13b

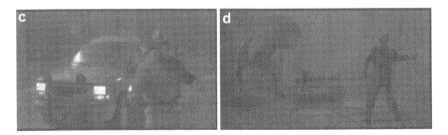

Figs. 7.13c, 7.13d   *Jurassic Park* (1993)

(D)

The fifth use of reverses also employs a two shot, reverse shot strategy to show Gennaro being taken by the *T. rex*. In this instance it is the reverse shots (Figs. 7.14b and 7.14e) that appear to be from the same shot. The main variation here is that the shot preceding the second reverse (Fig. 7.14d) begins wide and tracks into a medium close-up of Gennaro as he reacts. This type of push-in shot—another variation of Spielberg's 'ominous' track-in—simulates the *T. rex* point of view, prolongs the moment and generates tension. A key consideration in the design of the coverage for this and the previous instances is the limited appearance of the *T. rex* in the reverses. Figures 7.13b, 7.13d, 7.14b and 7.14e capture the *T. rex* from outside the circle of action yet the reverses for both are taken from inside the circle on Grant (Fig. 7.13c) and Gennaro (Figs. 7.14a and 7.14c–d) and exclude the *T. rex*. This choice likely reflects how budgetary concerns and Spielberg's general production thrift (Chap. 3) impact directly on choices made in coverage and the look of the film. Spielberg has commented: 'When I made *The Lost World* I limited the amount of special-effects shots because they were incredibly expensive. If a dinosaur walks around, it costs $80,000 for eight seconds. If four dinosaurs are in the background, its $150,000' (Total Film 2004). Excluding the digital *T. rex* from both reverses reduces cost but also directly influences how the reverses are constructed. This is evident in the following final wide reverse instance where Spielberg chooses to utilise the live-action *T. rex*.

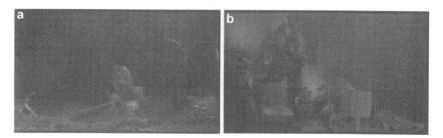

Figs. 7.14a, 7.14b

The Wide Reverse and Extended Variation 211

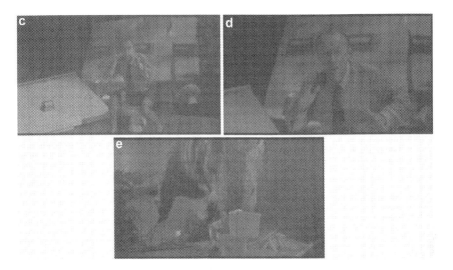

Figs. 7.14c, 7.14d, 7.14e *Jurassic Park* (1993)

(E)

This final reverse in the *T. rex* sequence (Figs. 7.15a and 7.15b) is a conventional exchange that recalls the kind of typical shot, reverse shot coverage used for dialogue scenes. The reverse technically breaks classical convention by 'crossing the line' with the camera placed on either side of the axis-of-action line between the *T. rex*, Grant and Lex. Yet the issue of improper eye-lines is negated by making both shots as over-shoulder compositions thus showing all characters in the frame, which again confirms spatial orientation. Figure 7.15a is also notable for providing the only angle that reveals the 'fourth' wall, the only side of the scenogaphic space not seen during the entire nine minute sequence. Except for the reverse at Fig. 7.12c where the *T. rex* is introduced, Figs. 7.15a and 7.15b are the only other shots where the *T. rex* is seen in both the shot and the reverse. As noted, in all other reverse arrangements the *T. rex* appears in only one of the two shots. Using the live-action 'animatronic' *T. rex* head for this scene permits Spielberg to 'revert' to shooting both angles from outside the circle of action.

This suggests that there are a number of elements influencing, and I argue—*compromising*—the way Spielberg deploys reverses and wide reverses in *Jurassic Park* and in the nine-minute *T. rex* sequence in particular. More specifically, there are three implications: a reduction in the use of wide reverses and/or matching over-shoulder reverses because of the increased number (and greater associated cost) of effects shots; a negation of the kind of 360-degree revealing of space due to the offshoot restrictions of soundstage shooting and a distinct pattern of creating a type of master or main shot and then cutting animation-enhanced reverses into that shot as seen with the masters at Figs. 7.13a, 7.13c, 7.14a and 7.14c–d. In the case of *Jurassic Park*, it can be seen that computer animation and studio-based shooting *restrict* Spielberg's preference for designing coverage that maximises the revealing of scenographic space.

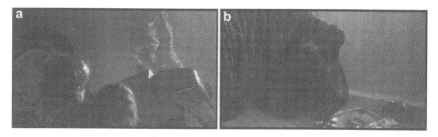

Figs. 7.15a, 7.15b *Jurassic Park* (1993)

Single-Shot Reverses: Ten Examples

> Tracking action without cutting is the least jarring method of placing the audience into a real-time experience where they are the ones making the subtle choices of where and when to look.—Spielberg. (Breznican 2011)

In contrast to all of the previous examples studied, the single-shot reverses construct scenographic space *with* camera movement and *without* editing. Spielberg's concern about where the audience should be looking recalls his earlier comments relating to deep space compositions and in this instance he achieves deep space and 'dynamic' compositions with a moving camera. Jean Mitry (1997) echoes Spielberg's 'real-time experience' by claiming that the moving camera legitimises scenographic space.

> ...the moving camera has made it possible to 'actualize' the represented space, since the space in which we effectively move can only be a space actually present. Things are 'in the process of happening', since we follow them in their very mobility, according to their continuous development. We move until them and therefore act (or feel as though we are acting) at the same time as them. (p. 188)

Not only does the moving camera assist in defining space, it does so in linear time and this combination powerfully encourages the perception of a more 'real' unfolding. While Spielberg may claim that this type of shooting is 'least jarring', he actually utilises this shot sparingly and certainly less frequently in comparison to the simple and complex configuration reverses and single reverses. Nevertheless, these single-shot reverses still effectively create a space that varies between 180 and 360 degrees. They can be divided into four variations: a combination track and pan producing a 180-degree reverse vista, a reverse pan also creating a 180-degree vista, a 360-degree pan creating a 360-degree space and a 360-degree track that also creates a 360-degree space. There is also a fifth variation utilising reflections that appears less frequently across Spielberg's films and will be examined at the end of this section.

1. Duel

With its elaborate, overt camera movement, the single-shot reverse from *Duel* (1971) seemingly qualifies as an example of artistic motivation. Beginning behind Mann in his car, the 22-second shot pans and tracks alongside and past first the car and then the truck until it completes a 180-degree reverse with the front of the truck filling the frame (Fig. 7.16a–f). The shot does have plot significance; this is the first time that Mann encounters the truck so the unmotivated nature of the camera movement emphasises the shot's subjective study of the truck and the importance of the truck itself. The examination initially reveals the truck to be dirty, old and therefore seemingly benign. Yet throughout the shot, the camera remains at the same height and angle—approximately that of Mann—so that the tilt up at the end of the shot emphasises the truck's relative size, inferring the potential for menace. The design of the shot also accentuates the location as a 'real' space—this kind of shot would not have been possible on a soundstage in the 1970s using frontal or rear projection techniques. This is in contrast to the example discussed later from *War of the Worlds* (2005), which includes a similar shot convincingly created partially on a soundstage and made possible through advances in digital effects. Figure 7.16a–f is staged such that it simultaneously reinforces the space as real but then also reveals the space the camera will occupy at the end of the shot (the area in front of the truck) as well as the space behind the car it originally occupied at the beginning of the shot, again undermining authorial presence. As we have seen with the cut reverses, this shot reflects Spielberg's willingness to give the camera omnipresence, moving around the two vehicles at will while in this instance, still preserving the importance of off-screen space by not revealing the truck driver. While the lack of motivation in a camera movement generally results in a higher degree of self-consciousness, this is tempered in this instance by the significance of the subject and function of the shot—the introduction and examination of the narrative's antagonist.

Figs. 7.16a, 7.16b

The Wide Reverse and Extended Variation 215

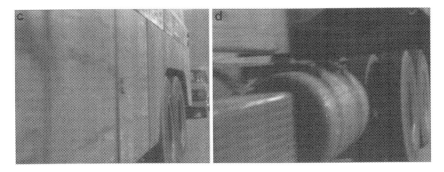

Figs. 7.16c, 7.16d

Figs. 7.16e, 7.16f   *Duel* (1971)

2. A.I. Artificial Intelligence

While the *Duel* example uses a follow track and pan to capture a 180-degree reverse, the variation in *A.I. Artificial Intelligence* (2001) employs a counter track, pan combination (Fig. 7.17a–d). As Monica turns her head to the left, the camera tracks to the right past her and simultaneously pans to keep her in frame, the shot ending with a 180-degree reverse view. The design of this shot also lays claim to consideration as artistically motivated particularly in view of the inherent contradiction suggested by the camera movement that appears motivated by the character's head turn, yet draws attention to itself by travelling counter/in opposition to character movement. The shot's uniqueness—this is the only time it appears in the film (unlike *Minority Report* (2002) where it is used repeatedly) —also signals the importance of the moment. Another intended effect is that it creates a sense of 'unbalance', that something is not right (reinforced by an accompanying 'swishing' sound effect) and at the same time operates as a visual alternative to point-of-view cutting. The tight framing implies emphasis and reinforces the significance of the character's changing gaze (as turning head) while the camera panning and tracking in tandem replace editing by combining the conventional, classical point/glance shot, and the cut to point/object view revealing what is being looked at, all in one flowing shot. The end frame gives us Branigan's reverse shot (Fig. 7.17d) where object and subject are combined in the same frame. It also gives us the reverse perspective of the first frame so again the last frame reveals the now empty space formerly occupied by the camera position that created the first frame. The temporal immediacy of the movement means that the audience sees the object at exactly the same time as the character, recalling Spielberg's 'real-time experience' advantage of the tracking camera. The shot avoids the temporal delay associated with conventional point-of-view construction where the audience usually experiences the character's view after the character. The shot creates a cognitive parallel between audience and character that has implications for character identification and audience empathy.

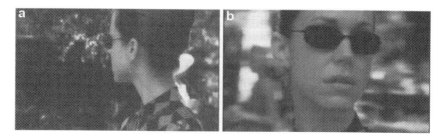

Figs. 7.17a, 7.17b

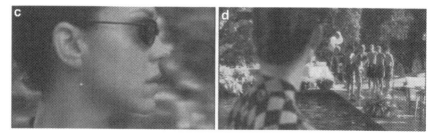

Figs. 7.17c, 7.17d   *A.I. Artificial Intelligence* (2001)

3. Minority Report

Examining all of Spielberg's films reveals that he has utilised the single-shot to reverse shot track, pan described above, sparingly—I detected only 12 instances across all of the films he has directed. Yet the shot appears six times in one film, *Minority Report* (2002). This example, the semi-circular track around the seated protagonist (Anderton) (Fig. 7.18a–d), is not especially innovative in terms of classical narrative. This kind of staging with a camera tracking around a seated figure or figures (often in discussion) appears frequently in mainstream cinema and television, the intention being that it add visual energy to what would otherwise be an overly static composition. Bordwell (1977) notes 'A moving vantage point supplies a dense stream of information about objects' slants, their edges, their corners, their surfaces, their relations with other objects'. Spielberg makes it unique by keeping the protagonist relatively small in the frame, thus prioritising space, and then moves the camera from an oblique frontal shot of Anderton (Fig. 7.18a) around him in a semi-circle until the shot ends behind his right shoulder (Fig. 7.18d). This provides a panoramic vista of the apartment across more than 180 degrees and ends with the home movie playing in the background. This simultaneously; introduces the next section of the scene, directs the spectator's attention to the home movie, and motivates the cut that continues the following sequence.

As with the *A.I.* example, the shot ends (Fig. 7.18d) in a point/object, over-shoulder point-of-view composition that again temporally matches the audience perception of the home video with Anderton's own experience in turn again encouraging character/audience identification. The beginning of the shot follows a close-up of Anderton selecting some kind of a video file and therefore functions initially as a classically conventional re-establishing shot of his position seated at the desk. As mentioned, the end of the shot sets up the next section of the sequence by including the beginning of the home movie, essentially disguising the point at which the tracking shot ends and the next shot begins. This smooth, visually efficient integration of the start and end of the shot into the rest of the sequence downplays its unmotivated nature and therefore relatively high degree of self-consciousness, seemingly cleverly subjugating it to narrative information that additionally has the effect of suppressing 'evidence' of authorial presence.

Figs. 7.18a, 7.18b

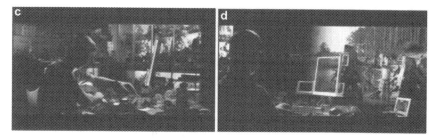

Figs. 7.18c, 7.18d   *Minority Report* (2002)

4. Catch Me if You Can

This example (Fig. 7.19a–d) begins with a wide shot framed behind and over the protagonist's (Frank) right shoulder and then tracks around to the left, the frame slowly tightening until the shot ends with Frank in close up.[5] The shot is loosely motivated by the passing of the newspaper to Frank (Fig. 7.19a, Frank is at the left edge of the frame) and the camera tracks around to see him reading and reacting to what he has been told. The shot is conventionally classical in the sense that plot demands are prioritised and it is the only instance of the ten examples in this section where the consideration of space is secondary. The primary function of the shot is communicating plot information. The close-up emphasises that the newspaper article and verbal information told to Frank has captured his attention and this contributes to the cause/effect chain by motivating Frank to initiate a new scheme.

Yet the design of the shot is intriguing in that it creates a kind of double reverse with the first framing at Fig. 7.19a finally reversed at

Fig. 7.19d but then there is another reverse within this with Fig. 7.19c an over-shoulder, revealing what Frank is reading with this itself also reversed by Fig. 7.19d. So the one rotating tracking shot establishes the location and characters, reveals the plot information present in the newspaper without an insert close-up and then ends on a close-up of Frank that visually imparts to the audience the significance of the information for the character. This remarkable visual efficiency additionally displays another variation in that it combines the tracking reversal with the camera pushing in on the subject, the push-in here similar to that noted in Fig. 7.11b–c and 7.11d–e as commonly used by Spielberg as a punctuation device.

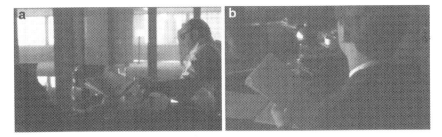

Figs. 7.19a, 7.19b

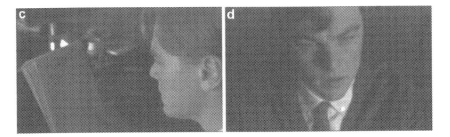

Figs. 7.19c, 7.19d   *Catch Me if You Can* (2002)

5. Munich

The fifth example is taken from *Munich* (2005) and the shot introduces the first target earmarked for assassination by Israeli agents (Fig. 7.20a–d). The noticeable camera shake in this wide, 180-degree reverse track suggests the shot was captured with a handheld camera, which introduces yet another variation to this shot type. The shake in itself implies point of view—invoking the classical convention that the camera occupies the perspective of someone walking towards the speaker; yet this hypothesis is dispelled once the camera reaches him and turns around 180 degrees, changing into a reverse track. The shaking movement is also more noticeable because it occurs suddenly—with shots before and after this composed as smooth and steady thus making the movement in the shot stand out. This is further accentuated by the subject who speaks in Italian thus further emphasising the visuals and drawing more attention to the exaggerated movement in the frame. If we examine what the shot reveals, it initially functions as a traditional establishing shot (Fig. 7.20a) and then tracks forward until the speaker is captured in a close-up, accentuated by the rotating examination of him as he speaks. The shot ends with a reverse that reveals the initial camera position and completes the revealing of the scenographic space around the speaker. One can also consider the camera shake as a reference to documentary convention and the notion of direct cinema that implies an unmediated composition, a more 'real' showing. With this context in mind, Spielberg manipulates convention and intentionally misleads the audience by encouraging consideration of the shot as point of view. When this is proven not to be the case, the doubt and unpredictability encourage a sense of unease, reflecting the Israeli agents and their own sense of apprehension and anxiety. While on the one hand the shot initially clouds audience identification, perspective and comprehension, it at the same time unambiguously orientates audience understanding of scenographic space.

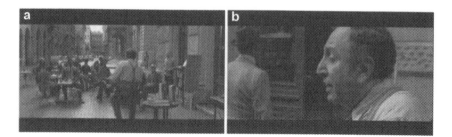

Figs. 7.20a, 7.20b

Figs. 7.20c, 7.20d *Munich* (2005)

6. Saving Private Ryan

The next reverse variation appears in *Saving Private Ryan* (1998) (Fig. 7.21a–d) and occurs early in the third act as the soldiers discuss plans aimed at defending a small bridge from the approaching Germans. The 36-second shot begins with a wide (Fig. 7.21a) of the main location and then tracks back as the soldiers approach holding them in a loose mid shot (Fig. 7.21b) until the group passes on the left side of camera. The track then alters to a pan left as the camera lets the group pass until only one soldier is left in medium close-up (Fig. 7.21d), the bridge and canal visible behind him. The first part of the shot establishes (or re-establishes) the main space in which most of the film's remaining action will take place while the final angle of the shot is an 180-degree reverse of the first angle and reveals the remaining plot significant space—the bridge that the soldiers must defend. Unlike the previous examples in this section, the camera movement here is motivated by the staging of the cast as they move towards camera and then pass by the bridge with the camera seemingly responding to their action. The camera's smooth motion implies a certain sense of order and calm that contrasts to the mostly handheld camera shots that dominate once the battle commences. Both the shot's expository function (as they walk, the captain explains how to make 'sticky bombs') and the motivated nature of the camera movement again assist to disguise the shot's additional function of privileging scenographic space. Spielberg begins the sequence in this location with an earlier, similarly staged shot that takes in the arrival of the Captain and the soldiers and that also ends with a view of the bridge, so the second revealing of the space with Fig. 7.21a–d functions to remind and further familiarise this space for the audience.

Figs. 7.21a, 7.21b

Figs. 7.21c, 7.21d   *Saving Private Ryan* (1998)

7. Empire of the Sun

The final 180-degree reverse example (Fig. 7.22a–g) from *Empire of the Sun* (1987) involves only panning but is notable for its co-ordinated combination of on-screen and off-screen space, novel staging and motivated camera movement. The shot begins with Dr Rawlins shouting at Jim who is off-screen (Fig. 7.22a), followed by the camera panning through 180 degrees to reveal Jim on the top floor of the building. The initial composition suggests conventional point-of-view construction with Dr Rawlins' left-to-right eye-line as a point/glance shot. Yet this is immediately undermined by the movement of the pan as motivated by the passing fighter plane with the camera following the aircraft until it reaches the building revealing Jim on the roof. Once the camera settles on the building (Fig. 7.22f) Dr Rawlins appears from camera right and continues shouting and waving at Jim. The coordinated complexity of the staging—cueing both actor and aircraft[6] such that the camera pan with it

The Wide Reverse and Extended Variation

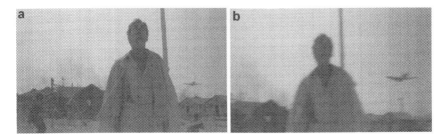

Figs. 7.22a, 7.22b

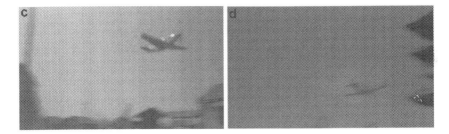

Figs. 7.22 c, 7.22d

Figs. 7.22e, 7.22f, 7.22g   *Empire of the Sun* (1987)

at the right time creates a visual energy that simultaneously—disguises the panoramic reveal of space—the 180-degree pan—that links both characters. Buckland (2006) has discussed Spielberg's use of off-screen space largely in terms of character entrances and exits as signalling off screen spaces (which he borrows from Burch (1973)), and this shot is an instance of this (though Buckland does not mention *Empire*). Intriguingly, Spielberg stages Dr Rawlins' movement so that rather than have him reappear from frame left in Fig. 7.22f—from the space that was revealed in the pan—he instead appears from the opposite side, from the space that has not been seen. His entrance from this side contributes to a sense of a complete scenographic space by implying the existence of this space off-screen to the right of frame. In this instance, Spielberg uses both on- and off-screen space to 'suggest' a complete 360-degree space with the aircraft passing on one side of the camera/audience and Dr Rawlins passing around the other side (Fig. 7.23, below). In this sense the action literally surrounds the audience, and this staging and shooting strategy recalls Eisenstein's conception of action that 'flows around' the spectator.

> In the theatre the *mise-en-scene* unfolds, in playing, across the space of the stage, that is, on one fixed place in front of the spectator, but in the cinema the action as though flows *around* the camera, that is, around the spectator. To get this effect, the camera can not only dissect out a view from inside the circular *mise-en-scene*, but can also as though flank it from the outside... (Nizhny 1979, p. 63)

Eisenstein discusses the film camera's ability to move both within and outside the space of the mise en scene. In other words, he notes how the camera can be positioned either inside or outside the circle of action. Remarkably, Spielberg achieves *both* with the single pan at Fig. 7.22a–e. The shot initially resembles a typical shot, reverse shot arrangement with Dr Rawlins' eye-line directed at a point behind the camera, thus positioning the camera inside the circle of action. Yet the pan and staging of Dr Rawlins so that he then reappears in frame—but now seen from behind (Fig. 7.22f–g) —means that the camera is now positioned outside the circle of action and captures both the foregrounded Dr Rawlins and distant Jim.

The Wide Reverse and Extended Variation

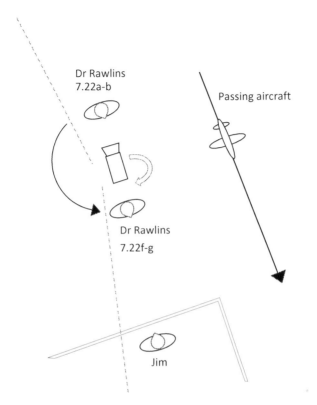

Fig. 7.23 Dr. Rawlins warns Jim – overhead view, *Empire of the Sun* (1987)

Yet the shot's creation of space is also problematic in that the staging acknowledges the camera's presence. In Fig. 7.22a Dr Rawlins' position is slightly favouring the right side of the frame so that logically the shortest route to Fig. 7.22f would be by entering from the left side. But he enters from frame right and as he does so he moves across the frame rather than diagonally into it, which suggests that he has moved *around* an object—the camera. On the one hand Spielberg uses the wide 180-degree reverse to construct space on one side of the 360-degree sphere and then expands the sense of this space by drawing attention to what is not seen—the other 180-degree space. The intentionality of the strategy falters simply through how Dr Rawlins enters the frame in Fig. 7.22f and in how the elaborate nature of the shot ends by drawing attention to the very artifice it seeks to supress.

226   J. Mairata

8. The Sugarland Express

The following three examples consider the construction of a 360-degree space by either single-shot panning or tracking. The well-known 360-degree in-car pan in *The Sugarland Express* (1974) (Fig. 7.24a–f) creates a seemingly uninterrupted panorama of space inside the police car. The shot's prioritising of space is again rendered largely transparent by the character dialogue

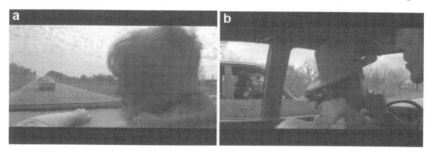

Figs. 7.24a, 7.24b

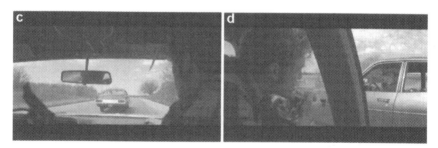

Figs. 7.24c, 7.24d

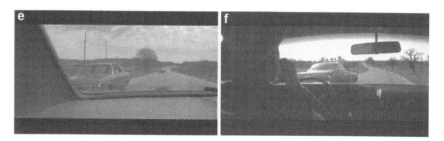

Figs. 7.24e, 7.24f   *The Sugarland Express* (1974)

and staging and the motivated pan that follows the chief's car in a clockwise direction as it circles around the protagonists (Fig. 7.25, below). Spielberg adds a reverse at the end of the long 360-degree pan with shot Fig. 7.24f and a perfect graphic match,[7] which now shows the protagonists from the perspective of the chief's car, effectively reversing the final angle at Fig. 7.24e.

Figure 7.24f as wide reverse also reveals the space occupied by the camera taking the 360-degree pan in a strategy similar to the end-shot reversal used in the ferry scene in *Jaws* (Chap. 6). The pan is also notable for its exploitation of a 'real' space with Spielberg designing a shot only then possible with location shooting—like the examples from *Duel*—in contrast to the multiple spatial restrictions that studio-based filming would have imposed. The proximity of the camera to the cast places the audience seemingly right inside the scenographic space—inside the circle of action—in a variation of the previous example from *Empire of the Sun*. This again recalls Eisenstein's 'flowing around' metaphor, which is literally illustrated by the interaction between the characters and Captain Tanner as his car circles around the fugitives and the camera.

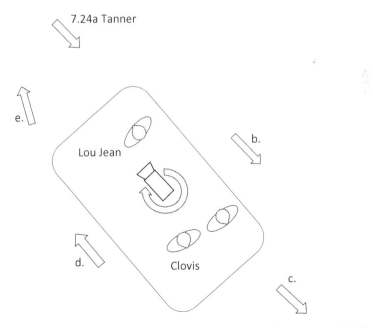

Fig. 7.25 Tanner speaks with Clovis—overhead view, *The Sugarland Express* (1974)

9. War of the Worlds

Contrasting to the 360-degree pan inside the car, the 360-degree track twice around the fleeing vehicle (Fig. 7.26a–i) in *War of the Worlds* (2005) utilises digital effects to still essentially construct a similar vista of scenographic space. In this instance the camera is positioned outside the circle of action in contrast to the *Sugarland* example where the camera was located inside the circle. The digital effects endow the camera with a greater sense of omnipresence as it revolves around the car, pulls back to let other cars pass by (Fig. 7.26f) and even seemingly enters the car (Fig. 7.26d). Such is the seamless blend between location and studio-bound space that it becomes impossible to determine where one or the other begins or ends. Also unlike the *Sugarland* example, the camera movement here seems largely physically unmotivated—the camera is not reacting specifically to elements of staging such as following a character or object. The movement is motivated more by character circumstance and services plot information relating to communicating the overall sense of panic and confusion experienced by the protagonists. The constant movement also assists in breaking up the long passages of expository dialogue and fractures the duration of what is essentially—at two and a half minutes—a long take, rare for a recent Hollywood action film, as Bordwell elaborates in relation to intensified continuity and decreasing ASLs. For all its technical virtuosity, the shot's relative distance from the characters—outside the circle of action—means that it lacks the immersive quality inherent in the comparatively simplistic in-car pan from *Sugarland* made some 30 years earlier.

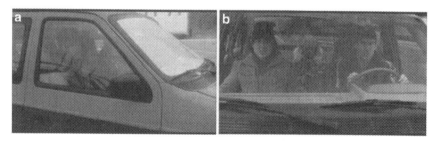

Figs. 7.26a, 7.26b

The Wide Reverse and Extended Variation 229

Figs. 7.26c, 7.26d

Figs. 7.26e, 7.26f

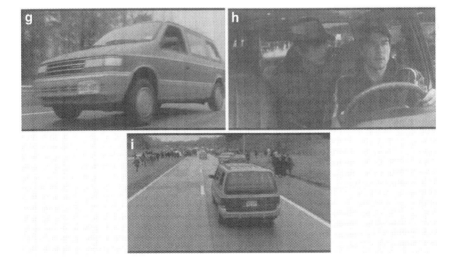

Figs. 7.26g, 7.26h, 7.26i *War of the Worlds* (2005)

10. The Terminal

The double 360-degree track in *The Terminal* (2004) (Fig. 7.27a–h) resembles the *War of the Worlds* example in that the camera also revolves around the subject but the *Terminal* instance is decidedly 'low tech' in its lack of digital effects elements. Yet this is an aggressive example of foregrounding space with the 360-degree wide-angle track around the characters (Viktor and Thurman) establishing and revealing the elaborate transit lounge set space in which Viktor, the protagonist, spends much of the film. Scenographic space is prioritised not only because of the 360-degree camera movement but also because the space is further emphasised by a continuing second 360-degree track around the characters. At the same time, the dialogue between Viktor and Thurman during the shot is largely redundant with the significant expository information having already been discussed at length in the previous scene in Dixon's office. This further underscores the staging of the shot as primarily about constructing space and showcasing the verisimilitude 'wholeness' and 'authenticity' of the location.

Figs. 7.27a, 7.27b

Figs. 7.27c, 7.27d

The Wide Reverse and Extended Variation   231

Figs. 7.27e, 7.27f

Figs. 7.27g, 7.27h   *The Terminal* (2004)

Optical Reflections as Reflected Reverses

Beyond the four variations of the single-shot reverse is a fifth type or subset that often appears in one scene (usually in one shot) in almost all of Spielberg's films and relates to the use of reflected images and their function in 'revealing' off-screen space. Hollywood has a long tradition of incorporating reflections—particularly using mirrors[8]—to enlarge scenographic space and Spielberg has clearly embraced this as device. Steven Katz (1991, p. 81) notes one instance in a scene in Jim's bedroom in *Empire of the Sun* where the use of a mirror effectively combines three shots into one. This efficiency in coverage and the ability to capture two (or more) reverse spaces with only one shot has undoubtedly motivated the staging of this type of shot. The three following instances from recent Spielberg films demonstrate a more demanding role for the reflected reverse—particularly in the latter two instances where digital effects work in tandem with the shot design to further enhance the significance of space.

Figure 7.28a–c from *Munich* (2005) shows the character walking towards camera in a canted, seemingly stylised composition with the camera tilting up from part of the car's rear window to follow him in a reverse angle as he passes by in Fig. 7.28c. The reflected image reveals an area approximately behind the camera while the tilt up as the character passes by presents a reverse field to that of the reflection thus presenting us with a simulated, wide 180-degree reverse. The shot displays an inherent narrational efficiency in that it re-establishes the target identified earlier (Fig. 7.20a–d) and that he is being watched—in one smooth camera movement. The shot initially seems subjective in its view of the reflection in the car window, its highly mediated perspective suggesting itself as characteristic of a point/object shot, but this is revised when Steve (sitting in the car) becomes visible in the tilt up in Fig. 7.28c. This largely unmotivated application of style—it is not point of view and there is no narrative rationalisation for shooting the reflection—also results in a momentary increase in the narration's level of self-consciousness. This is a likely reason why—as with the planimetric instance of 5.34b—Spielberg devotes little screen time to this type of shot and why it has not reappeared in his cinema.

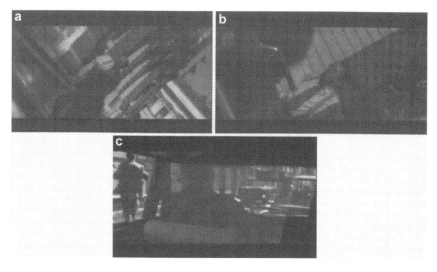

Figs. 7.28a, 7.28b, 7.28c *Munich* (2005)

Both stills Figs. 7.29a and 7.29b are taken from *War of the Worlds* (2005) and the 'reflected' image in both instances is of an invading alien vehicle. The reflection together with the characters' eye-lines reinforces the significance of the reverse, off-screen space such that it assumes greater importance than the on-screen space. Another variation on point-of-view construction, the composition, effectively presents the spectator with both the point/glance shot and the point/object shot together in one frame much like a vertical, split-screen effect. The reflections also assist in convincing the spectator that the computer generated images are 'real'—part of the profilmic—because of the way they appear (literally) more integrated into the scenographic space as reflection and then again in the reverse wide shot that shows the alien craft not as reflection but confirmed as 'actually' there. So the combination of reflected image followed or proceeded by a reverse view of that image both 'sells' the image as present and also helps to render transparent the cut across the two shots (point/glance and point/object), in turn creating the sense of a scenographic space ranging across 180 degrees.

Figs. 7.29a, 7.29b *War of the Worlds* (2005)

In *War Horse* (2011), Spielberg employs a reflected image taken from the eye of the war horse (Fig. 7.30a–b) to depict Emilie entering the barn, discovering the horse and then exiting—all in one shot. Here, the priority lies not with establishing space—though a reverse field is revealed—but with introducing Emilie as the next character to intersect with the horse. Spielberg avoids horse point-of-view shots throughout the film, instead conveying the horse's experience through the relevant characters' emotions in their dealings with it at any given time. Figure 7.30a is the nearest the film achieves to expressing the horse's perspective and the indistinct nature of Emilie's appearance also contributes a sense of expectation as the next act of the horse's journey commences.

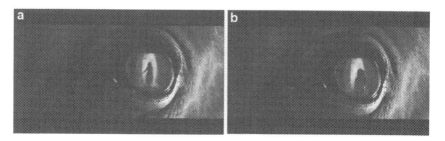

Figs. 7.30a, 7.30b   *War Horse* (2011)

All of the single reverses examined preserve the process of constructing a 180-degree scenographic space. They also all reveal the camera space occupied by each other's shot thus also preserving the sense of a suppressed narrator in a similar way to the examples examined in Chap. 6. The brevity of the two shots permits their insertion at almost any point in the narrative, further assisting the covert process of suppressing authorial presence. The single-shot reverses likewise build scenographic space across either 180 or 360 degrees yet it is when one considers their properties relating to suppressing evidence of the narrator's activity that they seem more problematic. Eight of the ten single-shot reverses do reveal the space occupied by the camera in an earlier part of the shot simply because the camera has moved to a reverse position during the shot [the reverse track from *Ryan* (Fig. 7.21a–d) and the 180-degree pan from *Empire* (Fig. 7.22a–g) are the exceptions]. This differs from the single and multiple reverses in Chap. 6 in that the edit from shot to shot assists in revealing the space taken by the camera. Without editing, the single-shot reverses generate the *sense* of a revealing of camera space through their movement. This is further complicated by the classical convention that style remain largely transparent and therefore that camera movement should be motivated by subject movement. Where camera movement lacks motivation, this can draw attention to style and the mechanics of narration, thus highlighting authorial presence rather than suppressing it. Part of the paradox here lies in also considering that the unmotivated shot often uses movement to emphasise plot related elements. The track, pan combination from *A.I.* (Fig. 7.17a–d) draws attention to the unfolding drama by the poolside while the double 360-degree track around Viktor in *The Terminal* (Fig. 7.27a–h) could be interpreted as style assisting in communicating his sense of confusion and of the protagonist as overwhelmed. Regardless of whether he uses a constructivist approach to cut together reverses, or alternately the uncut single-shot take, or the reflected reverse, Spielberg proves equally adept at ensuring that each fulfils an agenda that simultaneously promotes the construction of scenographic space and erases authorial presence. If we add consideration of Spielberg's appropriation of deep space compositions as examined in Chap. 5, then Bordwell's (1993) observation of how Eisenstein creates space could just as easily apply to Spielberg.

> On one hand he creates a diagonal view in order to draw the viewer deep into the scene's space. On the other, he creates an inverted perspective… which places the vanishing point out in front of the picture plane—that is, where the audience already is. Thus the action 'flows around' the spectators in two senses: they enter into it, and it comes out to meet them. (pp. 160–161)

The 'diagonal view' matches with Spielberg's large foreground, small recessed compositions that always maintain angled, deep space compositions while the wide reverses constantly intrude on the area seemingly occupied by the camera—and the audience—replacing it with scenographic space. Bordwell (2001) also notes Eisenstein's conception of '… breaking the barrier between spectator and spectacle…' and '… forging a unity between the consumer and the spectacle…' (p. 36). One clear implication of Bordwell's interpretation is of Eisenstein as claiming the spectator's experience as more immersive, more 'integrated' into the narrative. Many of the wide-reverse instances documented in this chapter demonstrate this strategy of positioning the camera and spectator in the scenographic space. Included are the panning camera in the earlier *Empire* (Fig. 7.22a–g) and *Sugarland* (Fig. 7.24a–f) examples but also the Chap. 5 (Figs. 5.8a–b and 5.9a–c) and 6 instances with Indi repeatedly running towards the camera (including Figs. 6.7c–d and 6.8a)—or even over it (Fig. 6.8e). All display aggressive illustrations of the action as driving toward the camera and/or flowing around it. When combined with the numerous angled or diagonal, deep space compositions the sense of a complete scenographic space becomes pervasive.

Notes

1. Excluding the two episodes he directed for the television series *Amazing Stories* (1985).
2. It also adds complexity and dimension to the character of Tanner.
3. *Duel* (1971), *Sugarland Express* (1974) and *Jaws* (1975) were all shot almost entirely on location (*Jaws* included some water tank shooting). *Close Encounters of the Third Kind* (1977) and most of Spielberg's subsequent films feature extensive studio use.
4. The third instance involves the *T. rex* menacing the children in the SUV. This is examined in Chap. 8.
5. A similar shot appears in the final scene of *Saving Private Ryan* but the composition is reversed, instead beginning with a close-up and ending with an over-shoulder wide.
6. The film is pre-CGI so this would have been staged as a 'live action' shot reportedly using scale model aircraft.
7. The implication of this type of cut for spectator cognition is examined in Chap. 8.
8. The historical use of mirrors in Hollywood is examined in Chap. 9.

References

Bordwell, D. (1977). Camera Movement and Cinematic Space. *Cine-Tracts*, *1*(2),19–26. Retrieved from http://library.brown.edu/cds/cinetracts/CT02.pdf

Bordwell, D. (1993). *The Cinema of Eisenstein*. Cambridge: Harvard University Press.

Bordwell, D. (2001). Eisenstein, Socialist Realism, and the Charms of Mizanstsena. In A. Lavalley & B. P. Scherr (Eds.), *Eisenstein at 100: A Reconsideration* (pp. 13–37). New Brunswick: Rutgers University Press.

Bouzereau, L. (Writer, Director & Producer). (2001). Steven Spielberg and the Small Screen [DVD supplement in S. Spielberg (Director), *Duel*]. Australia: Universal Pictures.

Branigan, E. (1975). Formal Permutations of the Point of View Shot. *Screen*, *16*(3), 54–64. Retrieved from http://screen.oxfordjournals.org/

Branigan, E. (1984). *Point of View in the Cinema*. Berlin: Mouton Publishers.

Breznican, A. (2011). Steven Spielberg: The EW Interview [Web Page]. *Entertainment Weekly*. Retrieved from http://www.ew.com/article/2011/12/02/steven-spielberg-ew-interview

Buckland, W. (1999). Between Science Fact and Science Fiction: Spielberg's Digital Dinosaurs, Possible worlds, and the New Aesthetic Realism. *Screen*, *40*(2), 177–192. Retrieved from http://screen.oxfordjournals.org/

Buckland, W. (2006). *Directed by Steven Spielberg: Poetics of the Contemporary Hollywood Blockbuster*. New York: Continuum.

Combs, R. (1978). Primal Scream: An Interview with Steven Spielberg. *American Cinematographer*, *59*(2), 111–113.

Duncan, J., & Shay, D. (1993). *The Making of Jurassic Park. An Adventure 65 Million Years in the Making*. London: Boxtree.

Fisher, B. (1993). When Dinosaurs Rule the Box Office. *American Cinematographer*, *74*(6), 37–44.

Katz, S. D. (1991). *Film Directing: Shot By Shot. Visualizing from Concept to Screen*. Studio City: Michael Wiese Productions.

Mitry, J. (1997). *The Aesthetics and Psychology of the Cinema* (C. King Trans.). Bloomington: Indiana University Press.

Nizhny, V. (1979). *Lessons with Eisenstein* (I. Montagu & J. Leyda, Eds. & Trans.). New York: Da Capo Press.

Pizzello, S. (1997). Chase, Crush and Devour. *American Cinematographer*, *78*(6), 38–54.

Sellors, C. P. (2000). The impossibility of Science Fiction: Against Buckland's Possible Worlds. *Screen*, *41*(2), 203–216. Retrieved from http://screen.oxfordjournals.org/

Total Film. (2004). *The Total Film Interview – Steven Spielberg*. Retrieved from http://www.totalfilm.com/features/the-total-film-interview-steven-spielberg

Windolf, J. (2008). Keys to the Kingdom. *Vanity Fair*. Retrieved from http://www.vanityfair.com/culture/features/2008/02/spielberg_qanda200802?currentPage=1

Film Title Editions

Spielberg, S. (Director). (1971). *Columbo: Murder by the Book* [Television broadcast, DVD (2004)]. Australia: Universal Pictures.
Spielberg, S. (Director). (1971). *Duel* [Motion picture, Blu-ray (2014)]. Austraila: Universal Sony Pictures Home Entertainment.
Spielberg, S. (Director). (1974). *The Sugarland Express* [Motion picture, Blu-ray (2014)]. Australia: Universal Sony Pictures Home Entertainment.
Spielberg, S. (Director). (1975). *Jaws* [Motion picture, Blu-ray (2014)]. Austraila: Universal Sony Pictures Home Entertainment.
Spielberg, S. (Director). (1977). *Close Encounters of the Third Kind* [Motion picture, Blu-ray (2007)]. United States: Sony Pictures Home Entertainment.
Spielberg, S. (Director). (1979). *1941* [Motion picture, Blu-ray (2014)]. Australia: Universal Sony Pictures Home Entertainment.
Spielberg, S. (Director). (1981). *Indiana Jones and the Raiders of the Lost Ark* [Motion picture, Blu-ray (2012)]. Australia: Lucasfilm Ltd.
Spielberg, S. (Director). (1987). *Empire of the Sun* [Motion picture, Blu-ray (2013)]. Australia: Warner Bros. Entertainment.
Spielberg, S. (Director). (1993). *Jurassic Park* [Motion picture, Blu-ray (2014)]. Australia: Universal Sony Pictures Home Entertainment.
Spielberg, S. (Director). (1993). *Schindler's List* [Motion picture, Blu-ray (2013)]. Australia: Universal Sony Pictures Home Entertainment.
Spielberg, S. (Director). (1998). *Saving Private Ryan* [Motion picture, Blu-ray (2010)]. Australia: Paramount Pictures.
Spielberg, S. (Director). (2001). *A. I: Artificial Intelligence* [Motion picture, Blu-ray (2011)]. United States: Paramount Home Entertainment
Spielberg, S. (Director). (2002). *Minority Report* [Motion picture, Blu-ray (2010)]. United Kingdom: 20th Century Fox.
Spielberg, S. (Director). (2002). *Catch Me if You Can* [Motion picture, Blu-ray (2012)]. Australia: Paramount Pictures.
Spielberg, S. (Director). (2004). *The Terminal* [Motion picture, Blu-ray (2014)]. Australia: Paramount Pictures.
Spielberg, S. (Director). (2005). *War of the Worlds* [Motion picture, Blu-ray (2010)]. Australia: Paramount Pictures.
Spielberg, S. (Director). (2005). *Munich* [Motion picture, DVD (2006)]. Australia: Universal Pictures.

Part III

Effect, Affect and Precedent

8

The Wide Reverse, Cognition and Affect

This chapter examines how Spielberg constructs his narratives through the lens of cognitivism and related emotion 'theory'. At the same time, this chapter is *not* designed to provide an exhaustive summary of current cognitive and affective theory. Rather, its purpose is to provide an introductory overview of some of the more pertinent concepts, debates and findings that are relevant to the consideration of style and its function in Spielberg's films.

I have examined how Spielberg innovatively manipulates classical style to construct wide reverses and the impact that these reverses have on how narrative is created. The next stage and first task of this chapter is to analyse how the wide reverse functions at the cognitive level and to determine whether it either enhances or hinders how spectators perceive Spielberg's narrative. The wide reverse examples examined in Chaps. 6 and 7 all involve substantial changes in visual perspective from one shot to the reverse and—in some instances—back again repeatedly. Does the requirement that the spectator must perceptually 're-absorb' such extreme visual changes lead to a degrading or enhancement of the spectator's ability to comprehend the intended narrative and effect? In other words, if the wide reverse functions to potentially distract the spectator, then it logically follows that it is being counterproductive by drawing attention to style and to editing in particular. This would then further undermine a key claim of the wide reverse, which is that it both preserves and functions within the conventional transparency of classical style. However, if the accumulated evidence implies that the spectator is not distracted, then this would further strengthen my contention that the wide reverse actually enhances the effectiveness of Spielberg's narratives for the reasons already considered.

A second related task involves determining how Spielberg's use of deep space and wide reverses contributes to the generating of emotion. This area is covered in *Part B—The Wide Reverse and Affect*. I conclude the chapter by re-considering the initial section of the sequence from *Jurassic Park* that introduces the *T. rex* with the focus now on its cognitive and affective properties. Before considering *Part A—The Wide Reverse and Cognition*, some fundamentals of cognitive theory relevant to the perception of film space require consideration.

Bordwell characterises the spectator's consideration of style as looking through the *how* to focus on the *what*—the narrative. Ira Konigsberg (2007) describes cognitive psychology as it relates to film studies as being concerned not with exploring content, but with the process—the *how*. As Bordwell (1989) broadly explains, '…cognitive theory wants to understand such human mental activities as recognition, comprehension, inference-making, interpretation, judgement, memory, and imagination'. Nöel Carroll (1996, p. 81) points out that comprehending the moving image is at the basic level essentially a biological process, as opposed to culturally learned. Joseph D. Anderson (1996, pp. 93–110) maintains that to understand how cognitive processing can help with comprehending how filmic narratives work, we need to study three key areas where cinema practice engages perception in ways that resemble how we innately make sense of the real world. (1) *Shot-to-shot transitions*: Anderson claims that editing from one field to another is easily processed because of its similarity to how we actually view the world, which is in sections, perceiving one space to the next. He notes that we tend to notice jump-cuts because of their inherent breaking of continuous movement—something that we do not experience in real perception. (2) *Orientational relationships*: the camera represents the spectator in the sense that it is our vantage point into the space of the film, just as we are always aware of our position in the real world—where we are and what is around us—so too do we understand that the camera functions to provide the axis for our orientation within the diegetic space in the frame. (3) *Hierarchical spatial comprehension*: this process is not dependent on camera position but on our ability to consider and relate different parts of a space so that we create a 'cognitive map', an overall understanding of the relation of objects to each other and to the space they occupy. Henry Bacon (2011) writes that we perceive the world as '…a mental construct based on a series of disconnected partial views gained as we gaze at our visual environment. Thus…we have an analogue with the mental construction of a film's diegesis' (p. 38).

Turning our attention to the classical continuity system, Anderson suggests that through a process of trial and error, classical continuity arrived at a system for presenting images that closely aligns with the 'rules' used in human visual processing. Todd Berliner and Dale Cohen (2011) also note that the classical continuity system has remained largely unchanged for more than 90 years due to filmmakers' '…intuitive understanding of space perception and the reactions of cinema spectators' (p. 61). Berliner and Cohen further explain the comparison between filmic continuity and 'active perception'. They explain active perception by citing psychologists Julian Hochberg and Virginia Brooks and perceptual psychologists Daniel Levin and Daniel Simons for their research into the role of constructive perception or constructivism. Constructivism in this context basically asserts that perception is essentially built out of a problem-solving process where the perceptual system rapidly constructs and revises versions of the environment based on sensory input.

Active perception refers to this process and Berliner and Cohen claim that the classical continuity system closely replicates the real-life constructivist process in three specific ways. First, classical editing and active perception both take non-continuous or fragmented images that the perceiver then makes sense of. They maintain that we perceive the world in a fragmented way, much like the individual shots in cinema that are then combined together to create complete space or spaces. Second, they contend that classical editing resembles active perception by presenting images in an orderly way and they give the example of traditional analytical editing where a wide or establishing view is then usually followed by tighter, more detailed information. Third, classical editing structures shots so that they create a causal logic.[1] If we see someone pointing or looking away at something we almost automatically turn to see what they are looking at—we seek an explanation for their gaze. Berliner and Cohen illustrate this by referencing the point-of-view point/glance, point/object pattern where the first shot is explained or answered by the second—a process that they argue is similar to that in active perception. Carroll (2003, p. 47) agrees, arguing that the desire to resolve the point/glance eye-line is part of 'natural behaviour', a view that challenges the position of scholars such as Daniel Dayan who claim point of view to be a code.

If we return to the rational-agent model examined in Chap. 3 and the precept that filmmakers intentionally construct narratives in ways that encourage spectators to perceive them in specific ways, we can also assume that some filmmakers are more successful at achieving this than others. The longevity and on-going popularity of Spielberg's films suggest him as a likely candidate for the former category. The next section examines Spielberg's unique style as embodied in the wide reverse in the context of its cognitive operation within the classical continuity system.

Part A: The Wide Reverse and Cognition

Of the eight complex and simple spatial configuration wide reverses examined in Chap. 6, all demand significant shifts in spectator perception. By this I mean that each 180-degree reversal requires that the spectator 'reconceive' the scenographic space as considered in the previous shot in a way more commonly associated with a change to a new scene. The process of perceiving a seemingly 'new' space or significant change in perspective is obviously normal and expected whenever a cut occurs to a new scene but is much less common—and less expected—within the same scene. First, we need to understand how a spectator cognitively processes the significant visual change that accompanies the wide reverse and the potential sensory disruptions that may attend such a dramatic change in perspective. Integral to understanding this process is a consideration of the impact of the cut itself on perception. If the spectator does not notice a cut then the implication is that their attention is consumed by the narrative. However, Tim J. Smith (2005) has noted that when spectator attention is unfocussed as a result of a lack of narrative cues, it then becomes '...vulnerable to capture by visual disruptions such as the whole field disruptions caused by a cut' (p. 81). One consequence of a noticed cut is that it briefly diverts some of the brain's resources to accommodating the unexpected information and Smith (2005, p. 176) cites studies that suggest this can have an impact on comprehension. More fundamentally, the implication of a noticed or disruptive cut within the classical context of continuity editing as practiced by Spielberg is that it suggests a potential rupturing of the carefully cultivated and preserved transparency of style.

In discussing the role of movement in retaining spectator attention within the diegesis, Smith (T. J. 2005) argues that it can be used to 'hide' a cut in two ways: by *attracting* or *directing* attention. Attracting attention is less perceptually complex in that it relies on 'capturing' attention through degrees of movement ranging from an object or objects moving across the frame, to gestures or eye-lines that are then 'answered' across the cut. The movement cues the spectator to expect the cut in anticipation of the progression of the movement into a new space or angle, and this anticipation dissipates the cut's visibility. Instances of this occur repeatedly in the opening of *Raiders of the Lost Ark* as reverses where Spielberg has Indi moving away or towards camera (Figs. 6.6a–b, 6.7c–d and 6.8a, 6.8e). Directing attention resembles Berliner and Cohen's third category where the spectator is required to make some sort of causal query, which is then resolved in the next (or later) shot, thus preserving spectator attention across the cut, again reducing the cut's visibility. Smith refers to these more specific causal cues as deictic cues and the point/glance shot is a typical example. Film editor Walter Murch (2001) claims that he prefers to edit in a way that mimics the spectator's inclination to blink, suggesting that this helps to reduce the number of noticed edits. While he can't perfectly anticipate when the audience will blink he structures his editing with a sense of the spectator's '...potential blink point' (p. 69).

So how are we able to examine the perceptual properties as cued by the wide reverse? This can be done in part by examining the conventional, shot, reverse shot arrangement. The classical shot, reverse shot commonly used for dialogue passages most closely visually replicates the wide reverse in that successive shots almost[2] reverse the perspective from the previous shot. Despite the often sustained role of editing in many shot, reverse shot sequences, its presence tends to go relatively unnoticed and this is largely due to the operation of a subset of 'attentional' cues known as associative cues (T. J. Smith 2005, p. 65). These are cues such as eye-line matching, the overlapping of visual elements, and aural cues such as music and dialogue across a cut. All infer that the cut to the next shot is taking place within the same place and time. Figure 4.1b–c is a typical instance with associative cues such as eye-line matching, similar backgrounds and dialogue across the cut. These cues combine with the classical convention of the shot, reverse shot pattern and the spectator's expectation via deictic cues that the first dialogue shot precedes a cut to a matching reverse. Figure 4.3a–b is another typical shot, reverse shot variation with fewer associative cues yet it still provides eye-line and aural (dialogue) cues. In both variations, Smith (T. J. 2005) would argue that the spectator's '…attentional capture is in agreement with their attentional set…' (p. 61). Because the spectator's expectation of a cut is realised, this then results in the cut being less disruptive or less noticed.

A related issue with regard to associative cues and the classical shot, reverse shot system that requires brief consideration involves the debate concerning the significance of eye-line matching. As discussed in Chap. 4, not 'crossing-the-line' during dialogue shot, reverse shot exchanges has operated for many years as the foundation 'rule' of the classical continuity system. Not having characters' eye-lines meet across a cut as in the simulated example at Fig. 4.3c–d is widely considered to be poor practice, in part—it has long been thought—because of the potential for spectator confusion relating to the spatial orientation between characters. As early as the mid-1970s film scholars such as Burch, Heath, Branigan, Bordwell and Thompson began to explore the variations in shot, reverse shot staging evident in the films of Yasujiro Ozu. Bordwell noted that while Ozu often observed the crossing-the-line rule, in his later films he also just as frequently chose to disregard it and Bordwell (1988, p. 98) suggests that this was Ozu prioritising graphic relations over eye-line matching (Fig. 9.25b–c). Yet the example from *The End of Summer* (1961) below displays a mismatched eye-line without any discernible trace of graphic matching other than centred framings. The suited businessman (Kitagawa, Fig. 8.1a) addresses the hostess (Fig. 8.1b) with both looking right-to-left rather than observing the classical 'rule' that would normally dictate that the businessman look left-to-right so that their eye-lines meet across the cut.

The Wide Reverse, Cognition and Affect   247

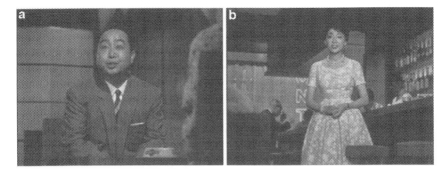

Figs. 8.1a, 8.1b   *The End of Summer* (1961)

Bordwell argues that the classically 'incorrect' eye-line in Ozu is not distracting and does not induce spectator confusion in terms of understanding where the characters are in relation to each other. Recent cognitive studies offer both supporting and opposing conclusions relating to the role of the 180-degree rule in assisting with spatial orientation and coherence and this debate is briefly considered in the following paragraphs.

Greg Smith (2012a, pp. 56–60) considers the 180-degree rule as evidence of a 'folk psychological' set of beliefs created by filmmakers (and scholars) to explain how to better present a coherent narrative for spectator perception. He claims to be 'suspicious' of the role of the 180-degree rule in enhancing perception and for evidence, points to comics where line crossing is common yet does not cause spatial ambiguity. Daniel Levin and Caryn Wang (2009, pp. 24–52) reference experiments with children that suggest spatial information is at least partially coded automatically. This basic process is combined with a variety of more advanced cognitive options that constantly refine spatial information. Levin and Wang point to the eye-line in classical continuity as an example of a 'foundational cue' but they also stress that spectators consider multiple cues. In a dialogue scene like the earlier Ozu example, these spatial cues could be drawn at least partially from T. J. Smith's associative cues and include elements such as character recognition including face and costume, overlapping audio and narrative elements.

Joseph Magliano and Jeffrey Zacks (2011) suggest that observing the 180-degree rule *does* play a significant role in bridging perception across visual discontinuities. Utilising functional magnetic resonance imaging (fMRI) to record brain activity, they conducted experiments relating to both continuous and discontinuous edits. While they noted that discontinuities in space and time produced 'minor' effects, discontinuities in action—such as the reversing of movement when the line is crossed—produced the greatest impact, in that it required higher level processing. As noted earlier, one potential implication of more complex cognitive processing is that other processes such as narrative comprehension may suffer. Berliner and Cohen (2011) contend that movement in the frame can itself function as a powerful continuity cue, distracting the spectator from spatial changes that result from a cut. Markus Huff and Stephan Schwan (2012) have found that observing the 180-degree rule contributes to less noticeable cutting. They characterise the 180-degree rule as a convention that spectators perceptually rely on to avoid a '…computationally demanding realignment…'. I argue that degrees of aberration in eye-line matching also likely play a role in determining consequence. The noted example from Ozu represents only a minor eye-line digression from classical convention in the sense that the eye-lines are only a few degrees 'out' and the characters' gazes more-or-less meet across the cut.[3] This is in contrast to the simulated example (Fig. 4.3c–d) where the characters appear to look in the same direction. This extreme arrangement is rare in classical cinema.

Spectators can anticipate a cut by following the direction of the character's gaze and often involuntarily shift their view to the side of the screen they anticipate the character will appear in in the new shot. James Cutting (2005) similarly argues that spatial information is not crucial, that orientation is achieved by both noting the characters and following the narrative. Cutting characterises the classical continuity rules as more like a 'guide' that do not need to be strictly adhered to, and he cites instances in *Stagecoach* (1939) and *Casablanca* (1941) where screen direction is mismatched across cuts. T. J. Smith (2012b, p. 16) also notes that match-on-action edits where graphic relations are aligned at the end of a shot and at the beginning of the next shot, as the most difficult type of edit to detect. This is an intriguing finding when considered in relation to Ozu's unique adoption of graphic matching as an intrinsic norm for some shot, reverse shot exchanges. It supports Bordwell's view that Ozu's mismatched eye-lines cause minimal perceptual disruption because it could be argued that the graphic matching effectively compensates or even surpasses matched eye-lines in reducing the spectator's perception of a cut.[4]

In explaining how narratives minimise the invasive potential of edits, T. J. Smith (2012b) isolates three areas: how spectators 'attend' to a shot, how attention is cued across an edit, and how expected continuity is preserved after the cut (p. 10). Smith notes that we tend to 'fixate' on an image using a combination of what cognitivists describe as bottom-up and top-down processes. The former deals with basic processing such as edge definition, colour and recognising motion while the latter involves more complex processing such as facial recognition and situational significance. If spectator attention is adequately activated and cued, then attention will be carried across the cut and will continue to be arrogated by subsequent cues. While Anderson's earlier assessment concerning the perceptual abruptness of jump-cuts seems valid in its logic, it does not explain why the instances of 'noise'—effectively jump-cuts—(considered in Chap. 4) do not seem to cause undue distraction for spectators. This may be explained by the narrative functioning as an attentional cue that can be seen to perceptually 'occupy' the spectator, distracting them from the visual discontinuity of the jump-cut.

Spielberg's wide reverses (as examined in Chap. 6) do tend to incorporate a substantial range of attentional cues. Of the four complex spatial configuration reverses, only one, the second shark attack scene establishes the main characters and the scenographic space—the beach in *Jaws*—without resorting to overt attentional cues. At the same time, it could be argued that these shots do carry narrative specific deictic cues relating directly to the previous scene in which the protagonist (Brody) reluctantly agrees not to close the beaches. This means that the initial shots of the following scene have a general anticipatory value in that the narrative information from the previous scene encourages the spectator to hypothesise about what will happen at this new beach location. The remaining sequences utilise deep space compositions with a distinct foreground as attentional cues (Figs. 6.2b–f, 6.5a–f). The four simple spatial configuration reverses also make extensive use of deep space compositions and foregrounding (Figs. 6.9c, 6.11d, 6.12a and a typical Spielberg three plane, deep space composition at Fig. 6.12b).

Wide Reverses and Associative Point of View

As mentioned in the introduction, scholars Hall and Neale (2010, p. 208), Morris (2007, p. 60) and Buckland (2006, p. 97) have all commented on Spielberg's extensive use of optical point of view (OP) in their discussions of *Jaws*. Stephen Prince (2012, p. 29) has also noted a persistent use of point of view in many of Spielberg's films claiming that it fosters a greater immersive effect. All the scenes considered in Chap. 6 include embedded instances of classical point-of-view point/glance, point/object constructions within the wide reverse system. One example of a more sustained point-of-view exchange is also used in *Jaws* as Brody nervously watches the water in expectation of an attack. T. J. Smith (2005, p. 65) has commented on the cognitive significance of the point, glance shot and character eye-line as a powerful cue for suppressing the perception of the edit. Because the point, glance shot involves a character looking at something off-screen, the audience is then cued to expect to see a new shot—the point/object shot. The spectator's expectation of the point/object shot acts as an attentional cue that results in the cut as less invasive because a new visual field is anticipated.

If we consider Branigan's definition of the optical point-of-view (OP) arrangement, which I have adopted, then Prince's observation in relation to the quantity of point-of-view usage by Spielberg appears to be more-or-less appropriate. Yet if we consider the wide reverse as often also operating as a kind of perspectival 'simulation' of point of view then its presence becomes ubiquitous. I label this variation on traditional point of view, *associative point of view* (AP). While I have established that the wide reverse functions to more effectively immerse the spectator in a number of ways, a further function relates to the use of over-the-shoulder compositions that retain a similar perspective to the character's point of view. These are effectively point/object shots and Branigan (1984, p. 110) describes them as 'less subjective' because they do not represent the character's OP but still retain the character's 'sightline'. The innovation in their use by Spielberg within the context of the wide reverse arrangement is that each simulated point of view is then reversed by another simulated point of view. For example, the Omaha Beach Landing sequence (Chap. 6 and Table 8.1 below) is structured around wide reverses that begin with an over-shoulder view of the German machine-gunner firing at the landing American soldiers in the background (Fig. 6.5c). Following a brief two-shot, the machine-gunner is then matched with a wide reverse and approximate over-shoulder of the American soldiers looking to the machine gun bunker now in the background (Fig. 6.5d–f). Each shot provides a perspective similar to that of an OP. The stylistic advantage of this AP is that it retains all of the perceptual advantages of the OP shot without bearing the costs. Among the advantages: the shots are not subjective and therefore also not self-conscious, thus permitting style to remain transparent; they offer the same immersive experience and potential for character identification that is usually associated with OP; and cognitively, the perspective view implies a character gaze that the spectator follows. Like the shot, reverse shot, the gaze in turn cues the spectator to anticipate an impending cut to the reverse, hence also minimising spectator registration of the edit. Table 8.1 shows the extent of AP and OP in the eight wide reverse examples from Chap. 6. Spielberg makes extensive use of AP in five of the eight sequences (sequence three, four, six, seven and eight). An added advantage of the AP is that it permits Spielberg to create a sequence that more comprehensively utilises a sense of point of view without actually resorting to an overuse of OP shots. Rather than the AP shots replacing OP, they work in *tandem* to enhance the visual effect. This is achieved while simultaneously revealing scenographic space via the wide reverse instead of restricting space as OP normally does. Of the wide reverse variations examined in Chap. 7, the integration of AP is even more pervasive. Nine of the ten single reverse instances incorporate AP while eight of the ten single-shot, long take reverses include AP.

As discussed in Chap. 6, a key function of the wide reverse is that it constructs a comprehensive scenographic space. In reversing the perspective of the previous shot, the wide reverse simultaneously introduces new space (that previously or subsequently behind the camera) and 'refreshes'

Table 8.1 Associative Point of View (AP) and Optical Point of View (OP) in wide reverses (Chap. 6)

---

1. Neary's close encounter (opening)
Number of shots:
In scene (part): (5)
AP: (0)
OP: (0)
2. Second shark attack
Number of shots:
In scene: (58)
AP: (0)
OP: (12)
3. Omaha beach landing
Number of shots:
In sequence: (77)
AP: (11) Figs. 6.5c, 6.5d, 6.5e, 6.5f, (an additional seven shots through the sequence)
OP: (6)
4. Indiana Jones escapes
Number of shots:
In sequence: (57)
AP: (19) Fig. 6.7b, 6.7d, (and 17 additional shots)
OP: (3) Fig. 6.6c, (and two additional shots)
5. The car ferry
Number of shots:
In scene (6)
AP: (0)
OP: (1-2) (one shot is ambiguous in terms of perspective)
6. Airfield attack
Number of shots:
In scene: (54)
AP: (9) Fig. 6.11d (and an additional eight shots)
OP: (6-10) Fig. 6.11a (and an additional five shots)
Note that four shots are ambiguous in terms of perspective and may also be OP.
7. Death notification
Number of shots:
In scene: (7)
AP: (5) Fig. 6.12b
OP: (1)
8. Establishing the arrival hall
Number of shots:
In scene: 21 (shot 22 (6.13g) is the first shot of the second scene and is AP)
AP: (10) (as over-shoulder reverses)
OP: (0)

the space already seen in the previous shot—now viewed from the reverse angle. This additional function recalls Hochberg and Brooks' (2007) concept of 'visual momentum' where editing is used to assist with spectator engagement. They argue that a scene can quickly become 'cinematically dead' for a spectator in that interest in the shot quickly dissipates. This can be reinvigorated by editing—by presenting a new shot and therefore a new perspective that reactivates spectator interest. Hochberg and Brooks use the example of montage where a sequence of shots assists with maintaining spectator interest because of the repeated shot changes. The wide reverse also achieves this by offering a renewed perspective without resorting to a change in location.

Like Hochberg and Brooks, other scholars [including Ed Tan (1996, p. 249), Patrick Colm Hogan (2007, pp. 41–58) and Colin McGinn (2005, p. 53)] have identified *interest* as a powerful attentional cue in relation to the spectator's engagement with narrative content. Hochberg and Brooks (1996, pp. 368–387) also note that the memory retention of an action is significantly improved when the action is perceived by the spectator as a 'purposeful act', i.e. when the action is given context within a story. Related to this is spectator recall of camera angles, which is 'significantly less accurate' than for recall of content according to Robert Kraft (1987, pp. 291–307). T. J. Smith (2012b) observes that continuity editing ultimately functions as a vehicle for storytelling '…it is about enabling the viewers to shift their attention to the audio-visual details currently relevant to them and the narrative' (p. 9). William Brown (2011) presents a more extreme position in that he argues Hollywood films so overwhelm spectators with sensory information that most of their perceptual processing is taken up by just following the story. Once spectators identify the characters that are the main causal agents, spatial coherence is maintained primarily by continual recognition of these salient characters and less by continuity editing or even arrangements like the shot, reverse shot.

> …a paradox seems to emerge in the case of intensified continuity: it draws our attention to the screen exogenously, but at the same time it also blinds us to the formal reasons *why* our attention is being drawn. Our mental capacities/cerebral bandwidth are more taken up with trying to work out what is going on (following the story/narrative). (p. 78)

Just as classical practice emphasises that narrative requirements dictate the role for style, so do cognitivists appreciate the determining influence that narrative has in spectator perception. Cynthia Freeland (2012, pp. 34–41) takes the functioning role of narrative a step further by citing research by J. David Velleman that considers the significance of emotion. 'Narratives are fundamentally linked to emotions, and emotions themselves often take on narrative form'. Sheena Rogers (2012, pp. 42–48) characterises the experience of narrative by summarising the spectator's perceptual and processing journey into three stages: basic psychological processes relating to attention and perception, including T. J. Smith's ATOCC[5]; engaging the spectator cognitively and emotionally; the combination of these first two stages together with acquired knowledge and cultural experience to '…generate intensely meaningful and affecting encounters with film'. Grodal (1997, p. 59) argues for a four step process beginning with simpler bottom-up processing; associations relating to memory; comprehending narrative significance and 'affect appraisal'; and a final step that includes voluntary and autonomic reactions, 'emotensities' and 'emotivities'.

Part B: The Wide Reverse and Affect

> One of the things we tapped into—not just Steven and I, but our whole sixties generation—is that we don't come from an intellectual generation. We enjoyed the emotional highs we got from movies and realized that you could crank up the adrenaline to a level way beyond what people were doing.—George Lucas (Shone 2004, p. 12)

Emotional engagement is an important element when viewing mainstream movies and Carl Plantinga (2009a, p. 5) believes experiencing emotion during film viewing is the *main* reason we watch cinema. Carroll (2013, p. 85) similarly suggests that movies are successful largely because of the way they appeal to emotion. How much we enjoy a film is often determined not by its degree of intellectual stimulation, but by how well it manipulates affect. Affect is a broad category that includes emotions, moods, feelings and sensations and involuntary responses like certain reflex or startle reactions. Unlike the undefined specificity of affect, emotions tend to intentionality in that they are often accompanied by a goal. Crucially, Plantinga (2009a) establishes the connection between affect and narrative comprehension when he elaborates on what spectator *interest* means '…I put a good deal of emphasis on the importance of narrative as the governing element in eliciting emotional response…', and 'Insufficient or inappropriate narrative development will counteract or even contradict our tendency toward emotional contagion and mimicry' (p. 116). A number of scholars emphasise the significance of engaging spectator interest: Carroll (2003, p. 60) notes that stimulating affect is an important requirement; Greg M. Smith (2003, p. 72) considers plotting, themes and character-generated empathy and sympathy as the main factors for eliciting interest, while Tan (1996, p. 249) identifies interest as an emotion and adds that triggering its onset induces the spectator to invest in the cognitive and emotional processing of the narrative. Tan (2005) further contends that interest is actually the dominant spectator emotion and that in mainstream cinema this is determined by the film's entertainment value.

Emotion

In describing cinema as an emotion machine, Tan (1996) comments 'The way the emotional response dovetails with the kind of emotion that the viewer has come for is a miracle of precision' (p. 251). Andras Balint Kovacs (2011) argues that '…our emotions, psychological states, and personal traits influence our perception of causal connections'. Kovacs adds that emotion is crucial in the process of understanding how a narrative develops and that a cycle exists in the sense that narrative progression, in turn, stimulates emotional variation, which then impacts on subsequent narrative understanding and so on. Understanding narrative depends on the ability of filmmakers to cue spectator emotions like curiosity, anticipation and suspense. Judgments and decisions about narrative components such as evaluating characters are largely based on emotional reactions. Plantinga's (2009a) 'cognitive-perceptual' theory includes both conscious and non-conscious responses, thus indicating that emotion is not always deliberate and can sometimes be generated from unconscious and automatic processes: 'I consider emotions to be mental states that are often accompanied by subjective feelings, physiological arousal, and action tendencies' (pp. 54–55).

A number of scholars also note the innate role of emotion in triggering action tendencies such as the so-called 'flight-or-fight' reaction. 'Our emotions are biological adaptations shaped by natural selection in order to protect and advance vital human interests' (Carroll 2013, p. 86). Tan and Frijda (1999) mention one function of emotion as orientating the individual toward some kind of potential threat. Grodal (2009, pp. 146–147) similarly conceives of emotions as activating 'tendencies to action', guiding the brain as to what is safe and what should be avoided. Carroll (2008, p. 149) identifies feelings or sensations that excite spectators by triggering inborn perceptual/hormonal mechanisms that drive the spectator into a heightened emotional condition. Zillman (2005, p. 170) notes the innate function of empathy as an inherent mechanism that allows a threat to be more easily identified if many or all in the group share the same fear. Carroll (2013), Grodal (2009) and Tan (1996) all identify the role of real-world emotion as providing potentially life-saving appraisals of situations where instant, emotive reactions such as fear induce action responses. Carroll (2013) claims that cinema addresses this ability to quickly process information by often representing narrative via the rapid replacing of shots through editing. The narrative control exercised by the filmmaker extends to what the spectator is supposed to feel. '…criterially pertinent variables stand out saliently in ways that make our emotive appraisal of it in the manner the moviemaker intends virtually unavoidable' (p. 89).

Yet emotion experienced in the cinema is not the same as that experienced in real life. Plantinga (2009c, pp. 88–89) argues that cinematic emotion differs from real or everyday emotions in two ways: the spectator realises that events cannot be altered and the experience is fictional, not actual. He adds that cinematic emotions such as fear include reduced degrees of anxiety because of the absence of the requirement for action tendencies—there is no need for the spectator to physically respond. This in turn allows the spectator to enjoy experiencing characters undergoing extreme levels of emotional distress. Plantinga (2009b) also isolates four types of emotion in film viewers that can exist individually or as a mixture: 'direct' responses such as surprise, curiosity, suspense and anticipation; sympathetic or antipathetic responses that relate to the experiences of characters, their goals and preoccupations, such as compassion/anger and admiration/disdain; an 'artefact' response to the film itself, admiration, impatience, amusement and 'meta-emotions' as spectator's responses to those of other spectators, such as pride, shame and so on. Anne Bartsch (2008) offers another definition for meta-emotions—in this case it is experiencing emotions about emotions. Tan (1996) describes six functional characteristics of emotion: (1) genuine emotion takes control precedence over other processes already taking place. (2) Emotion means there is a concern about something. (3) Stimulus specificity—each emotion has a specific situational meaning structure that reflects the emotionally critical characteristics of the stimulus. (4) Response to reality—the stimulus must represent some reality or other. (5) Response to change—emotion responds above all to changes in the situation. (6). Closure—an emotion has a strong tendency toward complete realisation of its appraisal and action tendency and is relatively immune to outside influences, such as conscious control.

Emotive engagement in a narrative depends on its ability to engage specific emotions in the spectator that then motivate the spectator to construct further emotions relating to future outcomes. Through his PECMA model, Grodal (2009) suggests that our processing of canonical narrative replicates the way our brain processes information in that spectator perception of narrative 'flows' from perception to emotion, cognition to motor action. Murray Smith (1995, p. 41) similarly identifies emotion as part of the 'flow' process of perception, cognition and action. Jens Eder (2010) proposes four stages: (1) 'Perceptual affects, sensations and moods' are generated by the spectator's processing of images and sounds; (2) 'diegetic emotions' created from mental models of the filmic world and the engaging of empathy and sympathy; (3) 'thematic emotions' from the larger narrative; (4) 'communication emotions' relating to a reflection of the broader process of textual comprehension as similar to Plantinga's narrative as artefact.

Given the significance of filmmaker intentionality in influencing how a narrative is constructed, one logical extension of this is that the filmmaker therefore also actively engages in predetermining how and when an audience experiences emotion. Carroll (2013, p. 91) contends that through narrative and style, filmmakers 'prefocus' or 'predigest' the desired range of emotions thus encouraging a selective 'emotive uptake' in the spectator, as well as directing attention. The narrative must also induce 'pro-attitudes' in the spectator. Carroll (2003, p. 70) defines this as the spectator investing in the character's situation, activity and future. Tan and Frijda (1999, p. 52) also emphasise the importance of the spectator as sharing in the feelings of the protagonist. They qualify this by categorising cinematic affect as 'witness emotions' in that the spectator's emotion closely aligns with real life except that they occur as if the spectator is an onlooker and cannot participate or act on the unfolding events. They further define the most common emotional responses to fictional cinema as 'F emotions' while those expressed as 'A emotions' relate to pleasure and admiration of the film itself.

Character

Empathising with characters is necessary because it assists with an understanding of character motivation and narrative function. Alex Neill (1996) defines sympathy as feeling for a character while empathy is feeling with that character. Neill argues that empathising with fictional characters is not significantly different from real-life empathy in part because as spectators, we still activate imagination and attempt to understand the character's point of view. Zillmann (2005) considers the role of morality in the processing of emotion, referencing Aristotle's Poetics and the 'rules', which instruct that the virtuous cannot end as miserable, while the wicked cannot be rewarded with happiness. Zillmann adds that the moral component of emotion is a key factor in explaining the enjoyment of any kind of drama. The greater the distinction between good and evil, the more intense the emotional response is likely to be once the conflict is resolved. Disposition theory contends that spectators experience the most enjoyment from liked characters that experience a happy resolution and disliked characters who receive their comeuppance. The reverse applies with minimal spectator pleasure where liked characters suffer and antagonists prevail (Oliver and Hartman 2010).

Murray Smith (1995, p. 75) notes that spectator identification—or 'imaginative engagement'—with characters, functions at three levels, which he describes as the 'structure of sympathy'. First, *recognition* relates to how spectators understand characters; second, *alignment* involves spectators perceiving the same information as characters. Smith mentions OP as an example of perceptual alignment. Third, spectators form *allegiances* with characters based on their morality. Smith claims that emotion is also an important component of allegiance. Carroll (1990, p. 96) and Plantinga (1999, p. 244) also believe that the spectator does not literally identify with the protagonist and therefore respectively prefer the term *engagement* and *character engagement* rather than identification in describing the spectator/character's affective relationship. In acknowledging the rejection of the strict concept of identification by Carroll (and Gregory Currie), Berys Gaut (1999) proposes two broad variations: imaginary identification, where the spectator imagines the position of the character, and empathetic identification, in which the spectator 'shares' the character's emotions by again imagining themselves in the character's situation. Gaut also refines the traditional notion of the OP shot as representing character identification by reconfiguring it as perceptual identification. This also relates to my earlier proposition relating the wide reverse to the perspectival equivalence of point of view as AP. Jens Eder (2010) claims that the spectator can perceive characters in two ways: from an 'external observer's perspective' where the spectator's emotions may diverge from that of the character and therefore the spectator is sympathetic or the spectator engages in 'relations of perspective' where the character's experiences replicate or 'approximate' those of the spectator's depending on the relation that a character has with another character. Eder further suggests that when spectator knowledge matches that of the character then the spectator feels partial identification with that character, and when character situations replicate the spectator's own experience then they can develop empathy.

Style

Mainstream cinema always features goal-orientated narratives and characters. Greg M. Smith (1999a) observes that 'In each cognitivist theory the dominant mechanism engaging filmic emotions depends on characters and their actions' (p. 105). He suggests that this can lead to an understanding of the emotion system that is too narrowly defined and does not take into account elements that may depend less on object, action or goal orientation. Because emotion can vary in intensity and focus, some emotional states may not conform to emotion prototypes and may therefore escape consideration even though they may still serve an important role in the emotion system. Smith instead argues for what he calls an 'associative network model' where emotions are determined based on numerous sensory inputs. These include the face, vocals, body posture, conscious cognition, non-conscious handling by the central nervous system and activity in the autonomic nervous system. Smith claims that because there are multiple channels of sensory input, the strength or intensity of emotion experienced can vary according to how many channels are activated and in what combination. Real-world situations are rarely emotionally unambiguous and so multiple inputs allow us to better negotiate and understand the complexity of a given situation.

An important component of Smith's conception of how emotion is generated is that relating to the role of style. Not only is emotion generated from character—including action, dialogue and vocalisation—but also from sound, music, lighting, editing, composition, staging and mise en scene. Using style as a foundation, Smith (2003) proposes a 'mood-cue approach'. This is a system where cues and 'emotion markers' are seen to be embedded in the narrative for the purpose of generating mood and emotion. In this system, emotion can be generated from character or style or both. According to Smith, cinema's primary emotive function is to create mood. Mood is a longer lasting but less potent emotional state. Mood is a preparatory state that facilitates the development of specific emotions that tend to manifest briefly in a concentrated burst before again reverting to the more moderated state as mood. While mood facilitates the onset of bursts of emotion, these bursts of emotion also assist in sustaining mood.

Mood is sustained in narrative through a succession of cues derived from faces, bodies, stylistic elements such as music, lighting, and so on. These cues are occasionally punctuated by emotion markers, moments in the film that result in these sudden but concentrated bursts of emotion.

Smith claims that these brief surges of emotion are not generated from the narrative but function exclusively to create immediate moments of emotion that are similar to the kind of involuntary reaction seen in the startle effect. He cites as an example a moment early in *Raiders of the Lost Ark* where one of Indi's assistants unexpectedly uncovers a giant stone idol and retreats in terror.

> ...this emotion marker neither hinders nor helps the protagonist's progress toward his goal, nor does it provide new story information. What this moment does do is provide a reliable burst of congruent emotion that helps maintain the sequence's suspenseful mood. This is the primary purpose of the stone idol scare. (2003, p. 46)

While the event can be seen to function emotively in the sense that Smith suggests, he significantly undervalues the other story and character-related functions of the idol scare. These include: expository elements relating to character, such as Indi as not affected by the stone idol, which underlines his masculinity and strength (as hero); that he calmly studies the idol also suggests that he is intelligent and knowledgeable; plot-related expository information that contributes to the sense of place and cues indicating that they are near their intended destination; the fear in the fleeing assistant suggests danger and tension; while the scare itself communicates an element of allusion-related genre orientation—that we are watching an action, thriller type of film. Smith further argues that Hollywood cinema tends to prioritise special effects and soundtracks over complex characterisation and narrative and that this is why consideration of emotion should not be limited to character and plot. While the role of style is undoubtedly crucial in generating emotion, Smith's inability to identify the plot and character elements relating to the idol scare suggests that he also underrates the complexity of Hollywood (and Spielberg's) characterisation and plotting.

Tan and Frijda (1999, p. 111) also note the flexibility of Smith's emotion system in that seemingly emotively opposite experiences can be connected and they illustrate this with the example of the thrill associated with the danger of the rollercoaster ride. This also recalls Bartsch's comments on meta-emotions and the concept of experiencing pleasure from fear. In contrast to Smith, Grodal considers style as a minor contributor to affect and actually warns against its potential for distraction if its role is prioritised. This also relates to Carroll's (2013, p.110) 'realistic heuristic' where character and narrative situation can be readily concomitant with the spectator's real-life experience.

The Face

The early resistance to the close-up of the face in primitive cinema is noted by Jacques Aumont (1997, p. 103). Initial instances were described as portraying 'dumb giants' and 'big heads', with the actor's absent body considered 'against nature'. This perception quickly changed. 'The close-up is a constantly repeated example of the power of the apparatus'. Bordwell (1985, p. 162) similarly notes the significance of the body and the face in classical narrative as likely 'focal points of attention' while Rogers (2012) comments that when looking at the space of a scene—it is always the area occupied by the face that dominates spectator attention. T. J. Smith (2005, p. 66) cites research that indicates that within a few months of life a baby learns to look at its mother's eyes. He adds that the colouring of the human eye with white (sclera) surrounding a dark centred pupil gives them a distinctive, easily perceived appearance that often makes them stand out not only from the face but from surroundings. The degree of empathy that the spectator feels with a character depends on the level of 'allegiance' that the spectator has with this character. Together with the close-up, Plantinga (1999) argues that point-of-view arrangements also function as powerful devices for generating empathy.

The Universal Theory of Facial Expression (UTFE) isolates between five and seven basic emotions: anger, fear, sadness, surprise, happiness, disgust and contempt. These expressions can be expressed as 'action units', arrangements of the facial muscles to express each of the basic emotions, and are presented essentially in the same way by the human face regardless of cultural origin. UTFE creator Ed Tan (2005) cautions that it is too simplistic to apply the theory directly to cinema because of its fictive nature, but also because of the variation in the way emotion is cued in different, non-mainstream types of cinema such as the art-film and documentary. Both Plantinga (2009a) and Eder (2010) describe a system of respectively 'proxemic patterns' and 'imaginative proximity and distance' that emphasises the role of the close-up in placing the spectator literally nearer to the character. This fosters the promotion of 'emotional contagion', the spreading of mood and emotion to the spectator.

Spielberg's preference for deep space compositions that simultaneously prioritise the face and background space—with the foreground object invariably a character's face—is evident in almost all of the scenes examined in Chap. 5. For those scenes where Spielberg chooses to mobilise editing rather than deep space, the prioritising of the character's face as close-up is still clearly evident. Neary's close encounter (Fig. 6.2a–f and Fig. 6.3) notably illustrates the significance of the close-up. Of the 47 edits that make up this four-minute scene, the camera angle at Fig. 6.2d is referred to a total of 12 times. This is in stark contrast to the other camera positions in the scene, which are reused no more than twice. I have already discussed how the first five shots of the scene establish Neary as the centre of the action. This is further reinforced by the use of the angle at Fig. 6.2d for Neary's close-ups (except when he looks up at the passing UFO) and is repeatedly returned to throughout the scene in a pattern that consists of a shot of something happening followed by a return to the angle at Fig. 6.2d for Neary's expressive reaction. This constant referencing to Neary ensures that the scene remains emotively orientated around his experience.

Music

> Of all the arts, music makes the most direct appeal to the emotions.—Elmer Bernstein, composer (J. Smith 1999b)

A detailed consideration of soundtrack music is beyond the scope of this study yet I acknowledge its significance here for two reasons: its role as the single most important stylistic device for eliciting emotion in mainstream cinema and the already noted (Chap. 3) career-long collaboration between John Williams and Spielberg. Between Spielberg's manipulation of style and Williams' orchestral compositions, the collaboration between the two could be seen as cinema's great emotive double act. Jerrold Levinson (1996) comments that a score composed specifically for a film is likely to be 'purely narrative in function' as opposed to a score made from pre-existing music. That Spielberg has never made a film that consists only of a pre-existing score—or that he rarely uses pre-existing music—further reinforces the level of creative integration he has with Williams.

Joseph Anderson (1996, p. 87) points out that the correlation of two senses—vision and sound as music—when combined together can produce intense affective properties. Carroll and Carroll (1986) cite Aaron Copland's five broad functions for music in cinema: to create atmosphere, to emotively underline the psychological state of the character, as a background element contributing to continuity, contributing to a sense of tension and assisting with closure. Levinson (1996) conceives of some 15 individual functions for music that include Copland's points and adds functions such as: foreshadowing a dramatic event; emphasising a moment, mesmerising the viewer and using music to distract the viewer from a technical element or elements. Carroll and Carroll note the complementary relationship between music and vision and how one is able to supplement the deficiency of the other. Music applies affect wherever it occurs in a film—unlike real-life perception where music is absent. Thus music contributes to the emotive 'prefocus' processing of narrative.

Understanding how spectators process music's affective properties is best achieved through a consideration of both cognitivist and emotive elements. Jeff Smith (1999b) identifies two processes in the spectator's emotional experience: *Polarisation* implies a kind of affective shading to the narrative, while *affective congruence* combines the affective value of the music with the affective properties of the image—the combination of the two creating a more intense emotion. This recalls Carroll's own comment that both elements when combined complement each other and create a more concentrated sense of affect.

The sound mix in a film clearly also plays an important role in cueing emotion. Charles Eidsvik (2005) has considered the role of background sound, or *presence*, in cinema. He has isolated five functions for background audio: identifying location, retaining ambient sound across cuts in the same scene to minimise distraction, effect sounds as substituting for actions—such as punches hitting bodies, background tracks heard in surround speakers as underlining character situation and unusual sounds to suggest psychological complexities.

Revealing The *T. Rex*

In understanding how Spielberg orchestrates the generation of affect, I return to the *T. rex* reveal sequence from *Jurassic Park* (Chap. 7) for its manipulation of style and integration of the single reverse. The complex, staged accumulation of affect in the sequence begins with Tim (the boy) at Fig. 7.11a–e and the simple, yet inspired visual cue of the vibrating water that captures his attention and also—crucially—engages spectator *interest*. Spielberg assists in the engagement of this process of interest in two ways: narratively,[6] by having the characters helplessly stranded in an area shared by the as-yet unseen *T. rex*, and stylistically with the close-up, OP arrangement and already discussed (Chap. 7) slow, 'ominous' reversed track-in movements that emphasise both Tim's face and the vibrating water. G. M. Smith would also likely characterise this moment as an emotion marker. The rising panic in the characters and the fleeing of Gennaro from the vehicle are followed by another emotion marker in the thud of the dismembered goat leg landing on the roof of the SUV now occupied only by the two children. Like the characters, we infer that the *T. rex* must have been responsible. This hypothesising also highlights the wider strategy that sees the spectator's range of knowledge matching that of the characters—Murray Smith's *alignment*. Gennaro's desertion of the children (and their very representation as therefore innocent and vulnerable) contributes to fulfilling Murray's next step: spectator *allegiance* with them. Plotting and style has efficiently provided the affective foundation for the arrival of the *T. rex*.

> Empathetic response also depends on affective congruence between narrative context, character engagement, various uses of film style and technique, and the psychological impressions and responses they generate. (Plantinga 1999, p. 253)

The detailed attention given to developing the situation also recalls Hochberg and Brooks' (1996) observation that action is better remembered when supported by a story. Following a brief, glimpsed reveal of the *T. rex* forearm and head, Spielberg reverts to a wide reverse (Fig. 7.12a–c) for the full reveal of the dinosaur as it emerges between the two SUVs. The wide reveal is held only briefly and is followed by a close-up of Malcolm and Grant (Fig. 7.12b), which is then affectively reinforced by the reverse AP view of the passing dinosaur (Fig. 7.12c). Spielberg emphasises the helpless disposition of all the characters by initially depicting the *T. rex*'s interest in the children from Grant and Malcolm's perspective suggesting that they—like the audience—are merely spectators in the unfolding events. This encourages sympathy for the vulnerable children and suggests Carroll's 'emotive focus', where the spectator is essentially channelled into fearing for all the characters—then specifically for the welfare of the children.

This distant perspective is then immediately contrasted by placing the camera in the SUV with the children as the *T. rex* investigates them. A series of close-ups of Tim, Lex and the *T. rex*—also from the perspective of the children inside the SUV—precipitates the intense attack scene (Fig. 8.2a–j, below). Spielberg uses a direct point-of-view exchange—or reciprocal point of view (Branigan 1984, p. 117)—between the children and the *T. rex*. This part of the scene has ten shots of which seven are OP. The other three shots (Figs. 8.2b, 8.2e and 8.2i) are composed as profile shots that frame the jaws of the *T. rex* across the top half of the frame in a diagonal with the outstretched arms of the children occupying the lower half. Figures 8.2c and 8.2d are wider and function partially to orientate and establish the perspective of each angle—the former from that of the children, the latter from the *T. rex*. The three profile shots also serve to orientate in that they reveal the *T. rex* in relation to the children in a spatially distinct way. This is in contrast to the point-of-view shots, which actively muddy their relative positions—particularly when the close-ups are used. Spielberg has the children looking directly into the camera, which usually increases the level of self-consciousness, although this is undercut by the brevity of the shots. The ten shots pass in approximately 12 seconds and the tightness of the framing in Fig. 8.2f–j generates a visual and emotive intensity that distracts from the more common, mechanical and highly self-conscious use of style that the reverse point of

The Wide Reverse, Cognition and Affect 267

view usually exposes. The screaming children, bellowing *T. rex* and ambient rain sounds contribute to the emotional impact and both the audio and the situational intensity assist in smoothing over spectator registration of the rapid cutting. As T. J. Smith (2005) notes '...the cut to another viewpoint matches the viewer's perceptual inquiry. As a result the cut is not an obstruction to the viewer's perception of the event but an aid' (p. 86). The scene is then punctuated by the reference to Grant in close-up (Fig. 8.2k).

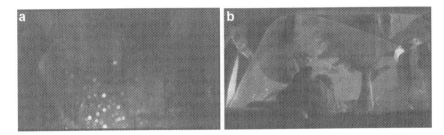

Figs. 8.2a 8.2b

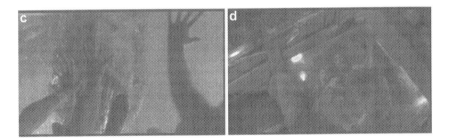

Figs. 8.2c, 8.2d

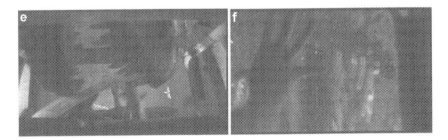

Figs. 8.2e, 8.2f

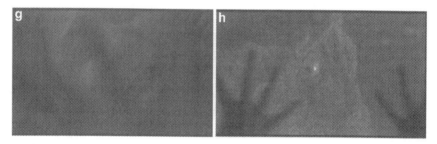

Figs. 8.2g, 8.2h

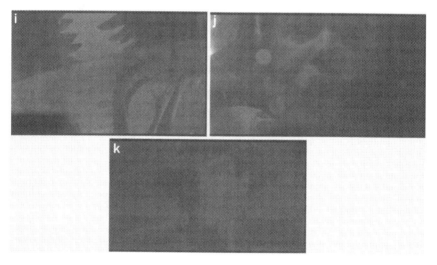

Figs. 8.2i, 8.2j, 8.2k *Jurassic Park* (1993)

Plantinga (2009a, p. 114) contends that emotional response is built out of the profilmic as referential realism when the world of the film conforms to perceptual realism in that things appear and behave as in real life. As Buckland suggests, the *T. rex* appears remarkably 'real' and perfectly integrated into the profilmic. At the same time, Spielberg does not dwell on it as novelty or spectacle. The narrative does not stop for us to admire this marvel of digital technology but instead incorporates the *T. rex* into the plot and cause-effect chain as it escapes the damaged fence and immediately threatens the children. As Spielberg and many successful filmmakers (and scholars) clearly understand, maintaining narrative relevance is a crucial tool in generating and sustaining affect. The frequent close-ups and repeated use of point-of-view arrangements are further supplemented by the associative point-of-view perspective as realised through the wide reverse. The congruence of these elements ensures that Spielberg is able to assemble a powerful set of associative and affective cues.

Notes

1. Berliner and Cohen describe the process of constructing shots to create perceptual coherence as analytical editing yet my understanding is that this term refers to the change from a wider view to a tighter one—as used in my explanation of their second point. The term constructive editing seems more appropriate to their definition of the third point (Bordwell and Thompson 2008, Ch. 6).
2. Almost in the sense that shot, reverse shot arrangements usually reverse the previous shot with oblique angles that are significantly less than the 180 degrees normally seen in the wide reverse.
3. My own anecdotal experience in teaching undergraduate production students is that, in the majority of cases, they fail to notice that they have crossed the line until the principle is explained to them.
4. Ozu's style is examined in the following chapter.
5. T. J. Smith has developed a system of attentional cues into the Attentional Theory of Cinematic Continuity (ATOCC).
6. As the principle screenwriter of *Jurassic Park*, David Koepp should also be included in the narrative aspect as a participator in the creation of spectator interest.

References

Anderson, J. D. (1996). *The Reality of Illusion: An Ecological Approach to Cognitive Film Theory*. Carbondale: Southern Illinois University Press.
Aumont, J. (1997). *The Image* (C. Pajackowska, Trans.). London: British Film Institute.

Bacon, H. (2011). The Extent of Mental Completion of Films. *Projections, 5*(2), 1–25.
Bartsch, A. (2008). Meta-Emotion: How Films and Music Videos Communicate Emotions About Emotions. *Projections, 2*(1), 45–59.
Berliner, T., & Cohen, D. J. (2011). The Illusion of Continuity: Active Perception and the Classical Editing System. *Journal of Film and Video, 63*(1), 44–63.
Bordwell, D. (1985). *Narration and the Fiction Film*. London: Routledge.
Bordwell, D. (1988). *Ozu and the Poetics of Cinema*. New Jersey: Princeton University Press.
Bordwell, D. (1989). A Case for Cognitivism. *Iris, 9*, 11–40.
Branigan, E. (1984). *Point of View in the Cinema*. Berlin: Mouton Publishers.
Brown, W. (2011). Resisting the Psycho-Logic of Intensified Continuity. *Projections, 5*(1), 69–86.
Buckland, W. (2006). *Directed by Steven Spielberg: Poetics of the Contemporary Hollywood Blockbuster*. New York: Continuum.
Carroll, N. (1990). *The Philosophy of Horror or Paradoxes of the Heart*. London: Routledge.
Carroll, N. (1996). *Theorizing the Moving Image*. Cambridge: Cambridge University Press.
Carroll, N. (2003). *Engaging the Moving Image*. New Haven: Yale University Press.
Carroll, N. (2008). *The Philosophy of Motion Pictures*. Singapore: Blackwell Publishing Ltd.
Carroll, N. (2013). *Minerva's Night Out: Philosophy, Pop Culture, and Moving Pictures*. Malaysia: Wiley Blackwell.
Carroll, N., & Carroll, P. (1986). Notes on Movie Music. *Studies in the Literary Imagination 19*(1), 73–81.
Cutting, J. E. (2005). Perceiving Scenes in Film and in the World. In J. D. Anderson & B. F. Anderson (Eds.), *Moving Image Theory: Ecological Considerations* (pp. 9–27). Carbondale: Southern Illinois University Press.
Eder, J. (2010). Understanding Characters. *Projections, 4*(1), 18–40.
Eidsvik, C. (2005). Background Tracks in Recent Cinema. In J. D. Anderson & B. F. Anderson (Eds.), *Moving Image Theory: Ecological Considerations* (pp. 70–78). Carbondale: Southern Illinois University Press.
Freeland, C. (2012). Continuity, Narrative and Cross-Modal Cuing of Attention. *Projections, 6*(1), 34–41.

Gaut, B. (1999). Identification and Emotion in Narrative Film. In C. Plantinga & G. M. Smith (Eds.), *Passionate Views: Film, Cognition, and Emotion* (pp. 200–236). Baltimore: The Johns Hopkins University Press.

Grodal, T. (1997). *Moving Pictures: A New Theory of Film Genres, Feelings, and Cognition*. New York: Oxford University Press.

Grodal, T. (2009). *Embodied Visions: Evolution, Emotion, Culture and Film*. New York: Oxford University Press.

Hall, S., & Neale, S. (2010). *Epics Spectacles and Blockbusters*. Detroit: Wayne State University Press.

Hochberg, J., & Brooks, V. (1996). Movies in the Mind's Eye. In D. Bordwell & N. Carroll (Eds.), *Post-Theory: Reconstructing Film Studies* (pp. 368–387). Madison: University of Wisconsin Press.

Hochberg, J., & Brooks, V. (2007). Film Cutting and Visual Momentum. In M. A. Peterson, B. Gillam, & H. A. Sedgwick (Eds.), *In the Mind's Eye: Julian Hochberg on the Perception of Pictures, Films, and the World* (pp. 206–228). New York: Oxford University Press.

Hogan, P. C. (2007). Sensorimotor Projection, Violations of Continuity, and Emotion in the Experience of Film. *Projections, 1*(1), 41–58.

Huff, M., & Schwan, S. (2012). Do Not Cross the Line: Heuristic Spatial Updating in Dynamic Scenes. *Psychonomic Bulletin and Review, 19*(6), 1065–1072. Retrieved from EBSCOhost MEDLINE Complete

Konigsberg, I. (2007). Film Studies and the New Science. *Projections, 1*(1), 1–24.

Kovacs, A. B. (2011). Causal Understanding and Narration. *Projections, 5*(1), 51–68.

Kraft, R. N. (1987). The Influence of Camera Angle on Comprehension and Retention of Pictorial Events. *Memory and Cognition, 15*(4), 291–307. Retrieved from http://link.springer.com/article/10.3758%2FBF03197032#page-1

Levin, D. T., & Wang, C. (2009). Spatial Representation in Cognitive Science and Film. *Projections, 3*(1), 24–52.

Levinson, J. (1996). Film Music and Narrative Agency. In D. Bordwell & N. Carroll (Eds.), *Post-Theory: Reconstructing Film Studies* (pp. 248–282). Wisconsin: The University of Wisconsin Press.

Magliano, J. P., & Sacks, J. M. (2011). The Impact of Continuity Editing in Narrative Film on Event Segmentation. *Cognitive Science, 35*(8), 1489–1517. Retrieved from EBSCOhost Education Research Complete.

McGinn, C. (2005). *The Power of Movies: How Screen and Mind Interact*. New York: Vintage Books.

Morris, N. (2007). *The Cinema of Steven Spielberg Empire of Light*. London: Wallflower Press.

Murch, W. (2001). *In the Blink of an Eye: A Perspective on Film Editing* (2nd ed.). Los Angeles: Silman-James Press.

Neill, A. (1996). Empathy and (Film) Fiction. In D. Bordwell & N. Carroll (Eds.), *Post-Theory: Reconstructing Film Studies* (pp. 175–194). Madison: University of Wisconsin Press.

Oliver, M. B., & Hartman, T. (2010). Exploring the Role of Meaningful Experiences in Users' Appreciation of 'Good Movies'. *Projections, 4*(2), 128–150.

Plantinga, C. (1999). The Scene of Empathy and the Human Face on Film. In C. Plantinga & G. M. Smith (Eds.), *Passionate Views: Film, Cognition, and Emotion* (pp. 239–256). Baltimore: The Johns Hopkins University Press.

Plantinga, C. (2009a). *Moving Viewers: American Film and the Spectator's Experience*. Berkeley/Los Angeles: University of California Press.

Plantinga, C. (2009b). Trauma, Pleasure and Emotion in the Viewing of Titanic, A Cognitive Approach. In W. Buckland (Ed.), *Film Theory and Contemporary Hollywood Movies* (pp. 237–256). New York: Routledge.

Plantinga, C. (2009c). Emotion and Affect. In P. Livingston & C. Plantinga (Eds.), *The Routledge Companion to Philosophy and Film* (pp. 86–96). New York: Routledge.

Prince, S. (2012). *Digital Visual Effects in Cinema*. New Jersey: Rutgers University Press.

Rogers, S. (2012). Auteur of Attention: The Filmmaker as Cognitive Scientist. *Projections, 6*(1), 42–48.

Shone, T. (2004). *Blockbuster*. London: Simon and Schuster.

Smith, M. (1995). *Engaging Characters*. London: Oxford University Press.

Smith, G. M. (1999a). Local Emotions, Global Moods, and Film Structure. In C. Plantinga & G. M. Smith (Eds.), *Passionate Views: Film, Cognition, and Emotion* (pp. 103–126). Baltimore: The Johns Hopkins University Press.

Smith, J. (1999b). Movie Music as Moving Music: Emotion, Cognition and the Film Score. In C. Plantinga & G. M. Smith (Eds.), *Passionate Views: Film, Cognition, and Emotion* (pp. 146–167). Baltimore: The Johns Hopkins University Press.

Smith, G. M. (2003). *Film Structure and the Emotion System*. New York: Cambridge University Press.

Smith, T. J. (2005). *An Attentional Theory of Continuity Editing*. [Unpublished PhD Thesis]. University of Edinburgh.

Smith, G. M. (2012a). Continuity Is Not Continuous. *Projections, 6*(1), 56–61.
Smith, T. J. (2012b). The Attentional Theory of Cinematic Continuity. *Projections, 6*(1), 1–28.
Tan, E. S. (1996). *Emotion and the Structure of Narrative Film: Film as an Emotion Machine*. New Jersey: Lawrence Eribaum Associates Inc.
Tan, E. S. (2005). Three Views of Facial Expression and Its Understanding in the Cinema. In J. D. Anderson & B. F. Anderson (Eds.), *Moving Image Theory: Ecological Considerations* (pp. 107–127). Carbondale: Southern Illinois University Press.
Tan, E. S., & Frijda, N. H. (1999). Sentiment in Film Viewing. In C. Plantinga & G. M. Smith (Eds.), *Passionate Views: Film, Cognition, and Emotion* (pp. 48–64). Baltimore: The John Hopkins University Press.
Zillman, D. (2005). Cinematic Creation of Emotion. In J. D. Anderson & B. F. Anderson (Eds.), *Moving Image Theory: Ecological Considerations* (pp. 164–180). Carbondale: Southern Illinois University Press.

Film Title Editions

Ozu, Y. (Director). (1961). *The End of Summer* [Motion picture, DVD (2007)]. United States: The Criterion Collection.
Spielberg, S. (Director). (1993). *Jurassic Park* [Motion picture, Blu-ray (2014)]. Australia: Universal Sony Pictures Home Entertainment.

9

Manifestations of the Wide Reverse in Mainstream Narrative Cinema

This chapter considers the issue of originality in relation to the wide reverse. This raises a number of questions: if instances of the wide reverse or variations exist in the films of other filmmakers, how similar or different are they in form and in the way they are applied to narrative when compared to Spielberg; could the work of these other filmmakers have influenced Spielberg's version of the wide reverse; and if it exists beyond Spielberg, from where did it originate?

Beginning with a brief examination of the origin of the wide reverse in classical narration, the bulk of this chapter is then divided into two sections. *Survey* identifies instances of wide reverses across a range of cinemas and eras, while the *Analysis* section contextualises their function in relation to the narration they appear in as well as comparatively with Spielberg's own systems. It is clearly beyond the scope of this study to consider all filmmakers and all films. As such, the rationale behind the choice of filmmakers and their films is based on the consideration of three limited categories. The first, *Contemporaries,* examines the so-called Movie Brats, the small group of filmmakers that emerged together with Spielberg in the early 1970s. This category also includes other directors that achieved prominence at approximately the same time in

Hollywood and who are often described as part of the 'American New Wave'. The second category, *Favourites,* examines those directors and films Spielberg himself has previously claimed to have admired and who may have exerted influence on his style, potentially contributing to the shaping of his wide reverse strategy. *Evidenced Instances* includes wide reverses or variations that I have noticed in films through my own viewing and that may logically have no connection to Spielberg but that are significant because of the application of single or multiple wide reverses.

Origin

In Chap. 6, I suggested that Spielberg's wide reverses likely evolved out of the similar shot construction found in the classical shot, reverse shot arrangement. Logically, to confirm this, exploring the development and evolution of the shot, reverse shot structure in classical narration would seem a possible strategy to pursue. Bordwell (1996) has proposed that the structure probably evolved through a process of trial and error. He cites the 'naturalist' argument that claims the shot, reverse shot simply reproduces how we would actually witness such a conversation if present and that the arrangement of shots simply reflects this.[1] At the same time, Bordwell also notes the 'arbitrary' explanation that posits the shot, reverse shot as entirely 'artificial' and that some other type of shot arrangement could have just as easily become the adopted convention. He goes on to argue that the likely explanation involves a mixture of both the 'naturalist' and the 'arbitrary'—and also includes what he describes as 'contingent universals'.

> …given certain uniformities in the environment across cultures, humans have in their social activities faced comparable tasks in surviving and creating their ways of life. Neither wholly 'natural' nor wholly 'cultural', these sorts of contingent universals are good candidates for being at least partly responsible for the 'naturalness' of artistic conventions. (p. 91)

Linked to this is Bordwell's reworking of the concept that meaning is culturally determined and contained in codes. He instead suggests that works produce a range of 'effects' of which meaning is only a component. This then frees up the potential for understanding how an artwork—or a system like the shot, reverse shot—actually functions.

Barry Salt's (1992) tracing of the development of the shot, reverse shot in classical cinema supports Bordwell's trial-and-error theory. What is intriguing about Salt's research is his identification of what is referred to in the United States as 'reverse scene' editing.[2] These are wide compositions that reveal a reverse vista through a 180-degree change in angle with the camera positioned outside the circle of action on the outer perimeter looking in (Fig. 4.2, Chap. 4). Not only is Salt identifying a typical Spielberg application of the wide reverse, the examples he discusses are from around 1900 and significantly *predate* the development of the shot, reverse shot. The earliest example he identifies appears in the short *Ladies Skirts Nailed to a Fence* (1900)[3] (Fig. 9.1a–b). The choice of a wide shot reversal in this instance is logically motivated by the scenario and the need for clarity by simply revealing the two men nailing skirts to a fence. Salt suggests that the reverse 'technique' used was inspired by lantern slides, which sometimes generated comedy by revealing action—for instance—on different sides of a fence in successive slides (pp. 55–56). Rather than relocate the camera for the reverse, Salt avers that the two women are instead moved to the other side of the fence so that we see the same side of the fence in both shots. One can speculate that this would likely have been done for convenience, it being

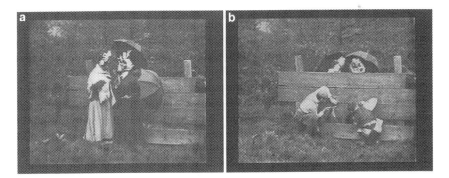

Figs. 9.1a, 9.1b *Ladies Skirts Nailed to a Fence* (1900)

easier to move the cast than the camera. Another explanation could have related to the possible unsuitability or a potential issue with the reverse vista. So while we are given the illusion that we see a different space in the reverse, the fact that only the two men are revealed further suggests that creating a new sense of scenographic space was not a priority.

Salt also discusses other early yet more complex examples of scene reversals structured around placing the camera on the outside of the scene looking in. *l'assassinat du Duc de Guise* (1904) is notable for its specially constructed set that provided for a fourth wall that enabled a reverse scene in an arrangement that was highly unusual for indoor shooting at the time. Salt points out the characteristic visual shift that sees objects initially in the foreground pushed to the background in the reverse—a commonly engineered deep space component of Spielberg's own wide reverses. Similarly, *The Romance of an Umbrella* (1909) features a reverse scene/wide reverse in an office that also would have required the dedicated construction of a 360-degree set. One clear implication, then, is that these filmmakers were consciously creating—or giving the impression of creating—a more complete scenographic space through the added versatility made possible by the combination of a 'complete' set, wide compositions and editing. According to Salt (1992) '…the sort of set-up where a scene is shown from two opposed directions in succession immediately caught on in a small way' (p. 94).

At around the beginning of the 1910s more complex variations started to appear, including early instances of the shot, reverse shot convention. Salt (1992, p. 94) uses the term reverse-angle as a kind of generic shot classification that includes all reverse cutting of more than 90 degrees and clarifies the differences between them by dividing these early instances into three variations. The first most closely resembles Spielberg's 'typical' wide reverse (Chap. 6) and is described as the '…camera far back from the actors looking in…' Salt observes that this arrangement was the least common of the reverse angle variations—its rarity likely due to the need for more complex sets for indoor shooting and a lack of function when used outdoors. Salt claims '…the use of the reverse scene was quite gratuitous, and added nothing to the exposition of the narrative from any point of view'. Salt's judgement seems to ignore the role for space itself in the application of these wide reverses. This devalues their potential function in contributing to a more comprehensive sense of the 'world' of the narration, itself most fully realised in its most recent iteration by Spielberg.

The second variation seems to more closely resemble the contemporary, conventional shot, reverse shot arrangement with the camera closer to the action but still depicting a 'behind-the-shoulders-reverse-angle'. The third, most common variation is still more conventional with the camera positioned at 'the-front-of-the-shoulder' showing each subject in a single, shot at a slightly oblique angle with 'correctly' preserved eye-lines that meet across the cut. Salt observes that 'continuity cinema' had become prevalent in the United States between 1914 and 1919.[4] Kristin Thompson (1995), in examining various national cinemas, also concurs, commenting that 'Shot/reverse shot seems to have spread quickly…' (p. 69). The superseding of this initial conception of the reverse scene/wide reverse by the now widely used, conventional form of the shot, reverse shot seems to have occurred because of a number of factors, including the pre-occupation with developing more tightly framed compositions—particularly where human subjects were concerned; the added set complexity (and hence time and cost) required for indoor 360-degree shooting likely discouraged its use; a general lack of understanding of the potential value or worth of depicting a complete view of scenographic space also contributed to its decline. These appear to have assisted in preventing the wide reverse from becoming established in any formalised way. Instead, a seemingly arbitrary range of applications of the wide reverse appears to have manifested itself across the work of various filmmakers working in different cinemas as the following section examines.

Section 1: Survey

Contemporaries

Consideration of Pye and Myles' (1979) late 1970s identification and grouping of the six movie brat directors—Martin Scorsese, John Milius, Brian de Palma, Francis Coppola, George Lucas and Spielberg, represents a reasonable starting point in the search for evidence of a shared style. In addition to the other commonalities among the six filmmakers, all but Coppola[5] were known during the early 1970s to socialise, informally assist and offer advice on each other's film projects (Pye and Myles 1979, p. 10 and p. 56). Together with Spielberg, the films of Scorsese, De Palma and Coppola all exhibit regular examples of an elaborate manipulation of style. Todd Berliner (2010) argues that Scorsese's early films display instances of 'stylistic incongruity' that recall Bordwell's definition for artistic motivation, underlined by Berliner's comments about *Taxi Driver* (1975) '...Scorsese creates idiosyncratic stylistic devices so pervasive and bold that they become a form of narration in themselves and draw inferences based on patterns in the film's style' (p. 153). Some of the overt devices Berliner identifies across the early films include the extended use of slow-motion jump-cutting, the use of non-diegetic music as counterpoint to the action and distinctive camera movement—techniques that are absent from Spielberg's films. De Palma's stylistic preoccupation in his earlier films included certain 'homages' to Hitchcock—such as the voyeurism in *Dressed to Kill* (1980) (typified by the art gallery sequence) and the revolving embrace in *Body Double* (1984), scenes that both thematically and stylistically reference *Vertigo* (1958).[6] De Palma's early films also usually included one scene shot entirely as a single shot, long take and the digital effects assisted example in *Snake Eyes* (1998) represents the culmination of this technique. De Palma has also occasionally incorporated deep focus compositions, typically achieved with the use of a lens dioptre. Neither Scorsese nor De Palma's work exhibits instances of wide reverses or demonstrates an unusual use of scenographic space. In contrast, Coppola's *Peggy Sue Got Married* (1985) displays an innovative manipulation of the reflected reverse, *One from the Heart* (1982) employs 'simulated' deep space compositions, while *Tucker: The Man and His Dream* (1989) elaborately manipulates scenographic space in multiple ways.

Favourites

With such an extensive career as a populist filmmaker, it is not surprising that Spielberg has accumulated a formidable quantity and range of quotes and comments relating to filmmakers he claims have influenced his own work. Besides the initial influence of his fellow movie brats (George Lucas in particular), Spielberg has expressed in earlier interviews an 'admiration' for the work of John Frankenheimer, Arthur Penn and Sydney Lumet, all directors originally from live television (Royal 1982). Singling out Frankenheimer's *The Manchurian Candidate* (1962), Spielberg claimed that after seeing the film '…I realized for the first time what film editing was all about' (Combs 1978). Also already noted (Chap. 3) is Spielberg's interest in Michael Curtiz and Victor Fleming—though this seems to be related primarily to their mode of production given Spielberg's comment that they lacked specific styles but were successful as 'craftsmen'. Spielberg's association with David Lean in the late 1980s included assistance with the restoration of *Lawrence of Arabia* (1962) and an aborted offer to produce Lean's intended film version of the Joseph Conrad novel, *Nostromo*. Spielberg has been effusive in his praise of Lean: 'Certainly *Lawrence of Arabia* was the film that set me on my journey' (AFI 2012). Yet Spielberg's comments on Lean's work tend to a preoccupation with the richness of his films as spectacle.

One difficulty with attempting to isolate and trace influence based on Spielberg's own comments relates to his tendency for generality. Bordwell (2008a) notes this issue together with the larger role of traditional practice in his own research in tracing the origins of a filmmaker's style.

> Sometimes norms are formulated as crisp rules, but most often they are rules of thumb and operate in the background, learned and applied without explanation or even awareness. (Filmmakers know a great deal more about their activity than they articulate). (p. 25)

This is further complicated by John Caldwell's (2008) research into how the film and television industry in California disseminates information about its own production practice. Information circulated among industry professionals may often significantly transform into something else when subsequently made available to the media and public. Caldwell notes that this is also then coloured by what he calls the 'inverse credibility law'.

> The higher one travels up the industrial food chain for insights, the more suspect and spin-driven the personal disclosures tend to become'. (p. 3)

This is not to imply that everything Spielberg utters is untrue or 'spin-driven'; rather his comments need to be considered in the context of the period of their recording and the nature of the media in which they appear. His high public profile and positioning as 'a signature' and commodity also undoubtedly influences what he says with the overriding requirement being that it be of a suitably general nature and appropriate for general consumption. This is reflected in the numerous so-called fan websites such as the internet Movie Database and www.listal.com, which purport to list Spielberg's ten favourite films complete with comments from him discussing the listed films. The significance of this information is further diminished by the knowledge that Spielberg has, over the course of many years, commented favourably on many different films, thus enabling the compilers of such lists to effectively 'cherry-pick' titles.

And yet his comments do occasionally suggest a potential link and influence with style in the work of others. Given John Ford's legendary disdain for discussing his own style (most infamously realised in his one-word answers to interviewer Peter Bogdanovich), a certain irony emerges in that it is when discussing Ford that Spielberg most clearly proffers insight into Ford's possible influence on his own practice.

> The way he stages and blocks his people [cast] often keeping the camera static while the people give you the illusion there is a lot more kinetic movement occurring when there is not. (AFI 2013)

This recalls Spielberg's own, similar staging strategy (Chap. 5) that sees him often moving actors around in the frame in scenes that also minimise camera movement and editing. The 'homage' to Ford is most generally (or perhaps generically) expressed in the opening scenes of *Indiana Jones and the Last Crusade* (1989), which offer the kind of Monument Valley-like mise en scene often associated with Ford.

In terms of staging and deep space, Spielberg also acknowledges the influence of Orson Welles, though his comments on Welles again tend to generalisation. Numerous other critics have noted the connection between the two. Writing about Spielberg in *The New Yorker*, Stephen Schiff (1994) asserts,

> And no one since Orson Welles has understood so deeply how to stage a shot, how to shift the viewer's eye from foreground to background, how to shuttle characters and incidents in and out of the frame at precisely the right moment... (pp. 178–179)

As discussed in Chap. 5, the greatest 'clue' to Welles' influence on Spielberg is suggested by Spielberg's similar fondness for tri-layered compositions in depth. Despite the compelling link to deep space practice, Welles never applies a wide reverse in his films and I detected only one distinct instance in Ford's *Steamboat Round the Bend* (1935).[7]

Stanley Kubrick is another filmmaker that Spielberg has spoken of at length. Their initial collaboration on what became *A.I. Artificial Intelligence* (2001) following Kubrick's death is well known. Kubrick's overt use of style is also well documented (Baxter 1997; Walker et al. 1999), particularly the repeated use of travelling shots with the subject frontally following a reversing camera and profiled tracking shots. Wide reverses are rare—I detected only one scene in *The Shining* (1980) and it is considered in the following section.

Of all the filmmakers Spielberg has acknowledged or claimed to have admired, it is the films of Alfred Hitchcock that display the greatest instances of wide reverses and variations. Joseph McBride (1997, p. 120) notes that Spielberg 'absolutely revered' Hitchcock's features and television series and that Spielberg was removed from Hitchcock sets on two occasions: during soundstage shooting for *Torn Curtain* in 1965 and again during the production of *Family Plot* in 1975. Quoting an apparent friend of Spielberg from his time at college, McBride records that in discussing Hitchcock, Spielberg '…would talk about camera movements and all this kind of stuff…' (p. 121). Spielberg's use of the '*Vertigo* effect' (simultaneously zooming in and tracking out) in *Sugarland Express, Jaws* and *Poltergeist* further suggests Hitchcock's influence on Spielberg's own style. Hitchcock does employ numerous instances of the construction of 360-degree scenographic space and does so by utilising both wide reverse variations and piecemeal, constructivist assemblages.

Evidenced Instances

This category is defined by the appearance of at least one instance of a wide reverse arrangement in a film by a director not known to have been considered or acknowledged by Spielberg in any of his *publicly* recorded comments. The frequency of detected reverses within a filmmaker's work ranges from the single instance in George Stevens' *Giant* (1956), to the contrasting, extreme case of the later films of Yasujiro Ozu.

Section 2: Analysis

The variation in the types of wide reverses detected in the survey has resulted in the identification of three specific categories. These are: *Incidental Use, Occasional Variation* and *Institutional Variation*. The first refers to those filmmakers in which a wide reverse construction appears rarely in their body of work. In each of these instances, the reverse functions primarily to service narrative demands and contributes to plot development. The construction of scenographic space operates submissively and appears incidental to the main function. This is (usually) the revealing of objects occupying the constructed space—much like the early example from *Ladies Skirts Nailed to a Fence*, which utilises a wide reverse to reveal the two men.

Occasional variation includes those filmmakers that have made use of wide reverses in more than one of their films and in a way that may involve variation in frame size and the ordering of shots. While these instances still prioritise style, they also suggest a greater prominence for space. Included in this category is an examination of Max Ophuls' use of mirrors to generate reflected reverses.

Institutional variation applies to only one filmmaker, Yasijuro Ozu. His unique, highly formalised system for deploying what is essentially another variation of the wide reverse can be seen operating in consistent patterns in all of his films from the early 1930s until his last film in 1962. Film scholars, including Bordwell and Thompson (Bordwell 1988; Bordwell and Thompson 1976), Stephen Heath (1976), Edward Branigan (1976), Donald Ritchie (1974) and Noël Burch (1979) have all studied Ozu's 'unique' strategy that partly functions around the 180- and 360-degree construction of scenographic space.

Incidental Use

Considered '…one of the great American filmmakers…' (Hopwood), George Stevens directed and produced a number of highly popular features in a range of genres during his four-decade long Hollywood career.

Paul Cronin (2004) notes that Stevens never received the kind of artistic recognition bestowed by the *Cahiers* critics on contemporaries like Nicholas Ray, Hitchcock or Ford. 'But in several crucial respects, Stevens—a director who rarely accepted studio assignments, preferring instead to initiate projects himself—can certainly be considered as the 'author' of his films' (p. ix). Having surveyed 11 of the 26 features Stevens directed, I observed only one example of a single shot, wide reverse and it appears in *Giant* (1956) (Fig. 9.2a–b). Stevens' preference for shooting large amounts of coverage is well documented '… Stevens was maniacal about reshooting the scene from every angle he could think of' (Bordwell 2006). *Giant* cinematographer, William Mellor, similarly commented that Stevens would shoot '…about three times the usual amount of film' (Cronin 2004, p. xi). Given Stevens' predilection for overshooting, we can assume that there would have been other instances where he likely would have shot wide reverses, most probably as reverse masters—though clearly the choice was made to not use them in any final cut. Regardless of whether Stevens did or did not shoot them, the wide reverse that appears in *Giant* functions to explicitly satisfy the plot requirements for that scene. In this instance, the wide reverse services part of a sequence set in a diner that involves a confrontation between Jordan Benedict (Rock Hudson) and the proprietor and that attracts the attention of all present. Figure 9.2a is a partial master shot and is repeatedly reused during this sequence. Figure 9.2b appears only once and it does elaborate on the scenographic space behind the characters from the previous shot as well as expose the space occupied by the camera—now replaced with a wall and associated set dressing. Its primary duty is to show that the altercation has captured the attention of all, itself emphasising the escalating seriousness of the unfolding situation. The wide reverse seemingly treats the reveal of space in a rigorously classical manner by making it subservient to narrative requirements. The exposing of the space occupied by the camera occurs largely as a by-product of the reverse shot rather than as part of a conscious strategy. The revealing (literally) of the 'fourth' wall and pictures is more a necessary requirement for preserving the studio set as a verisimilitude representation of a 'real' roadside diner.

However, placing the camera outside the circle of action looking in means that the reverse does also create a contrasting deep space, deep focus composition, which 'forces' the spectator to consider not only the objects in this newly revealed space but the space itself.

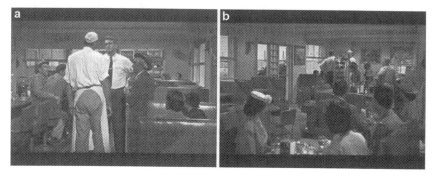

Figs. 9.2a, 9.2b   *Giant* (1956)

This one-off, isolated application of the wide reverse appears consistent with its use among the vast majority of films within classical narrative, both past and present. I have used the Stevens example as representative of filmmakers that have employed a wide reverse structure in one of their films and then rarely or never repeat its use. Contemporary directors from different national cinemas like David Fincher and Michael Mann (Hollywood), Takeshi Kitano (Japan) and Peter Greenaway (UK) still operate within the classical paradigm (with Greenaway perhaps more in the art-cinema domain). Yet they construct their narratives in varying ways and all have employed a wide reverse in at least one of their features. Of the films Fincher has directed, only one, *The Social Network* (2010), includes a single instance of a wide reverse and its application seems arbitrary. The location in which it appears—a rowing training facility—and the situation it depicts there does not actively benefit from its use other than to add variation to Fincher's application of coverage—similar to Bordwell's idea of the 'anthology' approach of varying style from scene to scene as he observes in Dreyer (considered later in this section).

A similar instance occurs in Greenaway's *Belly of an Architect* (1987) where the use of a single, wide reverse early in the film (Fig. 9.3a–b) functions to visually contribute expository information directly relevant to the plot. Greenaway's preference for 'flat' tableau-like or planimetric compositions (Fig. 9.3a, c) recalls Wes Anderson's own style with characters arranged in a perpendicular fashion across the frame in a highly formalised, theatrical-like presentation—or as Greenaway (1982) himself observes '…visually symmetrically balanced…' The composition also invokes painterly associations; Greenaway mentions a baroque influence partially reflected in the minimising of the human figure while also providing a ready opportunity for the inclusion of a geometrically matching reverse as in Fig. 9.3b.

Figs. 9.3a, 9.3b, 9.3c *Belly of an Architect* (1987)

Like Greenaway, Kitano also occasionally invokes planimetric compositions. The first three shots of *A Scene at the Sea* (1991) visually establish the locale, the main character and his occupation via a set of 180-degree reverses that begins with a wide shot of the seaside, a reverse tight two shot of Shigeru, (the protagonist) and his work colleague sitting in the cabin of a truck. Another 180-degree reverse wide from behind the truck looking out to sea effectively ties together the first two shots by revealing the kind of vehicle the men are sitting in (a garbage compactor) as well as the truck's beach car park location, which explains the vista from the first shot. Despite the recurring planimetric compositions in this film and in other Kitano films (*Sonatine* (1993) in particular), the wide reverse combination is not repeated.

Michael Mann invokes wide reverses in two separate scenes for *The Insider* (1999) with the second instance appearing in a Japanese restaurant location with the tighter reverse (Fig. 9.4b) cut into a profile master (Fig. 9.4a, c). This combination is relatively unusual for classical narrative with its convention for remaining on one side of the 'line' and in fact recalls Eisenstein's punctuation reversal or *impact reverse*—as I label it—first considered in Chap. 6. Mann shoots the entire scene on the same side of the line as Fig. 9.4a with over shoulder singles and wider two shots that preserve a similar oblique angle in a cutting pattern that is classically conventional. The insertion of the reverse (Fig. 9.4b) breaks this convention by crossing the line of action while the profiled framing of the two shots (Fig. 9.4a, b) also contrasts the angled, over-shoulder framing used for all other shots. One would expect that the anomalous appearance of the reverse and the profiled compositions fulfil some kind of narrative function (as I explain later is the case with Max Ophuls), yet this remains unclear. Each of the three shots are of the same length at approximately four seconds and the scene begins with a wider, angled establishing two-shot that runs for approximately 14 seconds. This is followed by reverses of eight seconds and 12 seconds and then shots of only two and three seconds, so using the reverse to quicken shot duration seems unlikely. Rather, the insertion of the reverse together with the profiled compositions suggests that these shots are more about providing visual variety to the over-shoulder reverses that constitute the bulk of the scene. Mann employs the reverse not to satisfy narrative demands or to construct space but to create an alternative composition, a fresh perspective. The implication in this instance is that the reverse is essentially servicing compositional variation with the revealing of space an intended but largely arbitrary by-product.

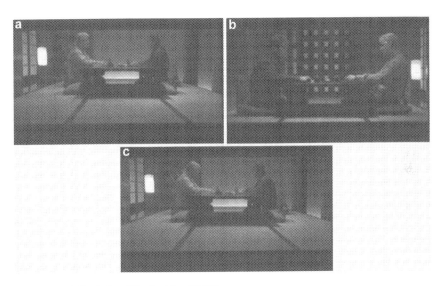

Figs. 9.4a, 9.4b, 9.4c   *The Insider* (1999)

In *The Shining* (1980), Stanley Kubrick uses a wide reverse to establish space and to visually structure the scene so that it begins wide and then conventionally tightens to singles for dramatic emphasis as the point of the scene is revealed. Figure 9.5a establishes the washroom space and then cuts to the tighter 180-degree reverse at Fig. 9.5b immediately after Grady (the waiter) identifies himself. Jack is surprised by Grady's information and Kubrick uses the line cross to the reverse, tighter angle to emphasise Jack's reaction in what is effectively another variation of Eisenstein's impact reverse. Kubrick briefly returns to the wide at Fig. 9.5c and then reverses again to the same shot as Fig. 9.5b for most of the scene and for the single, dialogue reverses.

Figs. 9.5a, 9.5b, 9.5c   The Shining (1980)

Jean-Luc Godard's *La Chinoise* (1967), like many of his films, undermines notions of conventional narrative construction by breaking the 'illusion' of the fictional spatial construct that makes up the world of the film. In this instance, Godard has actor Jean-Pierre Leaud acknowledge the filmmaking process by mentioning the crew and addressing the camera (Fig. 9.6a). Godard then confirms this acknowledgement with a 180-degree reverse that 'reveals' the camera complete with operator (Fig. 9.6b),[8] a shot that is repeated twice more during the scene. An element of Godard's playfulness lies in his refusal to then identify the second camera that is inevitably photographing the image of the first—the 'actual' camera.

Manifestations of the Wide Reverse in Mainstream Narrative... 291

Figs. 9.6a, 9.6b *La chinoise* (1967)

In his writings on the films of Buster Keaton, Noël Carroll (2007) identifies what he describes as a 'field reversal' in Keaton's *The General* (1926) (Fig. 9.7a–c). This is an instance of a wide reverse and Carroll suggests that the reversal is motivated by an intention to more clearly represent visually the nature of the 'gag'. In this case it is a following cannon, which threatens to fire at any moment.

> ...field reversal also gives the audience more data about the relative positions of the two objects, eliciting from the audience a felt sense of depth via the systematic permutation of screen configurations. (p. 114)

Carroll explains that this reversal is part of a wider strategy deployed by Keaton for constructing space to better convince the spectator of the implications of the situation. Carroll considers this in terms of an 'authenticity hypothesis' where the use of wide shots confirm that the stunts are actual '…[the] long shot confirms our sense of the real risk…' (p. 77). In the interest of preserving 'reality', Carroll notes that Keaton apparently abandoned impossible trick stunts because of the resulting implication that the actual, highly dangerous stunts might also be faked.[9] Carroll writes of the reverse as highlighting both foreground and background elements based on each being emphasised as it is reversed. This assists in a more comprehensive understanding of the relation between relevant objects—such as the danger presented by the following mortar through placing the camera on the same sightline or trajectory that it appears to be aiming at. Figure 9.7a highlights the foregrounded mortar and its target while the reverse at Fig. 9.7b emphasises where the fired shell is likely to impact. Not only does it visually represent the danger, but it also positions Keaton as caught in the middle in a way that only this angle can convey. The wide reverse and the 360-degree reveal of scenographic space also encourages the perception that Keaton is alone and that there is nowhere for him to hide.

> Keaton's cinematic techniques, then, make comparable cognitive experiences available to the audience by making the pertinent physical variable and their relationships salient, thereby affording the audience, non-reflectively and automatically, the kind of insight and bodily understanding of the physical environment that is presupposed by the character's successful concrete manipulations of troublesome objects. (p. 121)

Figs. 9.7a, 9.7b, 9.7c *The General* (1926)

Notions of genre specificity are also relevant here. Unlike Spielberg, who has worked across multiple genres, a mainstream Hollywood-centric director like Michael Bay tends to make films similar in type and constructs narrative using a fairly specific, unvarying visual style. Woody Allen operates at the opposite stylistic 'scale' with an approach that tends to downplay the significance of editing and visual style, preferring minimal coverage and few close-ups. Both 'types' of filmmakers conceive a different function for style and both are equally unlikely to see a role for the wide reverse.

Occasional Variation

Danish director Carl Theodor Dreyer made fewer than 20 features in a career that spanned almost 40 years. One of the most intriguing aspects of his work was his career-long experimentation with constructing scenographic space while operating within classical narrative convention. This is especially so for the later films in which he explored stylistic alternatives to the customary way of creating space while still operating within the broad conventions of classical narrative. Of particular interest is Dreyer's manipulation of space across different eras of narrative cinema beginning with the largely fixed camera of the late tableau period through to the introduction of sound and the well-established, dominant classical narrative form that mainstream cinema had evolved into by the time of his last film, *Gertrud* (1964). Bordwell (1981) observes that with his last three films, Dreyer essentially modifies but does not entirely dispense with the minimal depth, predominantly frontal compositions common in the earlier films.

> Instead of the missing fourth wall of customary filmmaking, the late films utilise a 'circular' mise en scene that insists on the total enclosure of the interior (p. 62).

Bordwell points to evidence of this in *Master of the House* (1925) where a 360-degree perspective of the main living space is slowly constructed across the film by having different scenes portray the same area from different angles thus cumulatively assembling a complete space. By *Day of Wrath* (1943), we see the manifestation of two wide reverses. Figure 9.8b is a 180-degree reverse of Fig. 9.8a and the next cut to Fig. 9.8c is another 180-degree reverse that returns to the first angle. This arrangement recalls the similar construction for *The Insider* and *The Shining* where the reverses (Figs. 9.4b and 9.5b respectively) cross the line of action and are more tightly framed. The change in frame size from Fig. 9.8a–b emphasises the cut, producing an impact reverse, but the extreme change in the shot size from a loose mid to a tight, medium close-up, two shot also invokes Hitchcock's 'smallest to biggest' contrast. Crossing the line into a tight two-shot adds emphasis because it creates a completely new composition with the characters' faces effectively exchanging places in the frame—producing a fleeting moment of intimacy that is abruptly curtailed as the shot then reverts to the 'distant' profile of Fig. 9.8c.

Figure 9.8a, c does not qualify as tableau-like in the sense of a 'primitive' cinema but it does recall Bordwell's conception of the Dreyer tableau where character is forced to compete with the surroundings. The characters in Fig. 9.8a seem almost enveloped by the bleakness from the heavy shadows, dark costumes and set decoration. This harshness is then further accentuated when juxtaposed with the reverse close-up.

> …the faces gain an unusual salience through their opposition to the tableau. Close-up or medium close-up, these shots shift us into another realm. Whereas in the tableau, the figure is subordinated to architecture, light and decor, in the facial shots the human countenance triumphs over the surroundings. (p. 51)

Bordwell points out that despite Dreyer's privileging of space and the on-going dialectic between it and character for prominence within the mise en scene, it is the deployment of the close-up that ultimately confirms the anthropocentric nature of his narrative. In the final analysis, then, narrative demands override those of space, thus aligning Dreyer's narration with conventional classical practice.

I argue that the comparison with Spielberg is intriguing in that for a filmmaker whose practice is so readily dismissed as conventional and

Manifestations of the Wide Reverse in Mainstream Narrative... 295

conservative, his application of the wide reverse demonstrates a more aggressively active role for space than seemingly less classically aligned filmmakers like Dreyer. There is no question that the facial close-up plays a crucial and recurring role in Spielberg's stylistic strategy. I have already considered the emotive significance of the face in Chap. 8 and examples such as the Neary close encounter and ferry scene (Chap. 6) both essentially terminate with close-ups. Yet many more wide reverse scenes do not resolve in this way, but instead privilege scenographic space. This is also seen in the deep space compositions examined in Chap. 5, where I point out that Spielberg is able to combine the facial close-up with a deep space vista together in the same shot.

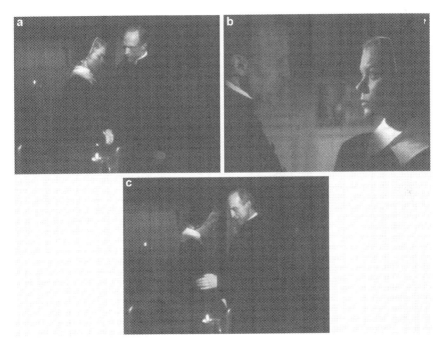

Figs. 9.8a, 9.8b, 9.8c *Day of Wrath* (1943)

Following on from the wide reverse in Fig. 9.8a–c, Dreyer repeats the same pattern again later in the same scene. The first instance involved the priest Absalon and his wife, Anne, while the second instance has Anne embracing her lover, Martin. Dreyer repeats the 180-degree reverse in the second instance to draw comparisons between the two events. As Bordwell observes, '…a narrative parallel arises from the jump in orientation' (p. 123). The repeated use of the wide reverse in the same sequence negates any sense of arbitrariness—Dreyer gives the reverses a highly specialised role in contributing significance to the narrative. At the same time, the reverses also service the construction of scenographic space, fulfilling Bordwell's claim that Dreyer intentionally creates a 'circular' mise en scene (p. 62). Having used the reverses twice in the same sequence in *Day of Wrath*, Dreyer chooses not to use them again, though he does employ a variation in *Gertrud* (1964) and a wide reverse is used to initiate the climax in *Ordet* (1955).

While Dreyer employs the wide reverse sparingly, he does utilise the reverse tracking shot repeatedly in the later films. *Day of Wrath* features four tracking shots that vary from 180 degrees to an elaborate 360-degree track during the final funeral scene. Figure 9.9a–c shows Absalon arriving to visit a dying priest and the shot begins with him entering the room (Fig. 9.9a) and tracks backwards while panning left to take in the room including the waiting nurse (Fig. 9.9b). The shot continues to pan and track back until it settles on the bedridden priest (Fig. 9.9c) at which point Absalon re-enters at frame right. The path taken by the camera ends in an approximate 180-degree reversal and the shot suggests similarity with Spielberg's own track reversals. Yet Dreyer employs a number of notable variations. Absalon's entry initially motivates the camera movement though it is unusual in classical narrative for that agent to then be left behind for most of the duration of the shot only to reappear near its end. The shot's seemingly anticipatory path recalls F.W. Murnau's extended tracking shot from *Sunrise* (1927), which takes a shortcut and arrives at its destination before the protagonist it was initially tracking. It is another example of Dreyer fusing classical practice with his own modification of it. For the brief body of the shot where Absalon is absent, Dreyer is actually prioritising space and the deliberate, unhurried motion of the camera's '…slow, stately cadence…' (Milne 1971, p. 26) emphasises this.

> The evocative quality of Dreyer's early films stems in part from the way that decors become narratively peripheral but visually prominent. (Bordwell 1981, p. 49)

Bordwell may be referring to Dreyer's tableau films but the concern with revealing space is certainly relevant with this reverse track. Again, the parallels with Spielberg's reverse tracks are self-evident though Spielberg's rigorous classicism forces him to cache his camera movements within a seeming sense of conventionalism. With Spielberg, any movement of the camera is inevitably and continuously motivated by character and/or subject movement.

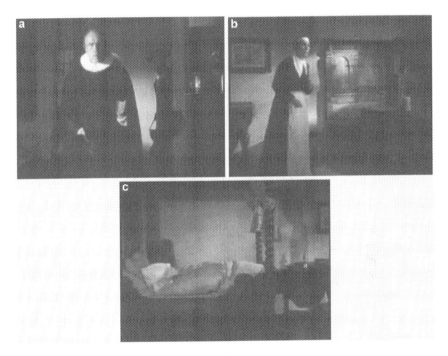

Figs. 9.9a, 9.9b, 9.9c *Day of Wrath* (1943)

Ordet (1955) also features Dreyer's characteristic, temporally measured 180-degree reverse tracks. An almost 360-degree track, pan combination occurs early in the film and functions primarily to establish the film's main living room space. Of more relevance to Spielberg's practice is a semicircular 180-degree track (Fig. 9.10a–c) that begins with Johannes on the right of frame and then slowly tracks around him and his niece,

Maren, until their positions are reversed in the frame. I examined Spielberg's similar version of this move in *Minority Report* (Fig. 7.18a–d) and noted that this particular camera shot has become relatively common in classical cinema, often employed to generate visual energy and depth in an otherwise static scene. Yet Spielberg displays more artistry in the way he merges the shot into adjacent shots and hence also reduces its degree of self-consciousness. As mentioned in Chap. 7, the end of the track fluidly introduces the video projection that continues the sequence. In *Ordet*, Dreyer follows the track with an abrupt cut to Mikkel entering the room. One assumes that this abruptness is entirely intentional, that Dreyer wants to stir us from Johannes' gloomy monologue with a sudden change. While this is entirely valid, the contrast with Spielberg's smooth transitions also continues to emphasise his key stylistic strategy relating to authorial absence—aggressively activating style while simultaneously cloaking its presence.

Figs. 9.10a, 9.10b, 9.10c   *Ordet* (1955)

The cinema of Alfred Hitchcock is well known for the prominent role often given to style in constructing narrative and evidence of this appears in almost all of his features. Examples include his experimentation with early sound technology and the amplification of the word knife in *Blackmail* (1929); the long takes in *Rope* (1951); the elaborate studio set for *Rear Window* and the zoom in, track out effect designed for *Vertigo* (1958). Each is an instance of the many creative applications he applied to style and mise-en-scene in the service of storytelling—always while operating within the paradigm of classical style.

As with Dreyer, Hitchcock's career spanned across both the pre- and post-sound eras though Hitchcock's earliest films were created after the passing of the tableau phase and already feature extensive use of close-ups. *The Lodger* (1927) includes the innovative spatial (and perspectival) device of having a ceiling appear transparent, revealing an upstairs room with the suspicious tenant pacing anxiously. By the early 1950s, and seen in *Dial M for Murder* (1954), Hitchcock is shooting some scenes with a kind of macro-constructivist approach that pieces together a set space with various angles that, when cut together, reveal a 360-degree view, similar to the process employed by Dreyer in *Master of the House*. With most of *Dial M for Murder* confined to the main living room area, Hitchcock sustains the repeated use of the same space by providing variation in camera positioning. This is achieved with a mixture of shot, reverse shot compositions of varying sizes, a high camera position looking down, as well as shots taken from a low, floor level camera looking up that gradually build a 360-degree view of the living room. Henry Bumstead, Art Director on two Hitchcock features, notes,

> One thing about Hitch, when you did a set for him, he shot the whole set, you know what I mean? Some directors, you do a nice set and they get themselves over in the corner and that's all you ever see, the corner. (Bouzereau 1997)

Despite Hitchcock's preference for the extensive revealing of space, wide reverses as single or two shot constructions are rare in his films. Only *The Man Who Knew Too Much* (1956) and *Frenzy* (1972) each contain a wide reverse with *Frenzy* saving its instance for the last two shots of the film. The example from *The Man Who Knew Too Much* (Fig. 9.11a–b) emphasises the emptiness of the hurriedly cleared space (Ambrose Chapel) while simultaneously revealing a 360-degree perspective. More commonly, Hitchcock shoots part of a scene from one wide establishing angle, follows this with tighter coverage of various sizes (which often also reveal previously unseen space) and then provides a wide reverse later in the scene. This occurs in the first hotel room scenes in Marrakesh and London and in the Marrakesh restaurant scene. The restaurant scene utilises multiple wide reverses but this coverage is motivated primarily by the arrangement of the two couples that sit facing each other. Hitchcock places the camera inside the circle of action between each couple with a composition that also reveals much of the restaurant in each reverse shot. An early scene in Midge's apartment in *Vertigo* (1958) uses a constructivist strategy to gradually build up space shot by shot until all four walls have been revealed. A scene in Gavin's shipbuilding office uses the same approach but doesn't quite reveal the entire space, instead exposing approximately 270 degrees of the area, and Hitchcock tends to vary the amount of exposure at somewhere between 270 and 360 degrees. Part of the efficiency of this piecemeal construction of space lies in Hitchcock's highly mobile staging. During the course of the scene, one character moves around the room simultaneously motivating camera movement, thus also revealing scenographic space.

In true classical convention, not only is the camera motivated by character movement, but space is in turn revealed by emphasising character prominence. The subservient role for space is further noted in Hitchcock's discussions with Truffaut (1983, pp. 210–212) where Hitchcock stressed the importance of resisting the temptation to 'open up' those films adapted from stage plays (such as *Dial M for Murder*). He argued that a large part of their success as theatre plays stemmed from their spatial confinement and that it was important to preserve this in the screen versions. This suggests a further de-emphasised role for space by acknowledging its potential to distort and even distract plot specificity. This further implies that the complete space in the living room set in *Dial M for Murder* is more about visual variation than the need to construct space. At the same time, Hitchcock occasionally employs unmotivated

Manifestations of the Wide Reverse in Mainstream Narrative... 301

camera movements like the long, single shot track across the dance floor that ends in a close-up of the perpetrator in *Young and Innocent* (1937) or the high, wide shot that cranes down to a close-up of Alicia's hand grasping a key in *Notorious* (1946). In each instance, the high degree of self-consciousness suggests authorial presence, much like Hitchcock directly addressing the audience to tell us 'Take note, this shot contains important plot information'.

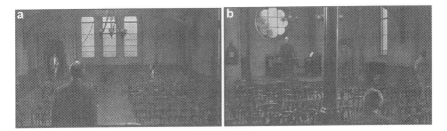

Figs. 9.11a, 9.11b *The Man Who Knew Too Much* (1956)

In *Vertigo*, Hitchcock utilises a relatively unmotivated 180-degree pan and track in Scottie's apartment (Fig. 9.12a–c) that begins at the fireplace and pans through to the reverse angle revealing Madeline sleeping in the adjacent bedroom. The shot is partially motivated by Scottie's (James Stewart) eye-line as he briefly peers left off-screen and the camera then pans around to reveal Madeline in a variation of Branigan's point/glance, point/object fusion examined in the *A.I.* example (Fig. 7.17a–d). Here the space in Scottie's apartment is revealed and simultaneously established via his off-screen glance with the smallest action of a character 'permitting' the camera to construct space. Like Spielberg, Hitchcock saves the greater exploration of space for those scenes with greater narrative significance. Instances include the reveal of Madeline in Scottie's bedroom, the exploration of Scottie's vertigo condition (as exposition) in Midge's apartment or the carefully constructed reveal of Mark's office in *Marnie* (1964), a set seen only once in the film but in which Mark's overt romance with Marnie begins, initiating a central plot device.

Figs. 9.12a, 9.12b, 9.12c *Vertigo* (1958)

The directing career of Max Ophuls is of interest here in part for his transition from making films in Europe to Hollywood—in itself not unusual during the 1930s as many European filmmakers fled to Hollywood—but that he subsequently returned to Europe to resume his career having made four features in the US.[10] Ophuls made use of wide reverses in both his American films and the later European ones. His style is noted for its protracted, moving camera compositions that often involve 360-degree tracking pans across ballroom floors—as in the double 360-degree pan, track in *La Signora Di Tutti* (1934), which he then caps with a remarkable 360-degree reverse whip pan. Other instances include the 360-degree pan, track on the dance floor in the *Palais de la Danse* in *Le Plaisir* (1952) or the elaborate ballroom montage in *Madam de...* (1953) that includes a 360-degree track, pan as the couple dance around the orchestra situated in the centre of the room, which is then followed by another 360-degree track, pan in the next sequence. Then there are the 360-degree tracking shots that occur elsewhere—such as the spiralling track, pan that follows the Raconteur (Anton Walbrook) and opens *La Ronde* (1950) and the other spiralling tilting up shot that follows Lucia (Joan Bennett) up the staircase in *The Reckless Moment*

(1949). Each of these shots seeks to construct a complete space, though the significance accorded space in each case differs considerably to the role space plays in Spielberg. The 360-degree tracks in *La Signore Di Tutti* frame their subjects tightly and comprehending scenographic space seems problematic, much like the almost 360-degree track, pan through the art gallery in *Le Plaisir*, which merely constructs a maze-like space and does little to orientate the audience. The dance floor track from *Le Plaisir* mentioned earlier that follows the dancing Monsieur Grandual also varies in composition between *Plan Americain* (tight full-shot) and a midshot. In all of these instances, the shot and its movement is unambiguously motivated by character action with the décor and architecture pushed literally into the background. Yet Ophuls scholar Alan Williams (1980) argues that this elaborate visual style has a tendency to overwhelm.

> …character 'identification' is often inhibited (the actors are frequently buried under layers of costumes and photographed through elaborate lattices); any possible feeling of 'realism' is reduced (the camera's presence is too obvious)… (p. 10)

The 360-degree coverage constructs space, but what kind of space? While Ophuls uses the 360-degree coverage to create a complete space, the roving camera in the process (according to Williams) draws attention to itself and therefore to the narrator—Ophuls (and *Le Plaisir* literally has a narrator in the form of the Raconteur who addresses the camera). The paradox here is that in creating a complete space Ophuls is actually baring the artifice, suggesting that Ophuls is not interested in reality but in creating what I would describe as a complete theatrical stage space. Ophuls creates a theatre area complete with a 360-degree scenographic space.

Four of his films do include wide reverse sequences comparable to those of Spielberg. *Caught* (1949) includes two wide reverse sequences. The first shows Smith and Leonora in a tense discussion while positioned at opposite sides of a large film projection room (Fig. 9.13a–b). Ophuls intercuts three reverses of each of the two shots and the wide framing and deep space composition results in each functioning essentially as reverse masters—a strategy seen repeatedly in Spielberg (Chap. 6). Lutz Bacher (1996) comments on the '…unconventional staging…' (p. 219) and the contravention of the 180-degree rule with each of the two shots photographed by positioning the camera on different sides of the axis of action. Any confusion that might result as a consequence of the mismatched eye-lines (they are both looking in the same direction—left to right) is alleviated by the wide framing of both and, as Bacher observes, results in a graphic match across the shots with both characters occupying the same frame space. This visually reinforces the confrontation between them while the oddness of the composition contributes a sense of uneasiness to the scene. The reverses also accentuate the distance between the two characters and Mary Ann Doane (1987) notes '…the deployment of space inscribes a hyperbolized distance between Ohlrig and Leonora' (p. 159). As with Spielberg's tendency to reserve the deployment of wide reverses for narratively significant events, Doane points out that the scene '…marks an important turning point in the narrative' (p. 162), as it lays bare the deteriorating relationship between the two characters.

Figs. 9.13a, 9.13b *Caught* (1949)

The second instance, also from *Caught* (Fig. 9.14a–b), appears during another confrontation scene—though the staging and positioning of the actors make the conflict more overt. Figure 9.14a functions as the master and the wide reverse exchange begins and ends with this shot. The reverse (Fig. 9.14b) is used twice and Ophuls also inserts an exchange of close-ups for both at the climactic point of the scene when Smith reveals to Quinada that he is married to Leonora. As with the previous instance earlier in the film (Fig. 9.13a–b), the wide reverses here also reinforce the adversarial relationship between the two characters. Ophuls maintains

Manifestations of the Wide Reverse in Mainstream Narrative... 305

the distance between them throughout while Smith's one step forward triggers the smooth insertion of a set of close-ups.

The similarities to Spielberg's wide reverses are striking. The deep space compositions, particularly in the first example, the aggressively foregrounded characters, the clear revealing of the 'fourth wall' and the space occupied by the camera in the previous shot—all regular components of Spielberg's practice—all are on display here. Yet there is a fairly subtle distinction in the way each director utilises the space created by the reverses. While Ophuls is well known for utilising a travelling camera that elaborately follows its subjects across studio sets, he seems less interested in creating a complete scenographic space. With the exception of the examples examined here and the 360-degree tracks mentioned earlier, he rarely reveals the fourth wall, unlike Dreyer or Spielberg who do so regularly. So the intention for Ophuls in deploying wide reverses is—in the best classical tradition—purely about servicing narrative requirements with the space between the characters literally connoting the nature of their relationship. This is borne out when we consider the remaining two instances of reverses by Ophuls.

Figs. 9.14a, 9.14b *Caught* (1949)

Bordwell (1981, p. 165) proposes the concept of 'sparseness' and quotes Meir Sternberg when describing one of Dreyer's key stylistic strategies in *Ordet* and the same concept applies to Ophuls and his use of wide reverses. Sparseness essentially holds that the less a stylistic device is employed within the context of a body of normative stylistic systems—in this case classical narrative—the more that device is foregrounded when it is actually deployed. As mentioned, Ophuls' *La Ronde* (1950) opens with an elaborate tracking shot that sets the stylistic tone for the first 20 minutes as the camera smoothly follows one character after another. The next 28 minutes largely dispenses with a moving camera but includes numerous oblique angles, tilted 'Dutch' framings and deep space compositions with foregrounded objects—often pieces of furniture—that confirms Williams' earlier cited criticism. All this ends abruptly with the square, perpendicular, visually 'severe' composition that depicts the couple in bed (Fig. 9.15a–b). Susan White (2008) notes the 'funereal' tone and exaggerated 'duality of the mise-en-scene', which is further emphasised by the front-on, planimetric-like framing that Paul Willeman (1978) describes as exuding 'a sense of symmetry' (pp. 70–74). Williams (1980, p. 40) cites Andrew Sarris' criticism of what he claims is the overwrought or 'decorative' décor in an Ophuls film and suggests that it's often underutilised when compared to Hitchcock and his integration of the set into the action. Sarris uses the example of staircases in Hitchcock and how they are often integral to the action while in an Ophuls film they are—as Williams interprets Sarris—'…weakly narrative…'[11] Yet it is clear that the wide reverse functions in part to emphasise the elaborate décor, giving it a role in Fig. 9.15b that sees the ornate clock obscuring the couple and aggressively separating them in a composition that visually represents the tenuous nature of their relationship.

Scenographic space is important but only in relation to mise en scene and how the art direction and decor inform us of the separation of the couple (White's duality), literally and emotionally.

> So it is with the gothic arches and metal grills and fences that play such a large part in so many Ophuls films: they both convey a sense of splendour and imprison his characters, conveying a suggestion of the world as a cage. (Harcourt 2002)

The revealing of the fourth wall also assists Ophuls' cause with the reverses showing the opposite walls, further contributing to the oppressiveness of the space and again suggesting a problematic relationship. While the 180-degree reverse framing does reveal the camera space and the fourth wall, the overtly unorthodox camera position behind articles of furniture also implies a subjectiveness that draws attention to the camera, implying authorial presence and creating a narrative that is highly self-conscious as Williams points out.

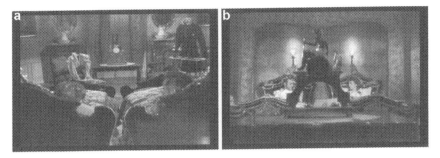

Figs. 9.15a, 9.15b *La Ronde* (1950)

The fourth single reverse appears in *Lola Montes* (1955b) (Fig. 9.16a–b) and its narrative function is consistent with that employed by Ophuls in the previous reverse examples, though in this instance Ophuls further emphasises the sense of artifice, suggesting an even greater theatricality. Again, we have a couple experiencing tension and so Ophuls places them at the extreme opposite ends of the carriage, repeating a similar staging strategy to that used in both instances in *Caught*. Like the first *Caught* reverse (Fig. 9.13a–b), Ophuls again chooses to cross the line resulting in both characters seemingly exchanging positions. The effect here is more jarring, partially because of the brevity of each of the reverses—each shot runs only approximately three seconds. The reverses also seem unmotivated and inconsistent with the rest of the coverage for the scene while the wideness of the framing for the reverses also appears disconcertingly exaggerated and contributes to a sense of artificiality with respect to the set—supposedly the inside of a travelling horse-drawn carriage. In this instance the revealing of the opposite wall and the space occupied by the camera in the previous shot both have the opposite effect and instead enhance the sense of artifice.

Figs. 9.16a, 9.16b   *Lola Montes* (1955)

Ophuls and Mirrors: Reflected Reverses

Kristin Thompson (1995) and Barry Salt (1992) both note the practice of employing mirrors to reveal reverse fields as appearing not infrequently in scenes in European cinema from the 1910s. Charles Harpole (1978, p. 222) comments on the use of mirrors to assist in creating deep space compositions, citing a shot in Ingmar Bergman's *Summer Interlude* (1951). Thompson references Erich von Stroheim's *Blind Husbands* (1919) (Fig. 9.17a–c) for its use of a mirror to not only reveal a reverse space occupied by a sleeping husband (Fig. 9.17a, b) but also the thoughts of a conflicted wife (Fig. 9.17c) (p. 75). The depicted space shifts from the medium close-up of the wife (Fig. 9.17a) to the reverse space of the sleeping husband (Fig. 9.17b) and on to a third undefined space—potentially inside the mind of the wife (Fig. 9.17c)—all without a cut.

Even more elaborate is Francis Coppola's mirror 'illusion' from *Peggy Sue Got Married* (1986), likely inspired by Jean Cocteau's *Orpheus* (1949) and the frontal shot of Orpheus walking towards a mirror (Fig. 9.19a). The Coppola film's first shot begins with a television filling the frame. As the camera tracks backwards the frame widens to reveal Beth sitting on the bed on the left of frame watching the television (Fig. 9.18a). Continuing to pull back, the camera reverses past Peggy Sue who appears to be applying make-up while seated at a vanity table (Fig. 9.18b). The camera stops and slowly tracks *forwards* towards the mirror as Beth comes forward towards camera to continue her dialogue with Peggy Sue (Fig. 9.18c). The camera appears in Fig. 9.18b, c to occupy an 'impossible' front-on position in that the camera itself should be visible in the mirror, seemingly positioned in approximately the same space occupied by Beth in Fig. 9.18c. In the best tradition of cinematic sleight of hand,

Coppola has in fact manipulated our perception of the space we believe we see. The reflected image does not reveal the space behind the camera because there is no mirror. We are actually viewing the space in front of the camera. Coppola perpetrates the deception by having an extra seated and doubling for Peggy Sue with back to camera in the foreground while the actress playing Peggy Sue (Kathleen Turner) is actually facing the camera just as Beth does in Fig. 9.18c. Coppola simulates the reverse angle space and deep space composition normally associated with a mirror shot by playing on our conception of what a mirror conventionally reveals.

Ophuls' application of mirrors to reveal reverse space tends to be more prosaic than these examples with one notable exception. Among the more straightforward instances are the reflected loan clerk from *The Reckless Moment* (Fig. 9.20a) and the suppressed reflection in *La Ronde* that presents a *Peggy Sue*-like frontal perspective in the restaurant with the camera and crew blacked out to avoid detection in the mirror opposite (Fig. 9.21a).[12]

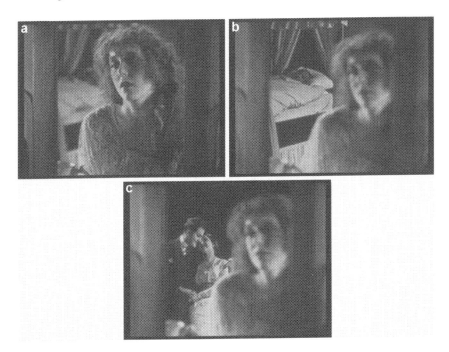

Figs. 9.17a, 9.17b, 9.17c *Blind Husbands* (1919)

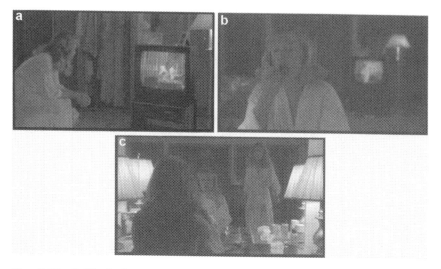

Figs. 9.18a, 9.18b, 9.18c *Peggy Sue Got Married* (1986)

Fig. 9.19a *Orpheus* (1949)

Fig. 9.20a *The Reckless Moment* (1949)

Fig. 9.21a   *La Ronde* (1950)

It is only in *Madam de…* (1953) that Ophuls deploys reflected reverses in combination with a single shot, reverse track. The reverse track concludes one of the most elaborate sequences in all of Ophuls' cinema and the montage sequence itself can be characterised as a showcase of style, with all of the main techniques used by Ophuls to construct space present in this single, seven-minute sequence. The sequence can be divided into six sections. Sections two onwards are constituted as single, long take shots, each linked by a dissolve:

1. Madam de and Donati are seated together. The wall mirror behind them reflects the ballroom and dancers on the floor as the off-screen space behind the camera.
2. Madam de and Donati now dancing.
   Dissolve to:
3. Madam de and Donati dancing—different costumes, different location. The orchestra is placed in the centre of the room and they dance around the orchestra—the camera is placed on the circumference of the circular track looking in at the dancing couple with the orchestra conductor featured distinctly in the background and he continually turns to face camera as the dancers and camera continue through 360 degrees.
   Dissolve to:
4. Madam de and Donati dancing at another ball, this one featuring numerous wall paintings and the camera holds them in one continuous tracking shot
   Dissolve to:

5. Another ballroom is established with an indoor fountain featured prominently. Madam de and Donati dance into frame and the camera follows them through 360 degrees, this time with the camera at the centre, looking out.
Dissolve to:
6. The orchestra is packing away. Madam de and Donati can be seen in the mirror dancing in the background (Fig. 9.22a). The shot continues as a single, shot reverse track that is itself reversed.

As one of the musicians (with bowler hat) exits frame left, the camera tracks and pans to the left to follow him. He pauses at the mirror to have his cigarette lit and Madam de and Donati can again be seen in the mirror (Fig. 9.22b). The musician continues and the camera pans and tracks with him until it finds the dancing couple (Fig. 9.22c) and pushes into a mid-shot as they continue to dance (Fig. 9.22d). At this point, Ophuls has staged the action as a 180-degree reverse track with the camera motion smoothly motivated by the departing musician. The shot continues, picking up an attendant as he passes through the frame to the right and now the camera reverse tracks and pans to follow his route (Fig. 9.22e). This continues until he reaches the chandelier near the group of still packing magicians (Fig. 9.22f), giving us a reversal of the original 180-degree track and ending the shot where it began—with the dancing couple again visible in the mirror. Not only does Ophuls manipulate the extravagant décor in the sequence to signpost shifting locales and temporal change, he also harnesses it to assist in constructing space. Ophuls moves the camera in a 180-degree reverse yet the addition of the reflected images means that we also see the off-screen space behind the camera with the dancers present in all of the reflected images. Ophuls manages to integrate staging, camera movement and design—the mirrored walls in this instance—such that all three elements contribute to constructing scenographic space.

Manifestations of the Wide Reverse in Mainstream Narrative... 313

Figs. 9.22a, 9.22b

Figs. 9.22c, 9.22d

Figs. 9.22e, 9.22f   *Madam de...* (1953)

Institutional Use

Only one adjacent (intercut), wide reverse exists in all of the surviving films directed by Yasujiro Ozu and it appears in *A Hen in the Wind* (1948) (Fig. 9.23a–b). Yet the unique systems for constructing space that he developed in the films of his mid and later career manifest intriguing similarities to the strategies employed by Spielberg—particularly in relation to the wide reverse. While Ozu's early films were stylistically (and culturally) influenced by his interest in Hollywood cinema, as evidenced by his early embracing of the classical continuity system, Ozu also began to evolve his own variations to classical convention. Initially, this involved the elimination of fundamental stylistic elements such as pans, dissolves, fades and, by the late 1940s, the complete absence of any moving camera shots. Bordwell (1988, p. 74) characterises this as Ozu reconfiguring style through the 'rearrangement' of extrinsic classical norms by necessarily observing specific fundamentals of classical narrative (the match-on-action cut) while at the same time substituting other classical conventions with his own variation—such as his rejection of the eye-line match. As for the wide reverse from *A Hen in the Wind*, Ozu creates a perfect 180 degree, wide angle reverse (Fig. 9.23a–b) to construct a 360-degree view of the small hospital room. The reverse comprehensively reveals the space occupied by the camera in the previous shot in a strategy that becomes common practice in Ozu's non-adjacent reverses where the 'fourth' wall is replaced by the wall of the set—adding to the perception of the space as an actual location rather than a studio set.

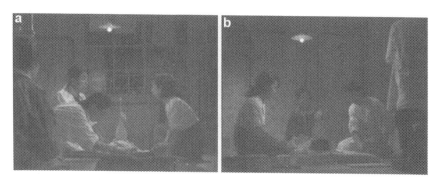

Figs. 9.23a, 9.23b   *A Hen in the Wind* (1948)

In his study of *Equinox Flower* (1958), Edward Branigan (1976, p. 91) isolates four principles that govern the construction of space by Ozu, these being: a 360-degree view of space, the changing of angles in multiples of 90 degrees, the perpetually low height of the camera [Donald Ritchie (1974, p. 12) labels this the 'tatami shot'] and the overlapping of space across adjacent shots. Bordwell and Thompson (1976) identify similar variations but expand Branigan's points to characterise Ozu's camera placement as operating either inside the circle of action looking out or outside the circumference looking in. Ozu's wholesale adoption of these processes is illustrated by their ready appearance in almost any scene from the later films. In *Tokyo Story* (1953), Shukichi and Tomi sit together in an establishing two shot (Fig. 9.24a) that places the camera on the outside of the circle and then matches this with a reverse master that preserves the camera's place on the outer circle looking in (Fig. 9.24d). In between, Ozu inserts two singles that now place the camera on the inside of the circle looking out (Fig. 9.24b, c). Note that the singles also involve 180-degree reversals from the shot they follow—Fig. 9.24b is a 180-degree reverse of Fig. 9.24a while Fig. 9.24c is a 180-degree reverse of Fig. 9.24b, d reverses the previous shot by 180 degrees. The two wide shots combine to reveal a 360-degree space while the reverse master also accommodates the appearance of the neighbour at the window in a composition that remains consistent with the overall formal patterning of the framing. Ozu does not privilege the neighbour's arrival at the window with a close up—the refusal to reframe objects is another element of Ozu's formal system and will be examined shortly. The ambiguous eye-lines of the two singles—both characters appear to be looking left to right—also illustrates another important element of a formal system that prioritises compositional graphic qualities over classical style's convention of converging eye-lines. As mentioned in Chap. 8 (Fig. 8.1a–b), Ozu preferences the matching of character symmetry and the perpendicular aspect of the background over the classical convention that preserves intersecting eye-lines and would normally also see the first close-up as an axial cut from the establishing wide to the single of Shukichi at Fig. 9.24c rather than the 180-degree reverse of Tomi[13] (Fig. 9.24b).

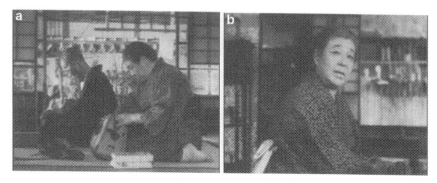

Figs. 9.24a, 9.24b

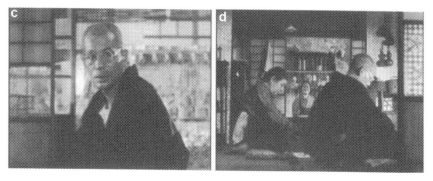

Figs. 9.24c, 9.24d *Tokyo Story* (1953)

A more graphically extreme (but still common) example of the prioritising of graphic elements within the framework of 180-degree reverses appears in *Late Spring* (1949) (Fig. 9.25a–d). Here, Ozu preserves the same wide, reverse shots as bookends (Fig. 9.25a, d) and fills the body of the scene with graphically matched singles (Fig. 9.25b, c). In this case the characters are arranged frontally,[14] creating perfectly matching compositions with even the wide reverses graphically matching each other through the angle of the characters seated at the table though Fig. 9.25d is framed slightly more loosely. Also repeated from the *Tokyo Story* example are the constant 180-degree shifts from shot to shot beginning with the establishing master (Fig. 9.25a), which is then reversed for the single of Aya (Fig. 9.25b). This is reversed 180 degrees again for Noriko (Fig. 9.25c),

Manifestations of the Wide Reverse in Mainstream Narrative... 317

with even the reverse master (Fig. 9.25d) a reverse of Noriko's single. Ozu also again places the camera inside the circle looking out for the singles and outside the circumference looking in for the wide reverses. Bordwell notes Ozu's refusal to reframe compositions for character movement while Branigan (1976) argues that '...reframing is not a slave to the narrative dominant or character movement...' (p. 82). Both imply the prioritising of space but it also seems likely that Ozu instead uses the wide reverses to not only complete the 360-degree space but also to 'preframe' the action with a wide composition that anticipates movement such as the arrival of the neighbour in Fig. 9.24d and Noriko's movement across the room to open the window in Fig. 9.25d.

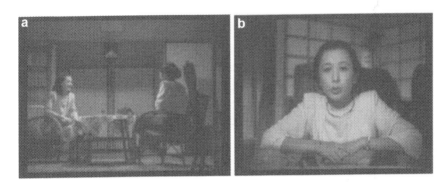

Figs. 9.25a, 9.25b

Figs. 9.25c, 9.25d *Late Spring* (1949)

Ozu's calculated development and refinement of the wide reverse as stylistic norm can be illustrated by comparing two of his films, *The Story of Floating Weeds* (1934) and the remake, *Floating Weeds* (1959). The plot of both films begins with the arrival of a travelling theatrical troupe that visits and performs in a small village. In the 1934 version, the troupe arrives by train but for the remake Ozu moves the village to the seaside and has them arrive by boat. To accommodate these kinds of changes to locations, coverage and staging requirements necessarily differ across the two films making specific stylistic comparisons problematic. Yet despite the 25-year gap between the production of the two films, there are some sequences in the 1959 version where Ozu reproduces scenes that closely resemble those of the 1934 version. One striking example is a scene in which an argument erupts between Kihachi and his son, Shinkichi. In the 1934 original, Ozu stages the altercation near the doorway of a small bar with the action framed in a wide shot (Fig. 9.26a, b). The two briefly struggle (Kihachi has back to camera in Fig. 9.26a) until Shinkichi shoves Kihachi away causing him to stumble back and fall to the right side of the frame in Fig. 9.26b. The next shot (Fig. 9.26c) is a reverse mid of Kihachi recovering and glaring at his son. Figure 9.26d is another reverse mid of Shinkichi's mother with her eye-line to Kihachi. Figure 9.26e retains the angle of the previous shot while the wider composition recalls the wider again establishing/master shot at Fig. 9.26a. Figure 9.26f is a 90-degree shift in angle with Shinkichi looking across at his mother in a loose mid shot. This is then reversed with her in a frontal mid shot with her eye-line to Shinkichi (Fig. 9.26g). The next shot to Kihachi at Fig. 9.26h represents another 90-degree angle change.

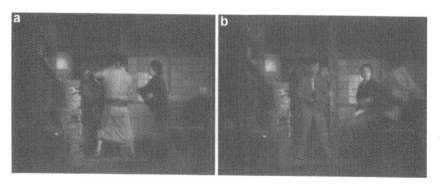

Figs. 9.26a, 9.26b

Manifestations of the Wide Reverse in Mainstream Narrative... 319

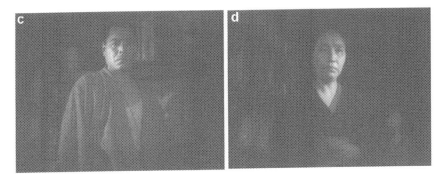

Figs. 9.26c, 9.26d

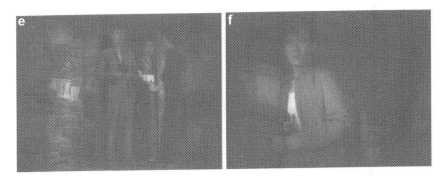

Figs. 9.26e, 9.26f

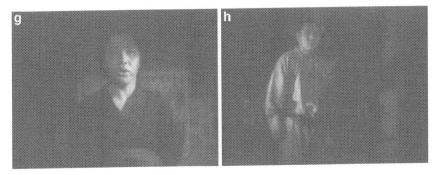

Figs. 9.26g, 9.26h   *The Story of Floating Weeds* (1934)

Examining the same scene as it appears in the 1959 version it is clear that there are a number of similarities but there are also key stylistic variations that set the remake apart from the original. On a first viewing the two scenes seem very similar with the location of the action—the entrance to the bar; the positioning of the camera for the establishing/master wide (Fig. 9.27a, b); the composition of the wide and the single shots (Fig. 9.27c, d, f, g); the staging of the actors and the action with the son shoving the father—all are almost identical to the original. The remake preserves Ozu's now well-established intrinsic norm for matching the singles graphically and both observe classical, matching eye-line direction—an uncharacteristic device for Ozu in 1959 as he had already long established a preference for dialogue scenes with unmatched or ambiguous eye-lines.

Despite the similarities between the two sequences there are two highly significant stylistic variations operating in the remake that relate to reversing the camera and the revealing of space. In the original, the first reaction shot of Kihachi after being pushed frames him in a midshot (Fig. 9.26c). In the remake, Ozu copies the 1934 version's establishing shot and action with the wide of Fig. 9.26e but gives us Komajuro's (Kihachi in the original) reaction as a 180-degree *wide reverse* (Fig. 9.27e) that also approximately matches the size of the establishing shot. Ozu also holds the wide reverse and uses it to deliver much of the plot related dialogue that is given to the singles in the original (Fig. 9.26f, g). Holding the wide reverse thus emphasises its importance narratively and in terms of the shot's extended screen time and effectively elevates the shot's significance to reverse master status. Working in tandem with Ozu's integration of the wide reverse into the scene is the pattern of 180-degree reverses already discussed in the scenes from *Tokyo Story* and *Late Spring*. While the staging of the actors is comparable across the two scenes, Ozu modifies the positioning of the mother for the remake so that she remains near Komajuro as opposed to the original where she was positioned largely near Shinkichi. The net effect of this is that for the remake Ozu is able to make each shot a 180-degree reverse of the previous one in contrast to the original

Manifestations of the Wide Reverse in Mainstream Narrative... 321

where he used a combination of 90- and 180-degree angle shifts. He effectively simplifies the way the scene is covered by eliminating the 90-degree angle changes. That Ozu recreates the scene from the original in an almost identical way but then heavily revises the patterning associated with the revealing of space suggests the importance and high narrative value he placed on the 180-degree reverse and wide reverse as a normative stylistic device and the crucial role afforded spatial construction in this later film.

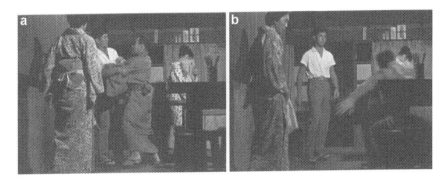

Figs. 9.27a, 9.27b

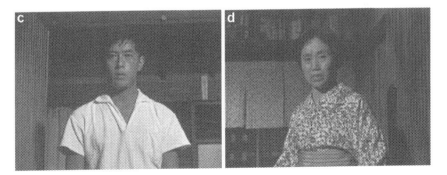

Figs. 9.27c, 9.27d

Figs. 9.27e, 9.27f, 9.27g *Floating Weeds* (1959)

Ozu rarely deviates from presenting dialogue scenes (and the later films are dominated by such scenes) without using 180-degree reverses patterned as in the examples examined earlier from *Tokyo Story*, *Late Spring* and *Floating Weeds*. Branigan (1976, p. 102) also points out Ozu's frequent manipulation of props such as bottles, glasses, ashtrays, and so on, and their seeming repositioning in the frame from one shot to the next as evidence of an intentional challenge to the traditional prioritising of classical continuity. He argues that this strategy instead reinforces the construction of a mise en scene that encourages consideration of all parts of the frame—not just the anthropocentric centre as is usually the case with classical compositions. Branigan further suggests that this attention to frame space is part of a larger 'spatial code' that allows spatial considerations to compete with narrative requirements, even to the point when discussing Ozu's transitions that '…at certain times the text is emptied of meaning and expresses only space' (p. 105). Bordwell and Thompson

(1976) similarly argue that in contrast to classical narrative where space is traditionally subordinated to narrative demands, characters and the cause/effect chain, in Ozu it is often foregrounded and competes on equal terms for spectator attention: 'Narrative causality is relegated to the status of only one 'voice' in a polyphony that gives an equal role to purely spatial manipulations' (p. 45).

So in late Ozu we have a filmmaker who has institutionalised a process of reverse shot structures into a highly developed formal system that elevates the communication and signification of spatial articulation in a way that Spielberg—or any other mainstream filmmaker—cannot appear to match. While Spielberg's manipulation of space does not constitute a dedicated, specific formal system in the fashion of Ozu, it is Spielberg's strategy of prioritising space while still operating within classical convention that makes his style intriguing. At one level, Ozu smoothly fashions his own style out of the modification of classical convention—as Bordwell has observed—and this explains why he retains some classical norms such as the match-on-action cut and the establishing wide. Like Spielberg, Ozu also constructs 360-degree vistas with 180-degree shifts and manages to do so without disorientating the audience, achieving this through a combination of match-on-action cutting, 'spatial anchors' and overlapping portions of the frame—identical strategies used by Spielberg in all of the wide reverses analysed in Chaps. 6 and 7.

Yet Ozu pushes the prioritising of space further with the already mentioned mismatched or ambiguous eye-lines, a consistently low camera height that draws attention to the artifice, and the groups of shots seemingly irrelevant to the narrative that appear between scenes and that have been described variously as: transitions and intermediate spaces (Bordwell and Thompson 1976, p. 63); contemplative space for the spectator to consider what has just occurred (Konshak 1980); 'pillow shots' in relation to the Japanese 'pillow-word' and suggestive of a decentring/non-anthropocentricism (Burch 1979); and Branigan's (1976) contention that the these shots are without meaning and '…express only space' (p. 105). I wish to argue that these 'intermediary' shots actually function in conjunction or as a component part of Ozu's wide reverse strategy that relates to revealing the 'fourth wall' and the space occupied by the camera. If considered in this light—as an extension of the desire to present a more 'complete' or 'real' space—the series of shots that open *An Autumn*

Afternoon (1962) (Fig. 9.28a–c) take on a different function to those suggested. Bordwell and Thompson's conception of the shots as transitory or intermediate is the most relevant in this revised version but the shots can be seen to also function in a slightly more nuanced way. The variation in the composition of the smoke stacks from shot to shot does denote a clear transition from exterior to interior with each shot bringing us nearer to them until they are seen from inside a building (Fig. 9.28b). Bordwell (2008b) notes that this continues in the corridor shot (Fig. 9.28c) with the shadows of the smoke stacks in evidence. This transition from one space to another is an important function of the series of shots but of greater significance is the transition from the 'real' exterior spaces to the artificial studio sets of the interiors. By visually associating the exterior shots with the interior sets and fusing both together at Fig. 9.28b, Ozu visually encourages us to consider—by association—that the studio sets occupy the same 'real-world' space as the smoke stacks and that they too are therefore 'realistic' and not merely studio spaces.

Figs. 9.28a, 9.28b, 9.28c *An Autumn Afternoon* (1962)

All of the scholars cited point out that Ozu's system is certainly not inferior to classical narrative but is instead positioned as an alternative. Bordwell and Thompson (1976, p. 63) also argue that the 'empty' transitions contribute to a sense of obliqueness and a lack of economy that retards narrative development. Further, Burch (1979) describes the performances in Ozu as 'presentational' (p. 183), acknowledging that the actors are often required to defer to compositional factors. Bordwell (1988) also notes that Ozu's foregrounding of spatial and graphic elements contributes to an '…impersonal narration system…' (p. 75) with even the performers subordinated to compositional requirements resulting in 'fixed', homogeneous performances—much like the rigid, emotionless acting style preferred by director Robert Bresson.

Ozu's high degree of stylistic invasiveness contrasts to Spielberg's classically cloaked manipulation of style. Ozu uses classical convention as the foundation for a formal system that elevates the significance of space and Spielberg also manipulates classical norms to articulate space to a greater degree than is characteristic of classical narrative. While Ozu pushes further and emphasises graphic relations at the expense of all other aspects of narrative communicativeness (in terms of the distractive influence it imposes on the narrative), Spielberg chooses to integrate his system of spatial manipulation within highly recognisable, largely inflexible conventions of the classical continuity system. This is a seemingly challenging undertaking given the constant necessity that he deal with the potentially stifling restrictive requirement that notions of space be seen to appear subservient to narrative demands. In contrast to its systematic use by Spielberg, the application of the wide reverse by filmmakers in classical cinema appears isolated and largely arbitrary.

Notes

1. This argument employs a variation of the invisible observer model.
2. According to Salt (1992), the term 'reverse scene' came into common usage in the US from around 1912.
3. *The Other Side of the Hedge* (1905) creates a humorous reveal through the use of a similar 180-degree reversal.

4. Salt (1992, p. 136) comments that instances of incorrect eye-line matches were still evident into the 1920s in European films that used the shot, reverse shot.
5. Coppola was the first film-school graduate to find success in Hollywood in above-the-line roles as writer and director. Also older than the other movie brats, his social and professional sphere extended more to fellow UCLA graduates Milius and Lucas than to the others.
6. There is a certain irony in that while Hitchcock does construct 360-degree spaces, De Palma's effort at 'mimicking' his style fails to duplicate this aspect of Hitchcock's craft.
7. The reverse depicts the steamboat making its way down the river in a brief, wide reverse vista.
8. Later shots also show the sound recordist and clapperboard in use.
9. This assertion by Carroll of the elimination of faked stunts seems ironic in this instance in that the subsequent explosion from the firing of the mortar would likely have been faked given the inherent inaccuracy of actually firing a mortar.
10. Returning to Europe was more unusual. Jean Renoir was one of the few major directors who also returned to Europe after the war.
11. Sarris must have forgotten about Ophuls' *La Signore Di Tutti* in which the hapless, wheelchair-confined wife plunges to her death down a staircase.
12. When viewed in motion, the table can be seen reflected in the mirror. In wider compositions the chandelier can also be seen reflected and parts of the camera and/or crew are visible (presumably unintentionally) in the mirror early in the shot.
13. Ozu does engage in axial cutting in his earlier films with the last instance occurring in *Record of a Tenement Gentleman* (1947) and his determination to replace it with reverses is illustrated in the comparison I make between one scene from *Story of Floating Weeds* (1934) and his own remake in 1958.
14. Noël Burch (1979, p. 174) has argued that the frontal compositions with minimal depth and an inherent 'flatness' are inspired by traditional two-dimensional Japanese art and architecture.

References

American Film Institute. (2012). *Steven Spielberg Interview* [Video file]. Retrieved from https://www.youtube.com/watch?v=ayJLeVDOCZ0

American Film Institute. (2013). *Steven Spielberg Interview* [Video file]. Retrieved from https://www.youtube.com/watch?v=DfUw4SN1Nig

Bacher, L. (1996). *Max Ophuls in the Hollywood Studios*. New Brunswick: Rutgers University Press.

Baxter, J. (1997). *Stanley Kubrick: A Biography*. New York: Carroll and Graf Publishers Inc.

Berliner, T. (2010). *Hollywood Incoherent: Narration in Seventies Cinema*. Austin: University of Texas Press.

Bordwell, D. (1981). *The Films of Carl-Theodor Dreyer*. Los Angeles: University of California Press.

Bordwell, D. (1988). *Ozu and the Poetics of Cinema*. Princeton: Princeton University Press.

Bordwell, D. (1996). Convention, Construction and Cinematic Vision. In D. Bordwell & N. Carroll (Eds.), *Post-theory: Reconstructing Film Studies* (pp. 87–107). Wisconsin: The University of Wisconsin Press.

Bordwell, D. (2006, November 15). *Shooting to Protect* [Web Log Post]. Retrieved from http://www.davidbordwell.net/blog/2006/11/page/2/. Bordwell Paraphrases William Hornbeck, Editor of *Giant*.

Bordwell, D. (2008a). *The Poetics of Cinema*. London: Routledge.

Bordwell, D. (2008b). [DVD audio commentary in Y. Ozu (Director) *An Autumn Afternoon*, Motion picture]. United States: The Criterion Collection.

Bordwell, D., & Thompson, K. (1976). Space and Narrative in the Films of Ozu. *Screen, 17*(2), 41–73. https://doi.org/10.1093/Screen/17.2.74

Bouzereau, L. (Writer, Director & Producer). (1997). *Making of the Man Who Knew Too Much* [DVD supplement in A. Hitchcock (Director), *The Man Who Knew Too Much*]. Australia: Universal Pictures.

Branigan, E. (1976). The Space of Equinox Flower. *Screen, 17*(2), 74–105. Retrieved from http://screen.oxfordjournals.org/

Burch, N. (1979). *To the Distant Observer*. Los Angeles: University of California Press.

Caldwell, J. T. (2008). *Production Culture: Industrial Reflexivity and Critical Practice in Film and Television*. Durham: Duke University Press.

Carroll, N. (2007). *Comedy Incarnate: Buster Keaton, Physical Humour and Bodily Coping*. Singapore: Blackwell Publishing.

Combs, R. (1978). Primal Scream: An Interview with Steven Spielberg. *American Cinematographer, 59*(2), 111–113.

Cronin, P. (2004). *George Stevens Interviews*. Jackson: University of Mississippi.

Doane, M. A. (1987). *The Desire to Desire: The Woman's Film of the 1940s*. London: The Macmillan Press Ltd.

Greenaway, P. (Writer & Director). (1982). *Introduction to the Film by Peter Greenaway* [DVD supplement in P. Greenaway, *The Draughtsman's Contract*. Motion picture]. Australia: Umbrella Entertainment.

Harcourt, P. (2002). Circles of Delight and Despair: The Cinema of Max Ophuls. *Cineaction, 59,* 4–13. Retrieved from http://search.proquest.com/docview/216885583?accountid=10344

Harpole, C. H. (1978). *Gradients of Depth in the Cinema Image.* New York: Arno Press.

Heath, S. (1976). Narrative Space. *Screen, 17*(3), 68–112. Retrieved from http://screen.oxfordjournals.org/

Hopwood, J. C. (n.d.). *George Stevens Biography.* Retrieved from http://www.imdb.com/name/nm0828419/bio?ref_=nm_ov_bio_sm

Konshak, D. J. (1980). Space and Narrative in 'Tokyo Story'. *Film Criticism, 4*(3), 31–40. Retrieved from EBSCOhost Academic Search Premier

McBride, J. (1997). *Steven Spielberg: A Biography.* New York: Simon and Schuster.

Milne, T. (1971). *The Cinema of Carl Dreyer.* New York: A. S. Barnes & Co.

Pye, M., & Myles, L. (1979). *The Movie Brats: How the Film Generation Took over Hollywood.* London/Boston: Faber and Faber.

Ritchie, D. (1974). *Ozu: His Life and Films* (2nd ed.). Berkeley: University of California Press.

Royal, S. (1982). Steven Spielberg in His Adventures on Earth. In L. D. Friedman & B. N. (Eds.), *Steven Spielberg Interviews* (pp. 84–106). Jackson: University Press of Mississippi.

Salt, B. (1992). *Film Style and Technology: History and Analysis.* London: Starword.

Schiff, S. (1994). Seriously Spielberg. In L. D. Friedman & B. Notbohm (Eds.), *Steven Spielberg Interviews* (pp. 170–192). Jackson: University Press of Mississippi.

Thompson, K. (1995). The International Exploration of Cinematic Expressivity. In K. Dibbets & B. Hogenkamp (Eds.), *Film and the First World War* (pp. 65–85). Amsterdam: Amsterdam University Press.

Truffaut, F. (1983). *Hitchcock Truffaut.* New York: Simon & Schuster, Inc..

Walker, A., Taylor, S., & Ruchti, U. (1999). *Stanley Kubrick Director: A Visual Analysis.* London: Weidenfeld & Nicolson.

White, S. (2008). [DVD audio commentary in M. Ophuls (Director), *La Ronde.* Motion picture]. United States: The Criterion Collection.

Willemen, P. (1978). The Ophuls Text: A Thesis. In P. Willemen (Ed.), *Ophuls* (pp. 70–74). London: British Film Institute.

Williams, A. (1980). *Max Ophuls and the Cinema of Desire: A Critical Study of Six Films 1948–1955*. New York: Arno Press.

Film Title Editions

Cocteau, J. (Director). (1949). *Orpheus* [Motion picture, DVD (2000)]. United States: The Criterion Collection.
Coppola, F. (Director). (1986). *Peggy Sue Got Married* [Motion picture, DVD (2002)]. Australia: TriStar Home Entertainment.
Dreyer, C. T. (Director). (1943). *Day of Wrath* [Motion picture, DVD (2001)]. United States: The Criterion Collection.
Dreyer, C. T. (Director). (1955). *Ordet* [Motion picture, DVD (2001)]. United States: The Criterion Collection.
Early Cinema: Primitives and Pioneers. (1895–1910). [Motion picture, DVD]. United Kingdom: The British Film Institute.
Godard, J. -L. (Director). (1967). *La Chinoise* [Motion picture, DVD (2005)]. Australia: Madman Cinema.
Greenaway, P. (Director). (1990). *The Belly of an Architect* [Motion picture, DVD (2004)]. United States: MGM Home Entertainment.
Hitchcock, A. (Director). (1956). *The Man Who Knew Too Much* [Motion picture, Blu-ray (2012)]. Australia: Universal Sony Pictures Home Entertainment.
Hitchcock, A. (Director). (1958). *Vertigo* [Motion picture, Blu-ray (2012)]. Australia: Universal Sony Pictures Home Entertainment.
Keaton, B. (Director)., & Bruckman, C. (Co-director). (1926). *The General* [Motion picture, DVD (2005)]. Australia: Madman Cinema.
Kubrick, S. (Director). (1980). *The Shining* [Motion picture, Blu-ray (2007)]. Australia: Warner Bros. Entertainment.
Mann, M. (Director). (1999). *The Insider* [Motion picture, DVD (2000)]. Australia: Touchstone Home Video.
Ophuls, M. (Director). (1934). *La Signora Di Tutti* [Motion picture, DVD (2010)]. United Kingdom: Eureka Entertainment.
Ophuls, M. (Director). (1949). *Caught* [Motion picture, DVD]. United Kingdom: Second Sight.
Ophuls, M. (Director). (1949). *The Reckless Moment* [Motion picture, DVD]. United Kingdom: Second Sight.
Ophuls, M. (Director). (1950). *La Ronde* [Motion picture, DVD (2008)]. United States: The Criterion Collection.

Ophuls, M. (Director). (1953). *Madam de...* [Motion picture, DVD (2009)]. Australia: The Madman Cinema.

Ophuls, M. (Director). (1955). *Lola Montes* [Motion picture, Blu-ray (2009)]. United States: The Criterion Collection.

Ozu, Y. (Director). (1934) *A Story of Floating Weeds* [Motion picture, DVD (2004)]. United States: The Criterion Collection.

Ozu, Y. (Director). (1948). *A Hen in the Wind* [Motion picture, DVD (2005)]. Hong Kong: Panorama Entertainment.

Ozu, Y. (Director). (1949). *Late Spring* [Motion picture, DVD (2006)]. United States: The Criterion Collection.

Ozu, Y. (Director). (1953). *Tokyo Story* [Motion picture, DVD (2003)]. United States: The Criterion Collection.

Ozu, Y. (Director). (1959). *Floating Weeds* [Motion picture, DVD (2004)]. United States: The Criterion Collection.

Ozu, Y. (Director). (1962). *An Autumn Afternoon* [Motion picture, DVD (2008)]. United States: The Criterion Collection.

Stevens, G. (Director). (1956). *Giant* [Motion picture, DVD (2003)]. United States: Warner Home Video.

von Stroheim, E. (Director). (1919). *Blind Husbands* [Motion picture, DVD (2003)]. United States: Kino International Corp.

10

Conclusion: Style by Stealth

If we return to my initial proposition that the early and continued popularity of Spielberg's films is in part due to his unique control of style and how he deploys it to construct narrative, we can now bring together all considered areas to determine the likely significance of style. At the same time, it is also important to bear in mind that the specific or unequivocal significance accorded style in contributing to the popularity of Spielberg's films in comparison to other factors is impossible to determine in and of itself. For example, *Jaws* was chosen by Spielberg as a film project because of its conceptual appeal. He found the story intriguing and believed it would make a good film. The subject matter was a key contributor to the film's success as evidenced by its popularity as a novel. Whether another director could have as successfully or even more successfully transitioned the subject matter from novel to film narrative is impossible to determine. We can point to the two inferior *Jaws* sequels as a partial indicator of how other directors fared in realising the concept as filmic narratives. Another evolving gauge may be glimpsed in the future remaking of some of Spielberg's most popular films. The 2015 critical and popular failure of the *Poltergeist* remake is one such example.

Then there are the cultural and industrial factors; the dominance of Hollywood cinema worldwide and the rise of the teenage audience in the 1970s (Chap. 1), the star system, the marketing of Spielberg's films and himself as entertainer, his position of power and control over the factors of production—some or all of these undoubtedly represent contributing influences. Even his uncanny ability to predict what kind of story will likely resonate with audiences only further distracts from the significance of style in his films. Thus it's not possible to categorically claim, for instance, that 50% of the popularity of *Jaws* was due to style or that it contributed to 70% of the success of *Saving Private Ryan*—and so on.

What this book has argued is twofold: that the extensive examination of Spielberg's narrative unequivocally reveals the operation of specific and unique stylistic strategies across many of his films and that it is possible to determine the related implications these identified strategies impose on spectator comprehension. Logically, greater or more coherent spectator comprehension as examined in Chap. 8 will likely lead to a more sustained level of narrative interest and therefore more intense spectator engagement.

Ultimately, Spielberg's use of style suggests a reconfiguring of classical practice and this is most clearly defined by the wide reverse. Returning again to Gombrich's problem-solution model, we see in early Spielberg, as rational agent, a filmmaker concerned with how to remedy the problem of studio shooting as perceived as inherently 'fake' or distracting. The (initial) solution: forgoing studio sets, always filming on location and then further exploiting the sense of a 'real' space with the wide reverse as stylistic device.

Several factors influenced Spielberg in his adoption of the wide reverse. Hitchcock's perseverance with rear projection into the 1970s and the New Hollywood rejection of such seemingly artificial, studio-bound shooting would have provided some impetus for change. I have already noted the probable influence of Welles in Spielberg's deep-space compositions (Chap. 5). Additionally, instances of the wide reverse from early in Spielberg's career demonstrate that this practice of fusing deep space and wide reverses can essentially be seen as fundamentally already fully formed in his television work. While the connection with filmmakers like Penn, Frankenheimer and Lumet is not initially clear, their films do display instances where the manipulation of scenographic space features prominently. Frankenheimer's innovative handling of a 'brainwashed' 'reality' in *The Manchurian Candidate* (1962)—a Spielberg favourite—underlined an interest in constructing an ambiguous space that could be both 'real' and imagined at the same time. Lumet undertook a similar strategy in *The Pawnbroker* (1964) with its initially unclear temporal and spatial flashbacks—techniques likely drawn from European art cinema.

It is not the specific impact of these filmmakers but rather the combination of the period in which they created their films together with the effect this exerted over the way they presented scenographic space that made their films influential. Central was the vigorous art cinema circuit in the United States during the 1960s that exposed American audiences to filmmakers like Antonioni, Bresson, Resnais, Truffaut, Godard, Bergman, Kurosawa and others. Crucially, while most readily utilised studio sets, they also made extensive use of location-based spaces that seemed innovative[1] because of their perceived connection to a more grounded neo-realist aesthetic. This preference for location filming for both interiors as well as exteriors quickly became an important component of the 'New Hollywood/Hollywood Renaissance/American New Wave' phenomenon. American '1960s auteur' directors like Arthur Penn, Dennis Hopper/Peter Fonda and William Friedkin reflected this new preference for extensive location photography in films like *Bonnie and Clyde* (1967), *Easy Rider* (1969) and *The French Connection* (1971).

This 'renewed' preference for the depiction of 'real' spaces quickly impacted on the classical 'traditionalists' and Hitchcock in particular. Despite the acclaim heaped on his work by the *Cahiers du Cinéma* writers led by Truffaut, the early 1960s saw some critics tiring of aspects of Hitchcock's mise en scene and Andrew Sarris, an early American champion of Hitchcock, wrote on the release of *Marnie* (1964):

> His fake sets, particularly of dockside Baltimore, have never been more distracting, and the process shots of 'Tippi' on horseback are appallingly dated. (Kapsis 1992, p. 123)

Hitchcock would persist with the 'appallingly dated' process shots until his final film, *Family Plot* (1976). Robin Wood (1977) suggests that this choice originated in Hitchcock's beginnings with UFA in Germany and his early fondness of an expressionist aesthetic that continued to inform his mise en scene as a '…distortion or deformation of objective reality…' (p. 12).[2]

It is intriguing to consider that this rejection of Hitchcock's unwavering method of representing space through process photography and rear projection likely contributed to Spielberg's determination to avoid process photography in his own filmmaking—particularly when considered in conjunction with the 'New Hollywood' shift. Set to direct *Duel*, Spielberg was expected by Unit Production Manager, Wallace Worsley, to use process photography for the car scenes as per studio practice for all television productions (Wasser 2010, p. 51; Awalt, 2014, p. 96). Arguing for the greater 'realism' possible with location shooting, Spielberg instead managed to shoot the film entirely on location, much as he had for large sections of the well-regarded TV pilot for *Columbo* earlier the same year. His following television work was also characterised by extensive exterior shooting while his first feature, *The Sugarland Express*, was also shot almost entirely on location. For *Jaws*, Spielberg was informed that the ocean footage would be shot using a studio-based water tank. Again, Spielberg managed to convince the producers to shoot the film at sea: 'It was a real sea and a real boat' (McBride 1997, p. 234). Some years later, while discussing his early determination to always shoot on location, Spielberg tellingly commented,

> The 70s was a time when the environment was crucial to the storytelling. (Biskind 1998, p. 263)

Shooting on location wasn't just about capturing a greater 'reality', although Dreyer had used this justification some 40 years earlier to shoot *Vampyr* (1932) entirely on location (Tybjerg 2008). But it was initially— for Spielberg—a determining factor. Like the original proponents of the reverse scene (Fig. 9.1a, b) from the 1900s who had realised that outdoor shooting *permitted* wide reverses, Spielberg was able to use wide reverses to *prove* that the space was 'real'. Location shooting allowed Spielberg the freedom to fully deploy his wide reverse strategy without being constrained by the visual limitations that process photography or studio sets would have imposed. As his career flourished and his control over his productions quickly grew, Spielberg was able to demand more elaborate, complete sets in which he could potentially incorporate wide reverses. This resulted in Spielberg shifting to studio interiors for some scenes with even the early *Close Encounters* making extensive use of studio-based sets. *Minority Report* gaffer David Devlin's observation underlines Spielberg's preference for sets complete with the 'fourth wall'.

> Alex McDowell built the Precrime offices as a fully practical set to give Steven the freedom he prefers – he doesn't like to be limited by having to piece together different locations to act as one. (Holben 2002)

Spielberg simply requests sets that permit 360-degree shooting. Examples of such interior sets can be found in almost every Spielberg film: the *T. rex* attack sequence from *Jurassic Park*, the elaborate town ruin and bridge in *Saving Private Ryan*, the multiple sets of *A.I.* and, most detailed of all, the transit terminal set for *The Terminal*, which Spielberg spatially establishes with two 360-degree tracks (Chap. 7). At the same time and in spite of all of the resources available to him, Spielberg is always mindful of maintaining a sense of referential realism and how best to achieve it.

> No matter how realistic the lighting looks on a soundstage, it still will look like a stage compared to the real thing. Personally, I like to be outside—or in practical interiors—as often as possible. (Pizzello 1997, p. 40)

When Spielberg speaks of 'the real thing', he is not referring to a reality or realism in the sense of a seemingly less mediated, neo-realism-like form. On the contrary, classical cinema has always depended on the elaborate depiction of its own highly codified, highly manipulated sense of a 'classical reality'. The wide reverse functions as a kind of stylistic, foundation device that operates on two levels. One relates to its origin in classical practice, the continuity editing system and the shot, reverse shot arrangement. Built out of these conventions, the wide reverse thus also exists within these systems. As device, it is essentially camouflaged because it is constructed from fundamental components of classical style and principally the spectator's comprehension of the shot, reverse shot and expectation of the perspectival shifts it entails. Thus, Spielberg utilises classical devices in a conventional way but then occasionally incorporates the wide reverse to complement and enhance cognition and affect. He also then integrates deep space compositions, which in the Bazinian tradition also suggest an additional level of perceived 'realness'.

Integrated into the wide reverse are the various additional effects that can be characterised as sets of *enhancements*. These are divided into three types: *transparency, punctuation* and *affective*. *Transparency enhancements* include the construction of a 360-degree space that encourages a 'hyper-real' perception of scenographic space, which implies its existence as autonomous rather than 'manufactured'; the revealing of camera positions [Dayan's 'revising' (Chap. 6)] in the subsequent and prior shots, which imply the lack of a narrator and again of the action as autonomous; constantly referenced spatial relationships between character(s) and object(s) in space with match-on-action cutting that suggests the action as unfolding regardless of whether the spectator is 'present' or not; and the 'shaping' of objects from one view to the reverse, giving them depth and a sense of dimension as per Branigan's (2006) complete objects (Chap. 6). There is a certain paradox in the sense that each of these stylistic techniques work to enhance classical narrative's traditional suppression of style. Added to these are the effects that simultaneously operate on the second level.

These can be considered as *punctuation enhancements* and include the cine tableau and the zones of action that clearly delineate space into safe or unsafe areas. *Affective enhancements* potentially include all of the above but specifically incorporate: the simple act of presenting the spectator with a wide shot brings with it an expectation that an analytical (or axial) cut is imminent, thus providing a strong associative cue that the wide reverse exploits; the accommodation of close-ups without extracting the face from backgrounds (the space, face duality), permitting a less self-conscious but still emotionally engaging formation; the repeated referencing of characters during the cutting of reverse scenes so that affective engagement is focused with that character; the application of associative point of view either independently or in tandem with optical point-of-view.

Spielberg utilises the wide reverse as a vehicle for deploying these enhancements in various combinations. The possible permutations also permit him to recalibrate the wide reverse in minor or major ways depending on the scene's narrative requirement. At the same time, he further *adds* to the range of options by also incorporating a choice of the many classical, stylistic norms such as the close-up, the slow track-in or the long take. All of this is seamlessly integrated into classical convention.

Crucial to the effective operation of Spielberg's stylistic strategies is his prioritising of story and plot. Kraft (1987), Hochberg and Brooks (1996), Tan (1996), G. M. Smith (2003), McGinn (2005) and Hogan (2004) all emphasise the importance of spectator interest and story in the successful operation of narrative. Related to an understanding of what works as story is an ability to construct narratives that audiences understand, enjoy and are moved by. Related to my earlier discussion on authorship and intentionality (Chap. 3), Plantinga (2011) invokes the role of 'folk psychology' as a major determining force in the process of understanding spectator response. Through the 'filmmaker-audience loop', successful filmmakers construct narratives based on assumptions of what they think audiences will understand and enjoy.

> I would argue that most folk psychologies share a universal core set of concerns and beliefs, and that mainstream filmmakers design narratives to appeal to those concerns and beliefs. (p. 32)

Bordwell (2010) similarly conceives of a classical tradition of filmmakers as making common-sense judgements about how best to communicate intended information in the most effective way.

> Filmmakers proved to be practical psychologists. Through tradition and trial and error, they were able to guide ordinary behavior in ways that created an aesthetic experience. (p. 15)

It is this combination of an innate sensitivity for what audiences want to see, an uncanny ability to commission the right material, and supreme control and mastery of style that makes Spielberg's narratives so persuasive. If we return to Salt's criteria for judging the value of a film mentioned in the introduction and the outstanding criterion relating to stylistic complexity as applied to Spielberg's cinema, the above surely satisfies this point. When Ed Tan describes cinema as a 'miracle of precision', he must surely have been referring to films directed by Steven Spielberg.

Notes

1. When combined with the new, compact camera technology and influence of the latest documentary techniques, both of which permitted a more mobile camera as noted in the introduction.
2. A more pragmatic explanation is that Hitchcock was widely known to dislike location filming.

References

Awalt, S. (2014). *Steven Spielberg and Duel: The Making of a Film Career.* Maryland: Rowman & Littlefield.
Biskind, P. (1998). *Easy Riders, Raging Bulls: How the Sex-Drugs-and-Rock and Roll Generation Saved Hollywood.* New York: Touchstone.
Bordwell, D. (2010). The Part-time Cognitivist: A View from Film Studies. *Projections, 4*(2), 1–18.
Branigan, E. (2006). *Projecting a Camera: Language Games in Film Theory.* New York: Routledge.
Hochberg, J., & Brooks, V. (1996). Movies in the Mind's Eye. In D. Bordwell & N. Carroll (Eds.), *Post-Theory: Reconstructing Film Studies* (pp. 368–387). Madison: University of Wisconsin Press.
Hogan, P. C. (2004). Auteurs and Their Brains: Cognition and Creativity in the Cinema. In T. Grodal, B. Larsen, & I. T. Laursen (Eds.), *Visual Authorship: Creativity and Intentionality in Media* (pp. 67–86). Denmark: Museum Tusculanum Press and the authors.
Holben, J. (2002). Criminal Intent. *American Cinematographer., 83*(7), 34–45.
Kapsis, R. (1992). *Hitchcock, The Making of a Reputation.* Chicago: University of Chicago.

Kraft, R. N. (1987). The Influence of Camera Angle on Comprehension and Retention of Pictorial Events. *Memory and Cognition.* 15(4), 291–307. Retrieved from http://link.springer.com/article/10.3758%2FBF03197032#page-1

McBride, J. (1997). *Steven Spielberg: A Biography.* New York: Simon and Schuster.

McGinn, C. (2005). *The Power of Movies: How Screen and Mind Interact.* New York: Vintage Books.

Pizzello, S. (1997). Chase, Crush and Devour. *American Cinematographer.,* 78(6).

Plantnga, C. (2011). Folk Psychology for Film Critics and Students. *Projections,* 5(2), 26–50.

Smith, G. M. (2003). *Film Structure and the Emotion System.* New York: Cambridge University Press.

Tan, E. S. (1996). *Emotion and the Structure of Narrative Film: Film as an Emotion Machine.* New Jersey: Lawrence Eribaum Associates Inc..

Tybjerg, C. (2008) [DVD Audio Commentary in C. T. Dreyer (Director) *Vampyr.* Motion picture]. United Kingdom: Eureka Entertainment Ltd.

Wasser, F. (2010). *Steven Spielberg's America. Cambridge and.* Malden: Polity Press.

Wood, R. (1977). *Hitchcock's Films.* New Jersey: A.S. Barnes & Company.

Index[1]

A
Adams, Ross Exo, 143, 144
Adventures of Robin Hood, The (1937), 59
Adventures of Tintin, The (2011), 8, 49n7
Allen, Woody, 4, 16n4, 293
Allusionism, 6
Altman, Rick, 7, 35, 49n11, 73
Always (1989), 30, 43, 49n6, 49n8, 49n9, 54, 55, 64, 65, 73n4, 127
Amazing Stories: The Mission (1985), 63, 74n9, 236n1
Amblin Entertainment, 4, 64
Amblin' (1968), 34, 38, 112
American Graffiti (1974), 2
Amistad (1997), 8, 34–35, 49n6, 49n9, 64–66, 82, 84
Anderson, Joseph D., 242, 243, 264
Anderson, Wes, 136, 137, 189
Andrew, Dudley, 56, 57
Angels with Dirty Faces (1938), 59
Antonioni, Michelangelo, 111, 333
Aristotle, 32
Artificial Intelligence (*A.I.* 2001), 8, 16n6, 30, 49n9, 64–66, 74n11, 127, 215–217, 235, 283, 301, 335
Aumont, Jacques, 45, 262
Auteur, 13, 55–59, 61, 62, 65, 66, 68, 72
Autumn Afternoon, An (1962), 324
Average shot length (ASL), 38, 42, 43, 93, 126

B
Bacher, Lutz, 303, 304
Back to the Future (1985), 36

---

[1] Note: Page numbers followed by 'n' refer to notes.

342 Index

Back to the Future Part II (1989), 36
Bacon, Henry, 243
Balász, Béla, 141
Barr, Charles, 122
Barry Lyndon (1975), 118
Barthes, Roland, 94
Bartsch, Anne, 257, 261
Battleship Potemkin (1925), 108, 110, 146n4
Bay, Michael, 293
Bazin, André, 25, 27, 33, 34, 36, 41, 42, 47, 55, 56, 58, 59, 71, 80, 121, 138, 139, 142
Beardsley, M. C., 53
Belly of an Architect (1987), 287
Belson, Jerry, 55
Bergman, Ingmar, 308, 333
Berliner, Todd, 243, 245, 248, 269n1, 280
Besson, Luc, 4, 16n8
Bettinson, Gary, 54, 55, 58
Bezhin Meadow (1937), 120
BFG, The (2016), 8, 30, 64, 66, 73n4, 74n10
Big Sleep, The (1946), 35
Billy Jack (1974), 3
Blackmail (1929), 299
Blind Husbands (1919), 308
Blockbuster, The, high concept, 3
Body Double (1984), 280
Bogdanovich, Peter, 4, 282
Bonnie and Clyde (1967), 111, 333
Bordwell, David, 9, 10, 23–28, 30, 32, 33, 37–40, 42–44, 46, 47, 48n2, 50n16, 55–58, 67, 68, 70–72, 80, 84, 89, 94, 96, 98, 99n1, 105–108, 110, 113, 121, 129, 136, 139, 146n5,
146n6, 153, 156, 158, 160, 181, 183, 186n2, 217, 235, 242, 262, 269n1, 276, 281, 284, 285, 293, 296, 305, 314, 315, 323–325, 337
Branigan, Edward, 27, 31, 32, 71, 87, 160, 167, 182, 184, 200, 205, 250, 266, 284, 315, 322, 336
Bresson, Robert, 325, 333
Brewster, Ben, 107, 184, 185
Bridge of Spies (2015), 8, 49n6, 49n9, 65, 66, 74n9, 81, 84, 127, 146n8
Brooks, Virginia, 243, 253, 266, 337
Brown, William, 253
Buckland, Warren, 46, 67, 157, 173, 194, 206, 224, 250, 268
Bumstead, Henry, 299
Burch, Noël, 33, 41, 46, 71, 72, 96, 107, 108, 224, 246, 284, 323, 325, 326n14
Burks, Robert, 118

C

Cabinet of Dr. Caligari, The (1920), 108
Cahiers du Cinéma, 56, 333
Caldwell, John Thornton, 9, 62, 281
Camera logic, 90
Capra, Frank, 36
Captain Blood (1935), 59
Carroll, Noël, 3, 6, 11, 16n10, 27, 41, 42, 47, 56, 109, 126, 159, 242, 244, 254–256, 258, 259, 264, 291
Carter, Rick, 63

Casablanca (1942), 59
Catch Me if You Can (2002), 7, 8, 49n6, 49n10, 65, 66, 127, 132, 218–219
Caught (1949), 303, 304, 307
Charge of the Light Brigade, The (1936), 59
Chinatown (1974), 2
Cinemascope, 111, 122
Cine-tableau, 153, 184–186, 191, 336
Citizen Kane (1942), 108
Close Encounters of the Third Kind (1977), 1, 16n6, 29, 30, 42, 60, 63, 64, 67, 68, 154, 197, 236n3
Cognitivism, 241
Cohen, Dale, 243, 248
Color Purple, The (1985), 8, 34, 49n9, 64, 74n9, 127
Columbia Pictures, 1
Columbo: Murder by the Book (1971), 138, 191, 334
Constructivism, 243
Contempt (1963), 143
Continuity editing
 axis-of-action, 80, 81, 151, 165, 182, 211, 304
 crossing-the-line, 83, 211, 246, 294
 180 degree rule, 45, 80, 182, 247, 248, 304
Cook, David, 2, 3, 5, 7, 9, 16n13
Cool Hand Luke (1968), 118
Cooper, Mark Garrett, 46
Copland, Aaron, 264
Coppola, Francis Ford, 1, 62, 279, 280, 308, 309, 326n5

Cowie, Elizabeth, 35
Cronin, Paul, 285
Cruise, Tom, 13, 65
Cukor, George, 108
Cundey, Dean, 205
Currie, Gregory, 53, 72, 259
Curtiz, Michael, 59, 60, 94, 281
Cutting, James E., 248

D

Dayan, Daniel, 158, 159, 244, 336
Day of Wrath (1943), 294, 296
Decoupage, 25, 48n2, 110, 138, 182
De Haviland, Olivia, 59
DeLong, Jordan E., 38
De Palma, Brian, 1, 279, 280
Detective Story (1951), 94
Devlin, David, 335
Dial M for Murder (1954), 299, 300
Di Caprio, Leonardo, 65
Digital logic, 36
Dirty Harry films (1973–1983), 6
Doane, Mary Ann, 46, 304
DreamWorks Pictures, 4, 16n7
Dreyer, Carl Theodore, 185, 286, 293, 296
Dreyfuss, Richard, 65
Dubin, Mitch, 70, 89
Duel (1971), 16n5, 34, 38, 126, 193–194, 213–215, 236n3, 334
Durgnat, Raymond, 183

E

Earthquake (1974), 2
Eastwood, Clint, 83

Easy Rider (1969), 333
Eder, Jens, 257, 259, 263
Eidsvik, Charles, 264
Eikhenbaum, Boris, 24
Eisenstein, Sergei, 57, 71, 110, 139, 224, 235
Elsaesser, Thomas, 3, 30, 32, 36, 48n3
Empire of the Sun (1987), 8, 43, 49n9, 64, 85, 222–225, 231
End of Summer, The (1961), 246
Equinox Flower (1958), 315
E. T. (1982), 7, 10, 30, 49n6, 54, 55, 64, 67, 68, 118
Evans, Robert, 62
Exorcist, The (1974), 2

F

Fabula, 32, 33, 39, 44, 47, 176, 179
Family Plot (1975), 283
Field, Syd, 31
Fincher, David, 286
Fleming, Victor, 55, 60, 281
Floating Weeds (1959), 318
Flynn, Errol, 59
Folk psychology, 337
Fonda, Peter, 333
Ford, Harrison, 16n9, 65
Ford, John, 4, 35, 56, 60, 89, 108, 282
Foucault, Michel, 57
Frankenheimer, John, 111, 280
Freeland, Cynthia, 254
French Connection, The (1971), 333
French New Wave, 39, 42, 111
Frenzy (1972), 299
Friedkin, William, 4, 16n11, 111, 333
Frijda, N. H., 256, 258, 261

G

Gaut, Berys, 259
General, The (1926), 291, 292
Génette, Gerard, 28
Genre, 5, 6, 8, 9, 16n8, 35, 41–43, 57–59, 69, 200, 261, 284, 293
Gerstner, David A., 54
Gertrud (1964), 293, 296
Giant (1956), 283, 285, 286
Gibbs, John, 40
Godard, Jean-Luc, 96, 111, 137, 143, 290, 333
Godfather, The (1972), 62
Gombrich, E. H., 24, 48, 109, 153, 332
Gone With the Wind (1939), 60, 108
Greenaway, Peter, 15, 286, 287
Griffiths, D. W., 36, 58, 107
Grodal, Torben, 53, 254, 256, 257, 262
Gunning, Tom, 28, 33, 40, 49n12

H

Hanks, Tom, 13, 65
Harpole, Charles, 106–109, 121, 308
Harry Potter films (2001–2011), 6
Hawks, Howard, 5, 56, 58, 60, 69, 89, 190
Heath, Stephen, 46, 71, 94, 159, 182, 246, 284
Hen in the Wind, A (1948), 314
Hitchcock, Alfred, 5, 15, 39, 40, 43, 56–59, 72, 73n3, 90, 118, 143, 157, 198, 280, 283, 285, 294, 299–301, 306, 326n6, 332–334, 338n2
Hobbit, The films (2012–2014), 6

Hochberg, Julian, 243, 253, 266, 337
Hogan, Patrick Colm, 61, 253, 337
Hollywood
American new wave, 111, 276, 333
Hollywood renaissance, 3, 7, 37, 111, 333
new Hollywood, 1, 3, 6, 7, 13, 38, 42, 84, 332–334
Hook (1991), 8, 34, 60, 65, 124
Hooper, Tobe, 67, 127, 128, 130, 146n6
Hopkins, Anthony, 65
Hopper, Dennis, 333
Huff, Markus, 248
Hulk, The (2003), 6

Incredible Hulk, The (2008), 6
Indiana Jones and the Kingdom of the Crystal Skull (2008), 64
Indiana Jones and the Last Crusade (1989), 282
Indiana Jones films (1981–2008), 16n9
Insider, The (1999), 288, 289, 294
Insomnia (2002), 84
Intensified continuity, 37–39, 48, 63, 69, 84, 89, 90, 93, 130, 138, 228, 253
It's a Wonderful Life (1946), 36

Jacobs, Lea, 184, 185
James Bond franchise, 6
Jameson, Richard, 43
Jaws (1975), 1, 2, 6, 16n14, 30, 38, 49n9, 60, 61, 64, 68, 118, 127, 129, 130, 135, 161, 163, 167, 169, 173, 174, 182, 183, 186, 196, 200, 227, 236n3, 249, 250, 266, 283, 331, 332, 334
Juggernaut (1974), 2
Jurassic Park (1993), 7, 8, 16n9, 30, 54, 97, 203, 206, 208–210, 212, 268
Jurassic Park films (1993–2015), 6

Kael, Pauline, 11, 58, 59, 67, 183
Kahn, Michael, 13, 69, 89
Kaminsky, Janusz, 63, 89
Katz, Steven, 84, 88, 231
Keaton, Buster, 15, 136, 291, 292
Kennedy, Kathleen, 13, 64, 65
King, Geoff, 3, 8, 11, 33, 34, 37, 54, 55, 58, 73n1, 111, 146n4
King Kong
1933, 207
1976, 6
2009, 6
Kitano, Takeshi, 15, 137, 286–288
Koepp, David, 64, 84, 269n6
Konigsberg, Ira, 242
Kovacs, Andras Balint, 255
Kraft, Robert, 253, 337
Kramer, Peter, 3
Kubrick, Stanley, 15, 66, 74n11, 118, 283, 289
Kuleshov, Lev, 14, 84, 109, 183
Kurosawa, Akira, 16n12, 111, 333

L

La Chinoise (1967), 290, 291
Ladies Skirts Nailed to a Fence (1900), 277, 284
Lanser, Susan, 31
La Ronde (1950), 302, 306, 307, 309, 311
L'arrivée d'un train en gare de La Ciotat (1895), 107
La Signora Di Tutti (1934), 302
L'assassinat du Duc de Guise (1904), 278
Last Laugh, The (1924), 207
Late Spring (1949), 316, 317, 320, 322
Lawrence of Arabia (1962), 281
Lean, David, 281
Lelouch, Claude, 111
Le Plaisir (1952), 302, 303
Levin, Daniel, 243, 247
Levinson, Jerrold, 264
Lincoln (2012), 8, 34, 49n6, 65, 66, 126, 127, 146n8, 186–187n3
Link, William, 138
Livingston, Paisley, 30, 54, 68
Lodger, The (1927), 299
Lola Montes (1955), 307, 308
Long Voyage Home, The (1940), 108
Lord of the Rings, The films (2001–2003), 6
Lost World: Jurassic Park, The (1997), 16n9, 64, 207
Lucas, George, 1, 4, 16n11, 16n12, 65, 254, 279, 280, 326n5
Lumet, Sidney, 111, 280, 332, 333
Lumiere brothers, 107, 121

M

MacDonald, Laurie, 64
Madam de... (1953), 302, 311, 313
Magliano, Joseph, 247
Manchurian Candidate, The (1962), 280, 333
Mann, Michael, 15, 185, 187n3, 193, 194, 213, 214, 286, 288
Man Who Knew Too Much, The (1956), 299–301
Marnie (1964), 301, 333
Marshall, Frank, 65, 67
Martin, Adrian, 43, 44
Master of the House (1925), 293, 299
McBride, Joseph, 10, 15, 67, 69, 113, 138, 283, 334
McGinn, Colin, 253, 337
McKee, Robert, 31
Medias res, 33
Mellor, William, 285
Metz, Christian, 72
Meyer, Leonard, 24
MGM, 2, 67
Mildred Pierce (1945), 59
Milius, John, 1, 279, 326n5
Minority Report (2002), 7, 8, 35, 49n6, 65, 115, 125, 215, 217, 298, 335
Mise-en-cadre, 110
Mise-en-scene, 30, 33, 34, 39, 40, 47, 106, 110, 142, 184, 202, 224, 260, 282, 293, 294, 299, 306, 322, 333, 334
Mitry, Jean, 213
Monaco, James, 11
Morris, Nigel, 8, 15n3, 34, 43, 164, 250

Movie brats, The, 1, 3, 6, 7, 10, 65, 106, 111, 275, 279, 280, 326n5
Mukarovsky, Jan, 24
Munich (2005), 8, 13, 35, 49n10, 64–66, 88, 90, 92, 94, 96, 126, 127, 146n8, 187n3, 219, 220, 232
Murch, Walter, 245
Murnau, F. W., 296
Myles, Lynda, 1, 279

Naremore, James, 57
Narrative, bulls eye schema, 47
Ndalianis, Angela, 36
Neale, Steve, 2, 5, 9, 56, 250
Neill, Alex, 258
Nichols, Bill, 68
Night Gallery: Eyes (1969), 113
1941 (1979), 7, 49n6, 60, 61, 127, 200, 201
Nolan, Christopher, 84
Nothelfer, Christine E., 38
Notorious (1946), 301

One from the Heart (1982), 280
Ophuls, Max, 15, 284, 288, 302–314, 326n11
Optical pyramid, 183, 191
Ordet (1955), 296–298, 305
Orpheus (1949), 308, 310
Oudart, Pierre, 158–160
Ozu, Yasujiro, 15, 26, 84, 99n3, 182, 186n2, 246–249, 269n4,
283, 284, 314–318, 320–325, 326n13

Panofsky, Erwin, 24
Papillion (1974), 2
Parkes, Walter, 64
Parson's Widow, The (1920), 141
Pawnbroker, The (1964), 333
Peggy Sue Got Married (1986), 280, 308, 310
Penn, Arhtur, 16n11, 111, 146n4, 280, 332, 333
Perkins, V. F., 9, 24
Philips, Julia, 15n1, 67, 74n8
Planimetric, 111, 112, 127, 135–138, 189, 232, 287, 288, 306
Plantinga, Carl, 14, 254–257, 259, 262, 265, 268, 337
Poetics, 12, 23–26, 35, 36, 258
Point Blank (1967), 192
Point-of-view
  associative, 14, 49n14, 250–254, 269, 336
  optical, 87, 152, 161, 204, 250, 252, 336
  perspective, 14, 202
Poltergeist (1982), 16n6, 67, 118, 283, 331
Post-classical, 35–37, 48
Preminger, Otto, 56
Premium Rush (2012), 84
Pretty Woman (1990), 65
Prince, Stephen, 250
Private Lives of Elizabeth and Essex, The (1939), 94, 95

348 Index

Propp, Vladimir, 32
Pudovkin, Vsevolod, 27, 70, 71, 84
Pye, Michael, 1, 279

R

Raiders of the Lost Ark (1981), 7, 10, 49n9, 64, 65, 68, 114, 116, 127, 131, 168, 169, 171, 173, 182, 185, 199, 245, 261
Reckless Moment, The (1949), 302, 309, 310
Renoir, Jean, 26, 36, 41, 108, 142, 326n10
Resnais, Alain, 333
Ritchie, Donald, 284, 315
Roberts, Julia, 65
Rogers, Sheena, 254, 262
Romance of an Umbrella, The (1909), 278
Rope (1951), 299
Ryan, Marie-Laure, 30

S

Salt, Barry, 15, 37, 38, 40, 42, 48n5, 49n13, 63, 67, 80, 83, 85, 90, 107, 117, 160, 183, 277–279, 308, 325n2, 326n4, 338
Sarris, Andrew, 39, 56, 57, 59, 72, 306, 326n11, 333
Savage (1973), 191
Saving Private Ryan (1998), 7, 11, 49n9, 49n10, 60, 65, 124, 127, 165, 166, 179, 182, 184, 221–222, 236n5, 332, 335
Scene at the Sea, A (1991), 287
Schatz, Thomas, 3, 5, 9

Schiff, Stephen, 282
Schindler's List (1993), 7, 8, 43, 63, 66, 124, 127, 202–203
Schwan, Stephen, 248
Scorsese, Martin, 1, 4, 59, 83, 279, 280
Scott, Tony, 96
Sellors, Paul, 207
Serpico (1973), 2
Shining, The (1980), 283, 289, 290, 294
Shklovsky, Victor, 24
Shot, reverse shot, 6, 13, 14, 25, 39, 45, 58, 79–94, 106, 151, 158, 190, 241, 276, 333, 335
Simons, Daniel, 243
Smith, Greg M., 247, 255, 259–262, 265, 303–305, 337
Smith, Jeff, 263, 264
Smith, Murray, 28, 257, 259, 265
Smith, Tim J., 244–250, 253, 254, 262, 267, 269n5
Snake Eyes (1998), 280
Social Network, The (2010), 286
Solomon, Stanley J., 10
Sonatine (1993), 288
Spielberg, Steven
  box office, 1, 2, 4, 5, 7, 8, 65
  influences, 3, 7, 8, 15, 26, 38, 42, 53–55, 63, 68, 69, 88, 111, 112, 160, 210, 275, 276, 280–283, 314, 325, 332
  output, 4, 191
  television, 1, 2, 4, 6, 7, 15n2, 63, 69, 85, 88, 111, 113, 120, 153, 191, 194, 217, 280, 283, 332, 334
Stagecoach (1939), 108, 248

Staiger, Janet, 5, 27, 28, 33, 53, 55, 66, 80
Starski, Allan, 66
Star Wars (1976), films (1976–present), 4, 6, 16n12, 37, 65, 207
Steamboat Round the Bend (1935), 283
Sternberg, Josef von, 36
Sternberg, Meir, 28, 29, 305
Stevens, George, 283–286
Sting, The (1974), 2, 16n3
Story of Floating Weeds, The (1934), 318, 319, 326n13
Stroheim, Erich von, 36, 117, 308
Sturges, Preston, 65
Style, 9, 23, 56, 79, 105, 153, 189, 241, 259–262, 276, 331–338
Sugarland Express, The (1974), 2, 6, 7, 11, 38, 54, 58, 64, 68, 114, 118, 119, 127, 141, 195–196, 226–227, 236n3, 283, 334
Sunrise (1927), 296
Superclassical, 36
Suture, 158–161
Syuzhet, 32, 39, 44, 48n5, 49n10, 175, 186

Tableau, 107, 108, 111, 136, 141, 184–186, 294, 297
Tan, Ed, 253, 255–258, 261, 262, 337, 338
Terminal, The (2004), 8, 34, 65, 66, 127, 180, 230–231, 335
Thanouli, Eleftheria, 35, 36
That's Entertainment (1974), 2

Thompson, Kristin, 10, 24, 27, 29, 31, 37, 38, 40, 42, 47, 49n15, 66–68, 94, 151, 246, 279, 284, 308, 315, 323, 325
Todorov, Tzvetan, 31
Tokyo Story (1953), 315, 316, 320, 322
Tolland, Greg, 58, 108
Tomashevsky, Boris, 54
Torn Curtin (1966), 143
Towering Inferno, The (1974), 2
Truffaut, François, 42, 56, 59, 111, 143, 300, 333
Trumbo, Dalton, 55
Tsui Hark, 4
Tucker: The Man and his Dream (1989), 280
2001: A Space Odyssey (1968), 207
Tybjerg, Casper, 62, 334
Tynianov, Yuri, 24

United Artists, 2
Universal Pictures, 2, 16n3, 73n2

Vampyr (1932), 334
Velleman, David J., 254
Vertigo (1958), 118, 165, 280, 299–301

Wang, Caryn, 247
War Horse (2011), 8, 30, 49n9, 64–66, 127, 233

War of the Worlds (2005), 7, 214, 228–229, 233
Welles, Orson, 25, 56, 58, 89, 108, 282
Wells, John, 62
White, Susan, 306
Wide reverses, 12, 14, 15, 25, 49n14, 70, 89, 90, 152–183, 186, 189, 194, 197, 202, 212, 235, 241, 244, 249–252, 275, 276, 278, 280, 283, 284, 288, 294, 302, 304, 305, 316, 317, 323, 332, 334
Willerman, Paul, 306
Williams, Alan, 303, 306
Williams, John, 13, 64, 87, 165, 263
Wilson, Colin, 64
Wimsatt, W.K., 53

Wölfflin, Heinrich, 24, 121, 146n3
Wollheim, Richard, 42
Wood, Robin, 333
Woollen, Peter, 54
Worsley, Wallace, 334
Wuthering Heights (1939), 108
Wyler, William, 58, 110, 139

Y

Young and Innocent (1937), 301

Z

Zacks, Jeffrey, 247
Zemeckis, Robert, 4
Zillman, D., 256
Zones of action, 46, 181, 336

Printed in the United States
By Bookmasters